To Eat Flesh
They Are Willing

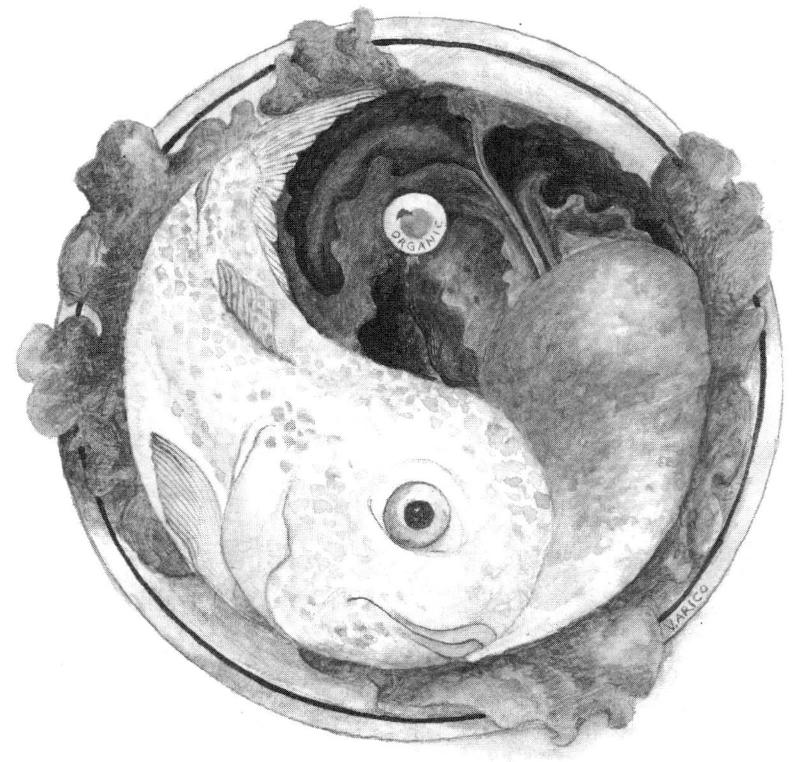

Are Their Spirits Weak?

To Eat Flesh They Are Willing Are Their Spirits Weak?

Vegetarians Who Return to Meat

Kristin Aronson, Ph.D.

PYTHAGOREAN
PUBLISHERS

NEW YORK   LOS ANGELES

Cover illustration and book design by Victoria Arico.

Grateful acknowledgement is made to poet Richard Grossman for permission to quote from *The Animals*, Graywolf Press, 1990.

A portion of this book was published previously in *Harvest of Compassion. Writings in Search of a Non-Violent World.* McCann's Journal of Poetry and Political Writing, Vol. III. No. I. Summer 1995.

Library of Congress Catalogue Number 96-92415
Cataloguing in Publication Data
Aronson, Kristin Janina, 1945-
To eat flesh they are willing are their spirits weak? : vegetarians who return to meat / Kristin Aronson.
p.   cm.
Includes bibliographical references (p.).
ISBN 0-9626169-3-1
1. Vegetarianism—Moral and ethical aspects.
2. Vegetarianism—Philosophy.
3. Vegetarians—Attitudes. 4. Ex-vegetarians—Attitudes. I. Title.
TX392.A665 1996   613.2'62'01

For further information or correspondence
please contact the author via the publisher:
PYTHAGOREAN PUBLISHERS Box 8174
JAF Station
New York, NY 10116

Manufactured in the United States of America.
Printed on durable acid-free recycled paper.

∞ The paper used in this publication meets the minimum requirements of the American National Standards for Information Sciences—Permanence of Paper for Printed Library Materials, ANSI Z39. 48-1984.

TO KIVA

Who Inspired It

"*In high truth
is there any difference between
'yes' and 'no'
between 'good' and 'bad'
is there any absolute distinction?"*

—Lao Tzu, *Tao Teh Ching*

Contents

Acknowledgments

I thank my colleague, Jim Munz, for teasing my mind with questions like, "If you had a pet Venus Flytrap, would you let it starve to death?" and for his image of plants on hooks; students Gary Meier, for taking my questionnaire to Thailand, and Wuttisak Thabthim for translating it into Thai and the responses into English; Departmental Secretary, Dale McAndrew, for artistic advertising; many librarians: Eva Wolynska (Central Connecticut State University), Paul Homer (Southern Connecticut State University), Vijay Nair (Western Connecticut State University), Mark Braunstein (Connecticut College), and the Reference Staff of the Lucy Robbins Welles Library, Newington, Connecticut; Giles Strekel for astute comments and Mark Reinhardt for advice; David Makinster for prose and poster; William Stephens and Stan Kundra for sources and story (respectively); Professor Mahlon Barnes for reading the manuscript and Theresa Sansone for transferring it to disk; Karen Lindquist for technical assistance, and especially vegetarian author Rynn Berry for being the "incendiary" whose words helped fuse the text.

~ DISCLAIMER ~

The material in this book is by its nature anecdotal. The tales
I collected represent the opinions of the tellers and are not presented
as "truth," even though all were told to me truthfully.

Preface

Variety is not life's spice, but its natural flavor. Vegetarians who, as a group, know much about seasonings but who can otherwise be clannish, ignore not only life's full cornucopia of foods but also life's full cornucopia of types. A type most ignored by vegetarians is the *former* vegetarian, perhaps because its members, who preferred and deserted what the constant held dear, cannot be taught or "converted."[1]

As former vegetarians may see themselves here, present ones may see what they fear, or what they fear they could become, and as the "former" may feel relieved, the latter may feel aggrieved that the issue was opened at all. But opening it is like opening a book—indeed, like opening *this* book. "It is variety that is the source of life, the sign of life. Why should we be afraid of it?"[2]

"Rich man, poor man, beggarman, thief; doctor, lawyer, merchant, chief." Here are women and men, rich and poor (but no beggars or thieves to my knowledge), three doctors, counting the chiropractor, one lawyer, and two merchants. Closest to the "chief" was a guest who ate buffalo at a Native American Sun Dance.

Without searching very long (or very far) for former vegetarians (and in a few cases, so-called vegetarians who eat some meat),[3] I found a hardhat construction worker (now a "farm wife"); a radical feminist community activist, champion of rights for gays, animals, women, and the disabled; a night-shift factory worker, now in retail sales; neither the butcher nor the candlestick maker but the baker (a vegetarian caterer); and one of a baker's dozen, a house sitter who was raised in a family of thirteen children.

One of the doctors, head of an urban hospital's Emergency Medicine Department, is also a practicing Buddhist; the other, a clinical ecologist, ate her pets as a farm child in rural Ohio. There is a professional film critic who also manages a bookstore; an importer with a master's degree in nutrition; one philosophy professor from Illinois who is also a professional dancer and another from North Dakota whose roots recall a Garrison Keillor yarn. There is a prize-winning chef of international renown; a massage therapist who ate snakes in China; a "doctor's wife" from Australia who runs a health clinic there; and two students, one from The National Gourmet in New York City, and another from Bangkok, Thailand.

There is a septuagenarian who works a seventy-two hour week and farms on the side; a brilliant biologist who teaches in private schools and shows science marvels live on national television; a free-spirited Rainbow Gathering goddess who thinks she may have to hunt her own food to survive in her old age; a graphic artist with a native habitat garden; and another artist, a "psychic," living in seclusion, recuperating. Also living in seclusion (for the past twenty years) in a shack with no plumbing or public utilities is a former New York City opera singer who went rural to raise goats. The lawyer, who is English, also has a Ph.D. in mathematics, and the chiropractor, a master's degree in philosophy. Rynn Berry, vegetarian scholar and strict vegan, is the book's foil.

Former vegetarians' formal educations range from grammar school to a double doctorate; their ages from twenty to seventy-seven.[4] Together they represent Catholics, Protestants, Jews, Buddhists, Taoists, athiests, and pagans, hailing from rural, urban, and suburban backgrounds throughout the country (and sometimes out of it). Many were vegetarian for more than twenty years before returning to meat; one lapsed after nine months. Each now eats flesh, and each, without prompting, introduced the term "spiritual" into the interview. Each was articulate, and to all I am grateful, for their stories, interwoven with my philosophy, are the soul of this book.

Introduction

The Sense of it All

ood is important, but it is not so much the mouth that should be open—it is the ears. We can be starved for what we do not or cannot bring ourselves to hear. So it is the auditory, not the gustatory, which interests me here. A vegetarian who listens to those who were, but no longer are vegetarian, is well-nourished; one who hears only what agrees with her beliefs is on a dangerously limited diet, perhaps even starved for the truth.

"It is opposition that brings things together," said Heraclitus two and a half millennia ago.[1] Opposites attract each other; but they also attract us to them, especially when we seek the truth, for truth is often found in opposition. I am a vegetarian, an avowed vegetarian, a vegan. So although I am interested in former vegetarians, I am not one. But because I am interested in vegetarianism, and most of all in truth, I am interested in those who oppose what I hold dear. Understanding why non-vegetarians become vegetarians is easy; but understanding why vegetarians become non-vegetarians is hard—if one is oneself a vegetarian.

"*Audi partem alteram*" ("Hear the other side") urged the medieval philosopher St. Augustine.[2] Even better is to hear why some change sides. When we listen, with no mission, to those who again eat meat, we put aside preconceptions, and sometimes misconceptions, because as much as we love our principles, we know that principles which do not have lives of their own are worse than dead: collectively they turn into ideologies or religions, and into the seeds of war.

I once heard an eminent vegan berate a beekeeper who tried to explain the ethics of his relatively humane system. The vegan's ears were plugged if not with beeswax then with the silt of pre-judgment. He heard nothing, talked over the defender's honest words, his head abuzz with stereotypes, and stung without mercy. Eavesdropping, I cheered on the beekeeper, but his words were never allowed to leave the hive: the vegan smothered him in an acrid cloud of arrogance.

Such deadly barbs of criticism, sometimes directed into others by vegans, are too much like the actions of flesh eaters whose diets they decry—cutting, stabbing, piercing, flaying. Indeed, inattention to others, refusing to listen, or hearing only what conforms to what one thinks one already knows, is really a form of power-over, and thus rooted in the same violence which leads to factory farms. The tongue is a most valuable organ; but the ears, an invaluable one.

My reason for listening to former vegetarians was not to find their "redeeming" features, for this would imply that vegetarianism is a religion, and that its apostates have fallen and need saving from sin. I will not argue that lapsed vegetarians can be good people, or that they can be spiritual. The question: Can former vegetarians be good people? is too easily answered, and thus uninteresting. Can former vegetarians be spiritual?, as a metaphysical question, is essentially unanswerable, although interesting to address; but I shall not try to prove anything. If I wished to demonstrate that meat eaters can be spiritual, too, I would have my work cut out for me in a spate of similar books I could write—proving that poachers can be spiritual, or corporate executives. But I have little to say about poaching and spirituality, and even less to say about spirit and corporate executives. I wrote this book because, as a vegetarian, I am interested in vegetarianism.

Thus I have no intention of answering the question posed in the book's title, although I shall ask what it means. Instead, I questioned former vegetarians to find out what their answers mean. To do my own soul-searching, I had to search the world, and because I could not travel widely, I explored people deeply. Unable to decide whether to write a vegetarian "Big Chill" or a philosophy book, I decided to do both. Hearing from those who lapsed told me why they did; I already knew what they did, so in that, there was no mystery, and hence no excuse for philosophy. The stories I collected are parables for our age. Whether the world is better or worse with former vegetarians in it, I shall leave for someone wiser than I to determine. The piece of the world which I perceive is too small for me to see final outcomes; but people were right to scale.

Few things surprise as much as innocence unveiled. Once, upon hearing of new "converts" to vegetarianism, or upon making them, I added them to the total, forgetting about decrease. Who would tally up births and forget about deaths? For every new vegetarian, there may also be a new former vegetarian, and for many who call themselves "vegetarian," there may be none. What had always seemed like a wave gathering momentum, suddenly I saw as part of an ebb and flow. The very concept of a lapsed vegetarian was somewhat chilling. Vegetarianism was something one added to, not subtracted from. There were plusses only, never minuses. There was every reason to be and none not to be one.

Are there more vegetarians today? I have not made a count, but have only discovered the defectors, the ones making exit out the back door, unnoticed by the throng filing in through the front. If for every gain, there is a loss, then vegetarianism is not strengthened by numbers, although it may be by intellectual force. I am not a census taker, but a philosopher; so I cannot provide audits. Instead I provide portraits, and interpret them.

Self-righteousness is a disease of the soul cured best by empathy. We need to heed those who revert, for they have much for our ears, and we for theirs, if they want to be talked or welcomed back.

But even if they do not, listening is good for us. Perhaps we will learn whether our hold on vegetarianism is a fragile or a tenuous one. Perhaps we can envision what we would do in their places. We can examine ourselves for traces of superiority. We can test to see whether we subtly, even unconsciously, thought something like I once did: "What I am is better, but they are not worse"—unaware of the contradiction. Some will be frustrated by the stories. Others (I hope) will be amazed. For anyone who doubts the sensitivity of a flesh eater after reading "A Spiritual Pragmatist," nothing, perhaps, will avail. If those who have judged former vegetarians as morally weak really listen, they will learn why empathy is a virtue not of the eyes, but of the ears.

Wisdom is not an orphan and does not spring to life by parthenogenesis. There are always opposites tugging away at each other, ideas and their antitheses, ambiguity and clarity, pro and con, in a kind of passionate propagation. Hearing how vegetarians lapse (ovo, lacto, pesco, pollo, and finally, lapso) both I and my theories have changed. Everything I have ever written about vegetarianism I wrote in response to lapsed vegetarians. In their stories, there were lessons; in the patterns of their lives, philosophy. Because philosophy and story are themselves opposed, in their coming together a new synthesis emerges, a philosophical anthropology in which ideas come alive.

Ideas do change the world, and are often generated by philosophers; but it is a mistake to think that philosophers' arguments change the world, for philosophical arguments are, by and large, of interest only to philosophers. What changes the world is insight. Insight is often attained by reading philosophy—between the lines, as it were. Insight is also gleaned from stories, from myth and poetry, and from art. I want to share philosophy and story to the end of provoking insight—in the hope that it will change the world.

The words of former vegetarians illuminate the elusiveness of a stark, divided universe of right and wrong, moral courage and moral weakness, inner peace and inner turmoil We all know vegetarians whose hearts are hard or misanthropes living on fruit only. We know that flesh eaters do not lack warmth of heart or loftiness of spirit. The stories in this book uncover the complexities of living consciously and carefully. In no way is it intended that lapsos are fallen angels or that flesh eaters lack wings.

Each story was an organic coil, a bud containing many truths about the ethics of vegetarianism, the spirituality of flesh eaters, and the moral ambiguities of diet and world view. My commentary, while not academic philosophy, is, nevertheless philosophical. Philosophers like to talk about arguments; for this book, I wanted to hear about lives. Because this is more than a book of arguments, it is less than a philosophy book; but because it is written by a philosopher, there is philosophy in it. There are people in it, too, because only in lived experience can we find a living truth.

1
Coming to Terms

"Definitions, contrary to public opinion, tell us nothing about things."
—S.I. Hayakawa

*S*ocrates thought philosophy would free the mind from the body; vegetarians think diet will do it. According to Socrates, we nourish the soul by denying the body; according to the vegetarian, we feed the soul by refusing to eat another's flesh. If we once refused to eat another's body, but now choose to do so, what have we done to our souls? Food, something so physical, may ensure something spiritual; food, something so immanent and natural, something transcendental.

For Socrates, the practice of philosophy demanded a theory of body and soul. Soul is better than body and opposed to it. Vegetarians who claim to attain the highest through the lowest, through lowly food, challenge his dualism to a duel. But in fact, it is not what we do but how we do it that matters. Socrates would prefer the abstemious flesh eater to the vegetarian glutton.[1] Likewise with vegetarians, it is not so much what we do as how we do it that defines us.

I have arrived at the paradoxical conclusion that some vegetarians (sometimes) eat meat, and that some people who do not eat meat are not vegetarians. Now more clear on what I mean by "vegetarianism," I am no longer stunned by the paradox: vegetarianism has less to do with diet than I thought and more to do with philosophy.

A vegetarian is a person who wishes to avoid eating animal flesh, and who avoids doing so on principle.[2] A person who wishes to avoid eating animal flesh, and does so, but not on principle, adopts a vegetarian diet, but is not a vegetarian. A person who, on principle, wishes to avoid eating animals, but who does not do so, adopts a vegetarian philosophy, but is not a vegetarian. If vegetarianism is a practice, we are vegetarian if we do not eat meat; if vegetarianism is a theory, we are vegetarian if we embrace the philosophy. But vegetarianism is neither a doing nor a thinking. It is a way of doing guided by thought. Thus more than a way of doing, it is a way of being.

If we were vegetarian, but abandon our vegetarianism, we are not ourselves anymore. We have changed universes; we are not where we were; we do not "live here" anymore. Vegetarianism is not just the decision not to eat meat; it is the decision to look at the world in a different way. Vegetarianism is neither a diet nor a philosophy; it is a *philosophy of life.*

Philosophies of life are not rooted in propositions, but in people. To be a vegetarian is to live in a certain way, not to argue in a certain way. Vegetarianism is not constructed logically, but lived expansively. Philosophies of life are things we grow into. They are not so much true as tried. If we choose a philosophy, but do nothing, we have still accepted it; but if we adopt a philosophy of life, and do not live by it, we have not chosen it at all.

I could perhaps call this "avowed vegetarianism"; but I have reasons for not doing so. The word "vegetarian" is now used so widely that it is becoming empty: on some readings, there can be no former vegetarians at all. Because, for many, "vegetarianism" is honorific, we say we are "largely" vegetarian, "mainly" vegetarian, "almost" vegetarian, "sometimes" vegetarian, "quasi" vegetarian. The prefixes seem innocent, but they are really negations of what they seem innocently to modify. With them we try to affirm what we actually have denied. One who craved meat, but unable to procure it, might inappropriately appropriate the label—a "forced" vegetarian.

A retronym is an expanded expression which now must do the work once done by a simpler one.[3] Examples are : "Classic Coke"; "organic food"; "unbleached flour"; "whole grain bread"; "free range chicken"; "wild animal"—and probably, "real life." If "vegetarian" continues to be used recklessly, it will soon require a retronym— "true vegetarian"; "real vegetarian"; "bona fide vegetarian"; "consistent vegetarian"; "complete vegetarian"; "genuine vegetarian." Because I would rather the term retain its original meaning, I refrain from qualifying it to distinguish it from what I take to be its misuses. If eventually a retronym is needed, it would only express what "vegetarian" has meant until recently when it has become socially safe (and even commendable) to identify with what was once a way of life requiring commitment—a marriage, not an "affair."

How we are to live is one question. How we are to live with ourselves is another. What is done can sometimes be undone; but how can what is lived be unlived? If vegetarianism is something we grow into, it cannot be unlived; but it can be outgrown. If vegetarianism is like a marriage, abandoning it is like a divorce. The divorced person may now be a monk, having renounced the way of the flesh and its temptations, but the former vegetarian has been tempted by flesh, and has found his way back to it.

If married, one does not say one is "single part of the time"—although many married people act that way. Divorced people do not call themselves "largely" married, "basically" married, "almost" married, "sometimes" married, or "married at home" although they may wish they were still wed. Yet after a divorce from vegetarianism, some feel faithful to it still, even while "cheating" with meat. They are "vegetarian at heart" or "vegetarian in spirit." Former vegetarians who speak this way are still in love with what they left, although no longer committed to it. Estranged from it, they become strangers to their former selves.

One can be more or less committed to one's vegetarianism (as one can be to one's marriage), but it is the commitment, not the vegetarianism (or marriage) which admits of degrees. One can be more or less "along" in one's pregnancy, but it is the process of fetal development, and not being pregnant, which shows the stages. Just as it is true that one is not more or less pregnant or married, one is not more or less a vegetarian. One is only more or less devoted to it. One is married—or not, pregnant—or not, vegetarian—or not.

My vegan friends laugh delightedly at locutions like "pesco" or "pollo" vegetarians: animal eating vegetarians. But we could say that those who renounce eating mammals are closer to vegetarianism than those who do not. So "near" vegetarian makes some sense, not in terms of degree, but in terms of distance. Can one ever eat flesh while a vegetarian? An affirmative answer is not out of the question. Some who reluctantly use meat medicinally or *in extremis* may be closer to vegetarianism than those who stop eating meat only because they want thinner bodies or thicker bloodstreams running through their arteries. A vegetarian to the letter may be "less" a one than a vegetarian in spirit.

One can also take one's vegetarianism seriously or lightly—although one is not more or less a vegetarian thereby. Some vegetarians are somber, dutiful, even dour; others, militant and missionizing; others, airy and spiritual. Still others are humorous, make their soup with laughing stock, and do not take the whole "bloody" thing so seriously. How we practice is a matter of style, not substance. A zealot is not more a vegetarian than an unassuming saint.

While some "vegetarians" experiment, others commit. Some even experiment with commitment. Fortunately, although a partner can abandon me, only I can abandon vegetarianism. It will never leave me, for it cannot; only I can leave it. Thus commitment to vegetarianism is safer than commitment to a person: it would seem to have at least twice the chance of success. Experiments may fail, however, and commitments be betrayed. More than one apostate spoke of "breaking" his vegetarianism as though it were a vow. Yet vegetarians often stubbornly refuse to acknowledge the divorce. Perhaps because they made their vows in private, they believe they need to pronounce nothing in public. No lapso announces: I am now free from my vegetarianism.

My definition of vegetarianism is not offered as a winnowing device to separate those who eat sheep and goats from those who don't, but rather as the ideal or paradigmatic case. Those who approach or approximate it can truly be called "vegetarians" (and can truthfully call themselves such) and those who fall short cannot. The closer we come to the ideal, the more right we have to the label, and the farther away, the less. If we listen to what former vegetarians now call themselves, we will see why we should start with a standard.

For some former vegetarians, feeling or believing creates reality. ELLY said: "I feel somewhat at an abyss between what I feel to be right and how I live. If someone offers me some meat, I'll say, 'No; I'm a vegetarian.' And I'm not being ingenuous. I really *feel* like a vegetarian because that is my preferred way of being. I feel I never really left; it feels the same. I still think of myself as a vegetarian because in terms of sentiment, I am. I hope to go back to a vegetarian diet; but I will always feel myself vegetarian."

NANCY said: "My heart is still vegetarian. I'm a vegetarian who uses meat only because she has to. If I didn't have to eat it, I would never, ever, *ever* gone back to it." JONATHAN said: "It has to start with one's sense of identity. Someone might say, 'I've had fish twelve times this year, so about once a month, and I feel I am a vegetarian though.' What if someone says, 'I have fish and chicken once a week; am I vegetarian?' They might *feel* they are vegetarian; so what's the criteria?"

JONATHAN considers himself a "middle of the roader" vegetarian. "Currently, I'm mainly lacto-ovo," he says. "That's currently, right now; that's the best way to put it, though with certain situations of travel, I've been eating fish." Others also consider themselves in the middle. JOHN said: "I've had a couple of situations of being a serious vegetarian. I would still describe myself as a 'borderline meat eater' or a 'borderline vegetarian.' I guess what I'm describing as a borderline condition persists to this day, where tomorrow I could wake up and never eat meat again." KIVA said: "I feel like I'm the middle person because I have been vegan and I've also gone back to eating some flesh foods. I feel like I'm trying to find some median between the two."

Sometimes the vegetarian identity seems to be split. JONATHAN said: "Technically, I am a partial vegetarian. I guess I call myself 'lacto-ovo-pesco' vegetarian, in the sense that day to day, I am mainly vegetarian. For ninety-eight per cent of my eating, I'm vegetarian, and that's a fact. For the two per cent that I'm having fish, I'm not a vegetarian, but two per cent out of my identity—I still feel I am really a vegetarian who will have some fish." LEONARD said: "I think I ate no more than two or three per cent animal foods in the last thirty years. I'm basically a vegetarian; I'll put it that way." JOHN said: "If there were more options, I could probably be vegetarian ninety-nine per cent of the time, perhaps even one hundred per cent of the time."

Some use the imagery of degree and distance, and others the imagery of distance alone. ROCKY said: "I would be more vegetarian if I had more support. Ten years ago I was closer to vegetarianism." BARBARA said: "I was just approaching that place [veganism] and was pushed away." JOHN would "make efforts in that direction" and then "step back from it." GAIL moved back and forth in a rhythm. She said: "I've had six waves of vegetarianism and six waves of eating some meat throughout my life."

Others prefer to speak in terms of diet rather than in terms of commitment to a philosophy. LINDA said when asked, she would reply, "No thanks; I don't eat meat. This is the way I eat," and added, "I'm a Yankee and we keep words to a minimum." KIVA said: "One thing I've always had a problem with was people saying, 'I'm vegetarian, but sometimes I eat chicken,' or 'I'm vegetarian, but I can't stop eating bacon bits on my salads.' And I would be like: 'You're not a vegetarian!' People would say, 'I'm a vegetarian' because it was the cool thing to be. I think it's better to be totally honest with yourself. You really have to say, 'I'm eating a vegetarian diet right now' or 'I'm eating a vegan diet right now.'"

PETER agreed: "I think the word 'vegetarian' ought to be used for people who don't eat meat, to be strict. And so when people ask me, I don't get hung up on the word. I say, 'I'm mostly vegetarian.' 'Pesco vegetarian'? I've never heard that before. That's good. But clearly that person is not vegetarian. Clearly. What's the point of calling themselves 'vegetarian'? It makes them feel like they're doing something good."

Many call themselves "vegetarian" because they never bring flesh into their homes. JONATHAN said: "I have never brought fish into my kitchen. It fits into your identity, because this is your house, your own sphere. You're living up to your vegetarian ideal in your own sphere. That's why you feel you are a vegetarian, because in your own refrigerator there's no flesh food, and your skillets are not defiled with the fleshy essence." ROLF called himself a "de facto" vegetarian at first, because he had not yet made the decision not to eat meat, but just gradually lost interest in it. He said: "After reading *Diet for a New America*, I decided to call myself a 'vegetarian.'" He now calls himself a "fair weather" or a "situational" vegetarian, because he will eat any meat, except veal, but only when it is served to him outside of his house, "as a social courtesy."

Sometimes expressed identity varies situation to situation. MARCIA said: "It depends on the company I'm in. I basically do consider myself vegetarian; but if I'm around someone who defines it more strictly, then of course I have to say I'm not. But for most people, I say that I am. I'm vegetarian because I don't eat meat or fowl. You want to call yourself 'vegetarian.' You want to identify with vegetarians, to encourage them." PETER said: "It depends on the conversation. If anyone is asking a serious question, my answer will be, 'I'm mostly vegetarian; I eat some fish.'"

Only one former vegetarian was stricter in her ideal of vegetarianism than I was. VICKY said: "I feel undeserving of the title 'ex-vegetarian.' I was a vegetarian only for a couple of years, between the ages of twenty-one and twenty-three or so; maybe it was longer. Anyway, it wasn't a lifetime occupation—more just an experiment. Maybe my gut feeling is you aren't really a vegetarian unless you can succeed in being one for life, not just play around with it; and furthermore, you aren't really a vegetarian if you eat meat voluntarily, even just now and then. One of my college painting professors used to speak disparagingly of certain students he called 'dilettantes.' 'What's that?' I asked, unfamiliar with the term. 'Sunday painters,' he said. I guess I feel like a Sunday-painting vegetarian."

What have we done when we've ended our vegetarianism? And what have we done to ourselves? It is hard to know what ending something is if we do not know what we are ending. Are we ending something we did, or something we were? The distinction between doing and being serves us well. We all know those who call themselves "Catholic" but who practice birth control (being without doing) and many who do Christ-like things without calling themselves "Christian" (doing without being).

Which locution is better: "being vegetarian" (following the diet, a doing) or "being a vegetarian" (claiming an identity, a being)? At first, calling vegetarianism a doing seems safer, because actions are determinate and real. But the *O.E.D.* cites "vegetarian crabs" (and insects)[4] and things other than animals are vegetarian—menus, entrees, and meals. While the first locution is about diet, the second, ideally, is about commitment, although it can also be about affiliation—and therein lies the confusion.

An affiliation implies an "ism" which is exclusionary; membership, with its insiders and outsides, comes much too cheaply. A commitment implies neither boundaries nor identification with something outside ourselves; if anything, it implies a taking in, an internalizing. "Being a . . ." is not the same as "being", *simpliciter*. My being is my identity, who I am rather than what I am. Thus my identity is different from what I identify with. A vegetarian in the ideal sense with which I began has taken something in; one who follows the leader or the crowd risks being taken in.

So if we do something, in this case, eat a vegetarian diet, we can say, "I am vegetarian." If we are something, in the sense of affiliation, we can say, "I am a vegetarian." But if we are referring to our identity or commitment, we can say, "I am living a vegetarian life."

It is only when we know the sense of "vegetarianism" intended that we know what we have done when we end it. On one extreme, we go on to something new; on the other, we no longer know who we are. Thus if our vegetarianism was an experiment, it fails; if it was our religion, we recant; if it was our passion, it fades away; if it was our diet, it is dropped; if it was our dream, we awaken; if it was our identity, we are in crisis. Some say they "fell out of it" as some people (usually those who do not know how to love at all) fall instantly "in love" and then instantly out again, only to "fall" for another. ("No promises.") Vegetarians, like lovers, can be fickle. Sometimes, like ROCKY, they say: "I really didn't care about it anymore. It didn't mean as much to me as it did. I just really didn't care"—as though vegetarianism were a rejected mate or pet.

When we are committed to vegetarianism, as we are in the ideal case, ending it is most like a divorce; it is not an accident that former vegetarians speaking of "breaking" it. What else do we say we break? We break dates, promises, hearts, and vows, sometimes making no bones about it; but it is bones that we again begin to break, on our plates, if not between our teeth, when we leave our vegetarianism. If we accidentally break a leg or a vertebra, we are not accountable; our body finds us innocent of its injury; but when we break our vegetarianism, we have broken our word, not to another, but to ourselves, and the bodies we have injured, now inside us, cannot be our witnesses. What is the sound of one vow breaking?

Often how subjects speak is an object lesson in confusion—but not always. When we give up our vegetarianism, our language can give us away. We say we "have" our meat, instead of "eating" it, as though what we want is to have our meat and *not* eat it, too. JONA-THAN, for example, used the former when referring to his eating flesh, but preferred the latter when referring to others. What we "have" we own; we possess; we have kept; we have not destroyed. What we eat disappears—as itself—and re-appears as us. We don't "have" it anymore when it becomes us, for having is relational, and we cannot be related to what no longer is. In restaurants, we commonly say, "I'll have the . . ." instead of "I'll eat the . . ." Either we are denying that we will be eating, or more precisely, what we will be eating; or perhaps we are only asserting that we own our dinners because we intend to pay for them. (If we are habitual meat eaters, we may pay in more ways than one.)

We may also deny what we carry home inside of us, before it has become us. When I told JONATHAN (who would not bring fish into his house) that when he went home, the fish was still in him, and he was in his home, so the fish was in his home, he denied it. When the light goes off in the refrigerator, does all food disappear? If no one is looking, does the world disappear? Is not seeing not believing?

No one likes the word "omnivore" anymore. It is "in" to be some kind of vegetarian, and to call all others "carnivores." But strictly speaking, no person is a carnivore, subsisting entirely on flesh.[5] There are probably millions of people who call themselves "vegetarian," whether closer or farther from the ideal, who are really omnivores. It is as though if we are closer to one pole than to the other, we identify with the nearest end of the continuum. But being vegetarian, unlike being over or under weight (in which case one can, literally, be more or less of what one really is) is not relational. We think there is a vegetarian continuum only because we believe that being closer to vegetarianism than to carnivorism makes us some kind of vegetarian; but this makes no more sense than to say if we are closer to white than to black we are not gray.

Because we can eat a diet that is *partly* vegetarian, we think we can be *partially* vegetarian. But if we eat vegetarian food eighty per cent of the time, we are not eighty per cent vegetarian. If we eat vegetarian food on weekdays, but not on weak-ends, we are not vegetarian Monday through Friday. If vegetarian food comprised half of one's diet, one would not call oneself "half a vegetarian" or "vegetarian half the time." To be clear, one should say one is relatively near or far from the ideal; but once a vegetarian, always some kind of vegetarian we seem to think, even if our vegetarianism exists only as the potential to become vegetarian again, as if it were not gone but waiting somewhere. In the wings? (Not chicken.) In limbo?

Logicians have a name for the fallacy of trying to conclude that if we don't know just where to draw the line, we cannot draw lines at all: the mistake is to think that just because the shades of gray are confusing we cannot tell black from white. Sometimes the error is called "The Fallacy of the Heap." We may drop rice or millet seeds one by one on the ground, and have trouble saying at which grain we have a pile; but this doesn't mean we can't tell a pile when we see one. Sometimes the mistake is called "The Fallacy of the Beard" because although we may not be able to see at just which point the stubble becomes one, we can recognize a beard when we see it. One straw won't break the camel's back, but too many are too much to bear. I began with a paradigm of vegetarianism to see how far away we can get from it before the camel stumbles.

If it is true that we can't always decide who is a former vegetarian and who is not, it is also true that vegetarians do not know what to call themselves either. In February, 1995, the *Hartford Courant* ran an article intriguingly called, "Even 'vegetarians' not immune to lower beef prices." According to *Washington Post* reporter Carole Sugarman, "Americans are saying one thing, and doing another." A 1993 poll of 4,700 people nation-wide found that "the self-reported vegetarians . . . ate only an ounce less meat a day than self-reported meat eaters." "People are reporting their intentions as opposed to their actions," said Mary Abbott-Hess, consultant to the National Livestock and Meat Board. "We eat for the body, the mind and the soul . . . when it all gets put together, it's very complex."[6]

Very complex, indeed. If someone says, "I'm a vegetarian, but I eat meat," we are confused. If someone says, "I eat meat, but I don't," we charge her with inconsistency. Likewise, it is not just odd to claim, "I'm a vegetarian, but I eat mostly meat," for this is contradictory in a way that "I believe in God, but don't go to church" or even "I am married, but unfaithful to my spouse" is not. But if someone says, "I don't eat meat as a rule, but I sometimes do, as an exception," we are relieved; at least we understand now. Taxonomers may be baffled, for their love is to label: is such a one vegetarian or not? But to classify is to calcify, and often to neglect nuance. Of course there are many who call themselves "vegetarian" who are not vegetarian; but how much does this matter?

It matters linguistically, if one loves the word, for one does not wish to see it emptied of its meaning. And if one sees vegetarianism as a "badge of honor" (as did KIVA and NANCY) it matters as a matter of pride. But the world is not necessarily a worse place if the label wears a bit thin, and may in fact be a better one (for vegetarians) if some in imitating "near" vegetarians themselves become "closer" ones. If we eat vegetarian food occasionally, we are not "occasional" vegetarians; but the committed vegetarian is more interested in what's on the table than in a label, in what she knows, rather than what she shows, in the spiritual rather than the superficial.

"Who is vegetarian?" and "Who is not?" are interesting questions, but the more interesting one is: "Who are we now that we eat animals again?" Workshops exist to assist the newly bereaved, but not the newly omnivorous. A vegetarian separated from her diet, a vegetarian now eating his potatoes with steak, a vegetarian without a sense of identity, may try to hold on to who they were, as many stay "in love" with a former mate for a time before their affection starves into attrition. On a new diet of meat we do not starve for want of nutrition: what starves is our love of vegetarianism.

We may live in denial for awhile, as we carve new identities with our knives and forks, or stake out new territory with steak, continuing to fool ourselves, perhaps, for just as long as it takes to build new bodies out of animal flesh. Indeed, one source of the persistent belief that we can be "partially" vegetarian is that our bodies do, in fact, cease by degree to be bodies made out of plants. While we are not less and less vegetarian, we are less and less made of vegetable foods. No longer feasting on the garden's variety, do former vegetarians become "garden variety" again, with no principles to set them apart? To eat flesh they are willing: are their spirits weak?

2

The Perils of Purity

Truth is never pure and rarely simple."
—Oscar Wilde

*"None of us is pure when it comes to animals . . .
a clean conscience is a figment of the imagination."*
—Andrew Linzey

Vegetarianism is not the answer to anything, and even if it were, the question would be too complicated to be answered with a single word. Nevertheless, some vegetarians seem to think they can stand under the shower of their commitment and be rinsed clean, as if the question were: What would make me pure? and its answer was "vegetarianism." If we think we can answer a complex question so simply, we have simply misunderstood the question.

No one who feels morally superior ever is, for the simple reason that righteousness is itself a moral taint. We may feel better, feeling that we are better; but the better we feel we are than others, the worse—and worse off—we will be. We can be corrupted by a good thing, by too much of a good thing, by taking a good thing much too seriously.

Isaac Bashevis Singer says, "When one becomes a vegetarian, it purifies the soul."[1] Indeed, some vegetarians see themselves (and other vegetarians) as spiritually refined. Rynn Berry, a confirmed vegan, said: "Meat eaters interfere with their spiritual development by incurring bad karma. Unfortunately, we in the West have no concept of karma; but we do have the notion of sin, so you would be accumulating sinful demerits, put it that way. You participate in karmic pollution. The Greeks have this notion of miasma or pollution: when you murder somebody, there's a miasma that lingers over that act. It's a pollution that cannot be absolved. So I think you become morally polluted. Someone who eats flesh cannot be considered spiritually pure. It's a stain that can't be washed away."

Rynn admitted that vegetarians can show "lesser" stains on their souls, but not this "greater" one. Yet if we are morally pure, we are without taint or pollution. Although what is pure is wholly what it is, purity is understood in terms of what it is not. It is defined in terms of what does not defile it; to be pure is to be unadulterated, like distilled water which evaporates without residue. Vegetarians, indeed, are often seen as abstemious, ascetic, and empty: pure. When Heraclitus cryptically stated: "The dry soul is wisest and best,"[2] he might have meant that any lingering miasma or pollution has evaporated away.

Meat eating itself is considered by some to be unclean, and those who forsake it, unsullied. Like children who wash scrupulously before meals, some vegetarians seem to expect a karmic return on their conscious investment, a reward for their sanitary habits. Sometimes they sound saint-like, even when silent. "If I sacrifice enough," they seem to say, "I'll be healthy. If I deprive myself, I'll be full." But it is unhealthy health which requires denial, and fullness can be the inflation of a false pride. Thus, ironically, the very thing we think scrubs us clean can be the thing which stains us, as if we washed with a soap laced with an indelible dye. The question then becomes: Which is the greater blemish—eating flesh, or being self-righteous?

Vegetarians commonly say that they do not judge others, yet they may feel superior to others, and to feel superior is to judge. To think we are better means we think others are worse: this is a simple matter of logic. To say, "Flesh eaters can be good, even so," is condescending; it is as though they must make up for their failing by being better in some other way. When we condescend, we put others below us, and the heavier the moral burden of proof we place on them, the harder it will be for them to look up, as we look down on them, from on high. Looking down on others is just as bad as having power over them, and for the same reason: when we admire vegetarians as "higher," we are still mired in hierarchy.

Freud thought that cleanliness was a tell-tale mark of civilization. Vegetarians perhaps believe, viscerally, if not cognitively, that flesh eaters are not so much below us as behind us, less advanced, more primitive, waiting to catch up. It is sometimes said that there are two kinds of people in the world—vegetarians and "pre-vegetarians." But if we think that we are relatively more civilized, then we think others are relatively more savage and unclean. If the vegetarian is the prototype of the perfect person, where the arrow of spiritual evolution is pointing, then others can only be left behind.

The connection between vegetarianism and sex—or rather the denial of sex—Freud would have been quick to note. Abstaining from flesh is not, of course, the same as no longer wanting it. But a vegetarian who is "pure" has supposedly wiped the lust for meat from his soul. There is an obvious parallel with celibacy. Some believe we are polluted by succumbing to the pleasures of the flesh; others that we are polluted by eating it. Yet forgoing flesh for which we long gives no one a moral edge, for it is only a form of repression, a monument to a buried desire.

That we sit down to our vegan dinners to decide that flesh eaters can be good people does not flatter us. How well we live our vegetarianism is more important than what we are or what others are not. With the examples of our own lives, we either draw people to us, or drive them away. We should want it said of us, "If more people were like ...., there would be more vegetarians"—and not the reverse. We should consider that it might be better to be an "open" flesh eater than a "closed" vegetarian. Vegetarianism practiced out of pride is simply not good for us.

Post-vegetarians talk much more freely about purity, self-righteousness, elitism, and ego than present ones, for they have no reason for *mauvais foi* (self-deception) or denial. They can look back at who they were from a distance which delineates details once too close and/or too painful to descry. Contrasting how they once spoke about their vegetarianism and how they now speak is edifying.

Some vegetarians say they feel "light." If eating plants (who live on light) makes us feel light, then how do we feel eating animals again? Do we begin to feel heavy? If we feel heavy, can we feel healthy? Can a former vegetarian ever feel *as* light again? ROBBAN said: "Initially, I began to feel a little lighter and a little cleaner." BARBARA said: "When I think of being a vegetarian, I think of 'light' and 'happy.' My body sings better as a vegetarian. There is something uplifting about it—feeling lighter. I feel I am singing or vibrating on a happier frequency. I'm open to the possibility that our bodies vibrate at very different frequencies, and I know from myself that there is a lighter frequency in my body when I'm eating vegetarian."

Others seem to have *seen* the light—a sacred, hallowed light—and speak of vegetarianism in religious terms. "My image of myself was that I was becoming more holy. I felt proud, self-sacrificing, self-righteous, holier-than-thou." (VICKY) "I felt very holy, and very, very good. That was my goal. My goal was to become enlightened." (ROBBAN) Sometimes vegetarians seek followers. "There was a real sense of trying to convert other people, of needing to proselytize, because I felt so strongly about it myself." (BARBARA)

Many spoke in terms of purity. JONATHAN said: "Meat eating would be like falling off the wheel of life: this was bad karma to eat meat. That would be a really serious moral slip. My image of myself was that I was becoming purer all the time, that there was an inner transformation going on which was definitely helping my spiritual development. It was a good feeling. It felt very right for me. I never had any feeling of having to backtrack or backpedal; this felt right. I felt I was becoming more spiritual." DAVID agreed: "I was purer. I think one of the karmic consequences of eating meat is that you're dealing with all these animals who are also striving to thrive and prosper in the world. There is a karmic consequence to eating meat."

PETER said: "My consciousness would be formed, in part, by what I ate. I would feel clean and pure." JOHN said: "I have worn the scarlet letter 'V' and it became almost like a cross I was carrying. Steak would have been the greatest failing, the greatest fall from grace into grease. There is a sense of philosophical purity that comes from vegetarianism."

Many lapsos felt they were once elitist and "above" others. KIVA said: "I think a lot of people who are vegetarians, who are very strict in a lot of their views, elevate themselves over people, in saying they are more aware; they are more intellectual; they are more ethical; they are more spiritual; they are more moral. I think that people use it to boost their own ego, and I think I did that to a certain extent. I knew something other people didn't know. It was also my badge, like my badge that made me different from everyone. Spiritually, I felt some hubris. I felt spiritually superior. There was a certain amount of pride, a certain amount of pride."

NANCY said: "I looked down on meat eaters in my idealistic youth. I thought they were stupid and ignorant. I thought [meat eating] was totally wrong, totally repellent." GAIL said: "I saw meat eaters as crass, a little crass. There was a little bit of distance. I didn't use it to climb up on a pedestal, or put down anybody; but I felt they were a little lazy intellectually, a little lazy spiritually, and a little lazy as far as thoughtfulness about their health." JONATHAN remembered "an initial burst of power that I got from switching" and BARBARA that she may have felt "the idea of eating meat was spiritually lower." JOHN said: "Almost any person who does it seriously has a sense of being apart from the mainstream. You can't help but feel that way."

Rynn said: "I'd rather the lesser stains than the greater stain. I'm not judging; well, I guess I am judging; but I don't consider myself self-righteous or superior." Others confessed what Rynn denied. BARBARA said: "There was a touch of self-righteousness about it" and LINDA revealed: "I felt a little bit smug, like I hadn't had meat in so many years, and I'm this wonderful person." JOHN, too, spoke of "the smug, superior sense of self" that he experienced, and said: "I was capable of being shrill and insufferable on the subject. It is the nature of that slightly superior sense of self that is inherent in vegetarianism. It is like the old comic books where there'd be a little angel on one shoulder, and a little devil on the other, and the devil's always the meat eater, and the angel's always the vegetarian."

Self-righteousness sometimes feeds on others' shame and guilt. TONY said: "Recently [at a dinner] a young vegetarian tried to make sure that anyone eating meat at the meal was going to go through all kinds of guilt. 'Dead things! That thing was walking!' they said. I guess I was probably as obnoxious as that. I rate a ten as being as obnoxious as everyone else." VICKY shared: "One of my boyfriends in college was the major influence in my becoming vegetarian. He was a converter—the kind of vegetarian that wants everyone else to be one, too, and doesn't mind making others feel damned guilty. He was the kind of person who could enjoy a raw sweet potato (with the skin on!) as if it were an apple. My housemates used to go to McDonalds and one was the obnoxious type of vegetarian who would tell you while you were eating, 'Oh, I don't eat *flesh*.' They say it in this way so you will be repulsed, and you know they intend you to get repulsed—but *they* might be a good person."

A vegetarian may be a rebel in search of a cause. For those who are young, incompletely formed in character, or insecure, identity with an "ism" can fill a great void. Indeed, the desire to be different which often accompanies the desire for affiliation, can mask a desire to be noticed, to be able to criticize, to aggrandize the self, and to belittle others. Here vegetarianism becomes not only a matter of elitism, but also a matter of ego.

TONY said: "We bring a large degree of ego into this, even if it's a healthy experiment. Vegetarianism seemed like a good course because the people were all pretty benign, but of course there were very egoistic people who were vegetarian for other reasons—like to be *different*—but not really follow a benign philosophy which I think would have great empathy toward other people, rather than being exclusive, selective, exclusionary as some vegetarians are. I was look-ing for something to grab onto, like we all do when we're at a certain age. We start to wear different hats and costumes. We're constantly looking for something. I was looking for an image; I had no image."

NANCY admitted: "I used vegetarianism as a badge of honor. I think people who have had a hard time fitting in, especially in high school and in junior high school, would use things that made them different, because if you're different enough, you can't be rejected." KIVA agreed: "It made me different from everyone else. I defined a lot of my personality, and an important part of my self-identity, that way because I was one of the few vegans in high school, and I was very different. I was the spokesperson for veganism." JONATHAN said: "You're more rebellious. On Thanksgiving, there was a lot of resis-tance to my not having turkey. It was the big conversation: 'He's not eating the turkey! He doesn't want to eat the turkey!'" FRANK said, somewhat darkly: "I think vegetarianism is sometimes a control is-sue, even for myself: it's a self-denial thing. Life is so out of control; if you can control one thing, you can get something from it."

After they begin eating meat again, lapsed vegetarians change —often dramatically. They seem to have mellowed, grown older and wiser, found the *meden agan* (the middle way), the Tao, the line of least resistance. They accommodate others, placing the relational before the radical, people before principles. They become more ho-listic, and often more humane. They make excuses not so much for who they are but for who they once were. Sometimes there is strug-gle, conflict, and guilt; but the process seems to be the dynamic one of growth, rather than a weakened wilting. They are not so much corrupted, like Yuppies, mocking their moneyless days, as they are awakened, like the Buddha, to the narrowness of their former ways. They do not argue that meat eating is right, but abandon right and wrong as divisive. They do not abandon ideals, but replace them, often going through a ruthless process of self-examination. They see the world they once inhabited as relatively small and tight, and move into an expanded one, thinking more for themselves, and less as they are told by others.

TONY said: "As I see it now, as I'm older, elitism is such a danger. The *I Ching* says, 'The gentle penetrating wind can go where nothing else can.' And to understand that is very important. When we're young, we all have this revolutionary quality and we choose rebellious ways. What we do, in essence, by soapboxing, is to alienate more people than we ever convert. As we get older, we find that the idea is not to alienate people if you believe something strongly, and believe in it for good reasons. The idea is to communicate rather than to alienate. The only way you can communicate is by being spiritually in a good place—being able to love people, as opposed to doing it because you hate people.

"When I was younger, abandoning vegetarianism would have made me feel like I had betrayed myself, like cutting my hair off after I had grown long hair. But older and wiser, I see it doesn't matter if you're bald or have a full head of hair. It really doesn't matter. I found that certain things were no longer important—long hair, short hair, eating meat, not eating meat, this, that, or the other thing. I see vegetarianism in two lights. I see vegetarians as spiritual, some quite humorous, and others doing it to be elitist. You come into the humorous category. These are the people who go through our lives not bothering anybody. They are very Felliniesque. I think what's really important is to create a harmony in the situation that we're in. If I create a harmony by eating meat, then it really doesn't bother me. I never want to get into an 'ism' again."

JONATHAN said: "I was never a zealot. I never took to haranguing people or putting people down, because, after all, I knew that I, too, was a non-vegetarian in the midst of my spiritual revolution, before I changed over. So I knew you could be spiritual and have all the feelings of purity without being vegetarian. Now the emotional charge has diminished. There's definitely been a shift; I've become more moderate. It would be nice to be living that ideal life. I do make compromises, but I accept it fairly well. Spiritually, you have to look at your whole life. Someone could be a vegan, but could be a nasty, cruel person. Someone could be slightly less perfect in diet, but live their life in the right way. I don't feel guilty. I don't feel that I'm less in tune. I feel better, actually, even if I'm taking on some spiritual negativity from eating this animal. Even if I am taking on a detriment from eating this flesh food, it is overridden by the positive energy I can generate."

NANCY said: "I still do proselytize about it, but there are certain parts of it, in the proselytizing, that I now see as false. We're all on the same path. Everyone who is seeking spirit is seeking spirit, and who is to judge the righteous path? Sometimes we have to change direction to get to the same spot, and if making too much of a diet makes you judgmental, then it is not the diet you should be on, because a diet should *open* you. It should make you inclusive; it should make you compassionate. It should make you non-judgmental, because that's what makes you spiritual.

"I hate judgment more than anything else. We can't see the whole picture. We see such a little teeny part of it. If you're on the path, you're on the path. That to me sums up everything. We change. I'm not the person I was twenty years ago. And then all the feelings I went through—the shame, the guilt, feeling almost like I had to closet myself. This is totally ridiculous. Like someone with a handicap is more than their handicap. Some are so quick to judge others on only part of what they are. Are we so fixated on only one aspect of becoming a spirit that we don't see the forest for the trees? Who's to say that someone who spends twelve hours a day doing environmental work who eats fish or chicken is any less spiritual than the person who doesn't eat meat and works in an office? I still have this shame and guilt. The badge of honor isn't there anymore, and I have to struggle with it. But we have to do what we have to do in life. There's a message that somehow the universe is making me have to make this choice."

KIVA said: "I had to really examine myself and realize how much part of my personality being vegan was and feeling like I've failed and betrayed myself. Now I feel I've come to terms with the fact that it is worse for someone to be one hundred per cent vegan and judgmental toward others, than for someone to eat hamburger every day and be very open to everyone. If I'm healthy, I can *be* more, and I need to be one hundred per cent in this world. I'd rather be healthy than morally better. You can only be so morally strong. If you define yourself as being a vegan, if that is who you are, then you'll set yourself up for a fall, and you fell if you finally decide to change."

ROBBAN said: "Sometimes I'll read a book, like *The Celestine Prophecy,* and get a little twinge of guilt, like I should be vegetarian, and I think, 'No!' Vegetarianism was highly recommended to me to balance myself physically and as the best way to get in touch with a higher spiritual level. I was doing it because it was the right thing to do. It had been recommended for my spiritual growth. Now when someone says, 'What's good for me is good for everyone,' I really take issue with it. I bought into that rigid way of thinking. It felt more like it was externally imposed than something I would have chosen on my own. It is better to live in the moment and in the situation, and do what's appropriate or what feels appropriate at the time. That makes more sense than to get into this rigid type thinking. There are rabid vegetarians and macro-psychotics, and there are people who are moderate—eating more or less like a vegetarian, and not taking it as a religion."

PETER agreed: "I am less concerned with my actions than with my consciousness, which isn't to say that I don't care about my actions, but I tend to be a little too solipsistic. I've incurred all sorts of karmic debt. Eating animals would not be one that would be high on my list. I respect vegetarians' sensitivities in these issues, but it kind of gets in the way of their lives. I think for some people vegetarianism comes out of a rigidity which is not healthy. There are certain people who force themselves into little holes, and are very unhealthy because of it. One of my friends in the macrobiotic community calls these people 'macro-neurotics.' And it's a perfect word. It's a *very* perfect word. They're not what they eat, and they're going to waste a lot of energy and time and money on matters of food out of proportion to its importance in life. There's an importance to those things—but it's taken out of proportion."

While GAIL admitted simply: "I'm not one to put myself in a real difficult situation for spiritual reasons" and called herself a "pragmatist," for BARBARA the transition was difficult and painful. "To me, the earth is a friend—the trees and the grass and the plants. I have the very strong feeling that by eating meat, I am betraying a friend, like I'm not doing my part to sustain the world that I love so much, my natural surroundings. When I was a child, my best friends were the trees and the rocks. Eating meat is like breaking that connection with my best friends. It feels like breaking clam shells as a child; you know, oh, dear, there's some kind of shattering going on there. I feel very uncomfortable. I feel very guilty about it. My soul is weeping; I can feel the tears, talking about this with you. I really feel that we've touched on the essence of my struggle."

VICKY said: "We all feel so guilty, we don't want to talk about it"; but others talked about it eloquently without remorse or shame. Both DAVID and ROLF ended vegetarianism for essentially philosophical reasons—DAVID to escape the snare of self-righteousness and ROLF the trap of taking the moral high ground.

DAVID said: "One of the things that made me fall from being a strict vegetarian was the realization that I felt self-righteous about it. And I realized I was completely wrong. It was really distorted and it was hurtful to have that perspective. From one side, I approach vegetarianism as a moral issue, and the moral issue caused me more pain than good because it established GOOD and BAD. There were *good* things to do, and *bad* things to do, and I realized that it had more negative effects on me than positive. It's painful to look back on it and think about the sorts of decisions I made on moral grounds, and how immoral what I did was. I'm embarrassed about that now. It shows a really immature way of looking at life and experience. As I've gotten older, I realize how complex relationships are, and that deciding things on simple moral grounds is not always right. It creates that good/bad line dichotomy that's really a painful thing. One of the problems of the spiritual life is creating this good/bad.

"I became increasingly disgusted with my self-righteousness. People who have strong concepts of good and bad are very important in our evolution as a culture and a community; but it can be *personally* very poisoning. If you look at some of these people, some of them led incredibly tortured lives. These people had really beautiful principles, but had very difficult lives. One of the aspects of a spiritual life is having a better understanding of our relationships, and trying to move to relationships that are less painful and more meaningful. People who have some artificial moral standard by which they live their lives—it will necessarily be a really difficult journey for them.

"Sometimes people make philosophical choices that do not show respect. It's a mental rather than an integrative process. Putting on my Buddhist hat, my Buddhist hat says that the real challenge in life is to live with real intimacy, to understand the effect of our relationships and actions in the world. Are they bringing about beauty and nurturance in our life, or are they bringing about pain?

"I feel that from a spiritual standpoint, I've grown. How many people say that? Not from eating meat, but because of the process I went through, and understanding how I got myself on the high moral ground. I don't have moral feelings on it anymore. Initially, it was a very good thing, but it was increasingly painful for me to do. I had to get back and re-explore why I was doing it. As a Buddhist, you have to give up your sense of individual pursuit, and have some sort of more global understanding, and embrace the aspect of our life, that is, all lives. So the issues become more complex."

ROLF said: "I've always been on guard against taking a moral high ground position on vegetarianism. I eat meat at least once a year to avoid the sin of purity. I think it's very dangerous to think of oneself as pure. An example of that might be Yogi Desai's belief, evidentially, that he had conquered his own sexuality, and was above that. I think it's a fatal moral flaw to think one has overcome something like that. There's a kind of self-righteousness that I have found in vegetarians that bothers me. I don't want to align myself with that. That would trouble me. I'm very distrustful towards anyone, including myself, when I find them taking the high moral ground. I always have to be on guard with that for myself.

"It's this distrust of purity that I have—the fear of making my behavior an accusation. I don't want to say 'No!' to nature and to the body and to the flesh. I don't want to get above it. I don't want to rise above it. I want to say 'Yes!' to it as fully and deeply as possible. At least the way I see it, my task in this world is to learn to love life in and through the flesh, and not to see it as preparation for something else. It may be—or may not be. I don't know; but to take it as it is. We live in the world. I think we've got to recognize that we are *animals* living in the world.

"Sometimes ethical thinking becomes shallow and sentimental, not wanting to accept the fact that destruction is part of life and essential to it. One of the things that makes me skeptical of the whole New Age Movement is that they want to think solely in terms of light and spirit, and not recognize the shadow, and the destructive side of ourselves and of nature. I think both have to be seen, squarely, and affirmed. There is a goody-goody sort of innocence —and I distrust morality based on innocence."

It is good that we do not wish to contribute to suffering, violence, and pain: there is nothing wrong with wanting to be good. Nor is there anything wrong with wanting to be better than we are. There is only something wrong with wanting to be better than others. It is not right to be self-righteous; one ought to feel bad catching oneself feeling so morally good. Not only meat, but also moralizing can be overdone; some prefer meat overdone to overdone moralizing.

When one is doing what most others do not do, when one believes that one is in possession of knowledge that most others do not have, it is easy to feel superior. But neither present vegetarians nor post vegetarians are pure. Philosopher Michael Allen Fox says that the purpose of morality is not to make us "perfect and pure";[3] but he could have said that the purpose of anything cannot be to make us pure because, as humans, we are not perfectible.

Vegetarianism is not, ipso facto, either good or bad, corrupting or redeeming. To think otherwise is either to place an impossible burden upon it, or to blame it unfairly. Vegetarianism in itself can make no one good, although it can make us feel good about ourselves, and sometimes make us healthy; but the way we practice vegetarianism can make us both good and healthy. Thus there is a virtue in vegetarianism—not in what it is, but in how we live it.

3

Vegetarianism and Virtue

"The fact that a virtue is good in itself is not enough;
it is necessary to take account of the vices that it entails
and the virtues that it excludes."
—Bertrand Russell

When Spinoza concluded his *Ethics:* "All things excellent are as difficult as they are rare," he wasn't talking about steak, but about virtue. And when anthropologist Marvin Harris took the expression, "Man cannot live by bread alone,"[1] to imply that we also need to eat meat, between the slices, as it were, he forgot that what we need in addition to our bread is virtue.

Ethics is about both character and action, about who we are and are becoming, and about what we do in the world. People and practices are not, however, as separate as they are in our philosophies. How we act makes us who we are. Our actions create our characters, and out of our characters, "characteristically," flow our actions. If we practice hard enough, we will become who we want to be.

Philosophers separate ways of judging actions and ways of appraising character ("act ethics" and "virtue ethics") and not without reason, for "What makes an action right?" and "What makes us good?" are different questions, separable, although not unrelated. A good person can sometimes do the wrong thing ("uncharacteristically") and a lifetime of wrong actions will not produce a virtuous person. The "ethical" vegetarian believes that meat eating is *wrong*. This is an act ethics stand. A virtue ethicist might claim that there is no virtue in eating meat, and that our choosing to do so is, under certain circumstances, a vice. Insofar as I am interested in people, I am interested not in "act" but in "virtue" ethics—a somewhat artificial distinction, but a fruitful focus. Morality, it would seem, can be either inorganic or organic.

Right actions may be done for the wrong reasons. Motives may be misanthropic; a mantle of apparent virtue may conceal hatred or rage, disgust, disdain, or rancor. Such actions may help the world, but they improve no one. Choosing vegetarianism, for example, as a way to distance and devalue others, or out of vanity or pride, does not make us good, although subsequent actions, such as boycotting factory farms, may bring good into the world. Ideally, we aim both to be good and to do good. Being good without doing good may involve *akrasia* (moral weakness); doing good without being good is a form of hypocrisy. If we are good, chances are that we will do good; but we cannot know whether anyone is good from actions alone.

Because I am interested in people, and not in acts out of context, I am interested in virtue, and because I am interested in vegetarianism, I am interested in whether vegetarianism is a virtue. I am not so much interested in whether meat eating is "wrong" as I am in whether it hurts our character. If we find that meat eating, under certain conditions, can corrupt us, and agree that whatever corrupts us is wrong to do, then we do not need arguments based on animal welfare, rights, or on pain and suffering to show that meat eating is wrong. We need only to show that by eating meat, we are not the best we can be.

So I do not ask: Is meat eating wrong to do? but Are people who eat meat wrong to do it? The issue isn't whether factory farms or rain forest ranches are bad, but what makes a person good. Can we be the best we can be and still eat flesh? Is flesh eating a character flaw? What kind of person does it make us into? Does it make us bad? If we were vegetarian, and revert to eating meat, have we taken a downslide? Are we morally weak? If we have a genuine choice in full knowledge, and eat meat, are we defective somehow?

Arguing that the industrialization of meat is wrong is easy. Arguing that modern meat endangers human health and ecosystems is easy. The more subtle issues are not in practices but in people, inside the meat eaters themselves—not in their stomachs or their guts, but in their very being. If a practice is wrong, are those who support it guilty? If we knowingly procure meat produced obscenely, are we complicit? If I admit there is something wrong with the system and support it, is there something wrong with me?

Virtues and vices of people are far more interesting than actions out of context. Whether you are an honest person is more important for me to know than the fact that you once lied, or even that, so far, you have always told the truth. Until I know the situation, and the act as you saw it, I know very little. You may have told the truth only because it was expedient. You may have lied to spare a life—and if you did, then I commend you, and condone your action. How we do things is more important than what we do: in *how* we do lies our virtue.

It is much harder to see how people are doing than what they are doing, and it is much safer to speak about actions in general than about people in particular circumstances; but it is not by doing kinds of actions, or even specific things, that we become virtuous. Eating meat or not, giving to the poor or not, recycling or not, tell us only about what we do, but not about who we are. Acts out of context shed no light on character.[2] The reluctant giver is not virtuous, although giving is a virtue. The brutally honest person is not virtuous, although honesty is a virtue. Virtue, as a standard or ideal, inspires acts; being or becoming virtuous requires traits. Virtue is defined, "dispositionally," in terms of what we are predisposed to do; it is what flows from our character. Virtue itself is a marker or ideal; being virtuous is what we live on the inside in response to the ideal on the outside. We do not become good by giving, but by becoming generous.

How are we to measure people? Or ought we to measure them at all? Although virtue ethicists make moral judgments, they do not pass judgment; but we can ask what traits, in general, make people good or bad. How we weigh our lives against the lives of others shows in how we choose our food, as unlikely as this first appears. How many psychologists start here? How many philosophers? How many priests? What we eat is taken to be a matter of personal choice (ironically, "taste") and/or cultural convention, and few of us make our food food for thought. Indeed, what we eat unconsciously and unconsidered, is food for naught. If we bring value judgments to bear on it, these are commonly found in restaurant reviews rather than in spiritual self-help books or personality primers. Finding the best eatery is apparently more important than finding the best philosophy; searching for fillet of sole more important than soul searching.

It is easy to think one is good when one does something which takes willpower. Being able to resist meat on moral grounds is considered a sign of character, for willpower is itself taken to be a virtue, a sign of personal and/or moral strength. VICKY said: "A vegetarian who is revolted at the thought of meat certainly has an easier time of living up to his ideals. An interesting thing about Dr. Doolittle is how he admits what a temptation meat is for him. He is particularly commendable because he overcomes his will."

Vegetarianism may be a response to high ideals. We say we live "up" to our convictions; no one used the metaphor of looking "down" on vegetarianism, but many talked of looking "up," seeing it as elevating us in some way. ROLF said: "Vegetarianism represents a higher consciousness than meat eating, taken by itself." VICKY said: "I looked up to vegetarians because they lived their values, and didn't just have values, as I did at the time. I had values, but I didn't always live them."

Former vegetarians often express an attitude of admiration for those who continue what they did not. JOHN said: "I found vegetarians quite admirable. Talk about stick-to-it-ness! When I read about a celebrity (as I often do in one of my lines of work) who is a vegetarian, I think, 'Hats off to them! Here's a better person. Here's someone who has apparently thought about something.' And in celebrities, that's always nice to see." VICKY said: "My view of people who practice a vegetarian diet is one of admiration. I found it difficult to be one, and I admire people who can keep it up." ROBBAN said: "If vegetarianism is part of being really, fully yourself, then I admire people who live up to what they believe in enough that they are consistent with it. When vegetarianism enables you to be more perfectly you, it's a virtue."

Being more perfectly oneself, or approximating one's own ideal of a perfect person may not, however, involve vegetarianism. A colleague wrote to me: "I remember reading a letter to the editor in *Vegetarian Times*. The author of the missive had been a vegetarian on ethical grounds. She then became a born-again Christian. Having taken Jesus as the perfect moral examplar, and given that Jesus was a documented omnivore, she thought it blasphemous to remain an 'ethical vegetarian.' After all, that would imply a moral shortcoming of Jesus."[3]

Some, like DAVID, look to a spiritual leader like the Buddha (who he believes ate meat) to justify their lapses from vegetarianism, and others look to Christian exemplars to find what they ought to be themselves. VICKY said: "Does Mother Teresa eat meat? Let's see what she's doing. She's a really good person . . . I wish that Jesus had said more about animals in the Bible, because I would follow his behavior." Those who wish to become good often look to those they consider better for inspiration; but if their moral mentors eat meat, they cannot consider vegetarianism, in itself, a virtue. Either the greats are less than great, or vegetarianism is not needed to perfect those of lesser virtue. Some say that the greats (like Christ and the Buddha) were vegetarian; but they do not close the issue, because some "saints," like Mother Teresa, eat meat.

We do not consider eating meat elevating, but often degrading; at best, it is considered invigorating. If we give in to meat, or give meat up, what do we do when we give up our vegetarianism? If meat eating involves a guilty pleasure because blood must be spilled to satisfy an appetite, then it may be a vice. Scanning the vegetarian literature, I found flesh eating called: "gluttonous"; "unclean"; "wicked"; "ruthless"; "selfish"; "savage"; "unfeeling"; "cruel"; "ugly"; "profane"; and "a desecration."[4] If meat eaters are "bereft of lofty motives"; if we "demean ourselves, coarsen our sensitivities [and] dull our feelings of sympathy with our fellow creatures,"[5] when we eat it, then what do we become when we return to it?

Some former vegetarians refer to their lapses in the language of The Seven Deadly Sins or other vices. We may "lust" for meat, whether or not we eat it. ELLY said: "I've always LOVED meat. I mean, I'm really someone who had to control herself from licking the Thanksgiving turkey. I could have thrown myself at that sucker— quickly, very quickly!" DAVID said: "There's an aspect of people who are meat eaters that is abhorrent to people who are vegetarian. There's a kind of gluttony. People who are called to vegetarianism say these people are 'gluttonous.'" GAIL confided that during one of her vegetarian phases, "The temptation to eat meat was gone," as though flesh eating were a vice: we do not say we are "tempted into" vegetarianism. LINDA called her decision to eat meat again "incredibly self-ish," and ELLY saw some meat eaters as "complicit and hypocritical, suffering from disconnect between what they do and the suffering that was imposed on animals as a result of that habit." If meat eating is a habit, it is considered a *bad* habit.

Some say they are not guilty. MARCIA said: "I admire people who are complete vegetarians, but I don't feel guilty. I just feel a little funny." JONATHAN said: "'Guilt' would be too strong a word. I mean, I do kind of let the thought float by that I should make an effort not to eat this at all; but I don't feel guilty per se." Others do. VICKY said: "Not being a perfect person, I don't always do what I think is the right thing. I don't do what my higher self really wants to, what I value. I sometimes experience pangs of guilt eating meat, knowing that it is just a lack of willpower that makes me do it."

ROCKY said: "When I was working at the factory, night shift, I still stayed vegetarian during that time. I was still very strong. I would try. I was doing my best." Whether eating meat is a vice is moot; but whether flailing is a failing is not. We feel less than our best when we fall short of our ideals: when vegetarianism is one of them, we blame ourselves for our weakness. *Akrasia* is a kind of embarrassment, a nostalgia for vanished virtue. Leontius, in Plato's *Republic*, exemplifies it when, unable to resist the degradation of gazing upon dead bodies killed in public execution, he gives in, crying, "Feast, you damnable eyes, feast!"[6] Unlike Leontius, lapsed vegetarians who feast on what some would call "corpses" do not do so only with their eyes.

Some would say that it is not reverting to meat, but our weakness, which is our defect. Others claim it is both. Rynn agrees with Brigid Brophy that meat eating is a sign of "moral cowardice"[7] and indicts "vegetarian recidivists" as if lapsing were a crime: "Former vegetarians are a lamentable lot. They may not be inherently lamentable, but they are lamentable from my viewpoint because it strikes me that they lack the moral fiber to remain committed to a diet that has ethical and moral implications. For me, reverting is inconceivable. Once one has tasted the ambrosia of meatless cuisine, one can never lapse from it. Once you are sensitized to the issues of animal slaughter and animal exploitation, I think it is morally reprehensible to give vegetarianism up. One has to consider always the life of the animal. Should an animal's life be sacrificed to placate one's cravings? It's all a question of character. It comes down to that." He added: "You can have a wonderful life, and a very productive life, and do good works, and be a morally upright person, but you still have to contend with this defect. So you cannot consider yourself an impeccable specimen of the human race."

Vegetarians are thought to lack neither dietary nor moral fiber; they are strong where others who would like to emulate them are weak. Ideally, theirs is the strength not of force but of courage.[8] Tough people prefer tender loin; tender people prefer tough bran. Courageous vegetarians show a tensile strength rather than a rigid consistency, as DAVID's story shows: "I heard a story about Baker Roshi, who is Suzuki Roshi's heir, who wrote *Zen Mind, Beginner's Mind*.[9] They were driving once in a car, and Baker Roshi said, 'Well, the one thing that I've missed, being a monk, is a good steak.' So they were driving along, and they stopped for dinner, and Suzuki Roshi, who was a complete vegetarian, ordered the largest steak on the menu. As it was explained to me, he was a very small man, a diminutive Japanese, and he went and ate the whole steak to their amazement, and didn't say a word about it. The mentor, who was a complete vegetarian, ordered steak!

"He was showing his disciple: Live a vital life! Don't live life like a coward! Don't hide behind some set of beliefs that is meaningless. Go ahead and eat your steak. See what your experience is. That's what the Buddha taught. What Suzuki was sharing with Baker Roshi was that he had this remnant in his mind, clinging to steak. Evidentially the teacher saw that there was some active process going on in his mind, and he was saying, 'Live life with courage. If this is what is moving your mind, go ahead and see what your experience is.' Buddha really encouraged people to live like outlaws, to do what was reasonable, but to try to deeply understand what their experience was once they did it. So Suzuki Roshi ate the steak that day."

Vegetarianism may be better for us; but we are not better in virtue of our vegetarianism alone, for how we are is more important than what we are, at least insofar as character is concerned. Vegetarianism is not a virtue in itself, because there are reluctant vegetarians, gluttonous vegetarians, "attached" vegetarians, rigid vegetarians. (The advertiser in a lonely hearts magazine who specified, "No smokers, drugs, vegetarians" probably knew a few of these.)[10] Vegetarianism may be a clue to our characters, and in this sense "telling"; but with our characters, we show, not tell. Some tell one thing, and show another. Some tell and show one thing, and hide another.

One vegan who presents himself to the world in words as a modern St. Francis, living meekly on his sprouts, pontificates on the delicate beauty of insects, but in his private life crushes them for no greater crime than partaking of his ornamental flowers, and even plotted to take the life of his neighbor's cat (and succeeded) for no worse crime than eating the birds he himself lured into his yard with feeders. Crushed insects and a cat caught in the sights of a shotgun are skeletons in the closets of vegans who have no bones in their larders.[11] It is said that by our fruits we shall be known; but if I know you eat persimmons and mangoes instead of chickens and cows, how much about *you* do I know? Food supplies calories, not character. Vegetarianism does not itself prove virtue.

Flesh eating may even improve character in some instances. I have a friend who once ate road kills—freshly dead squirrels. What for one driver was hit and run, was for him, an impoverished graduate student, dinner for one. He was not complicit in the animal's death, for he neither hit nor ran from it, but took what was already dead, and because he did not pay for it, encouraged no one to kill squirrels. Thus he was not even indirectly responsible for their deaths. Moreover, in Columbus, Ohio where the fate of a road kill is to sun-dry, flattened on asphalt, it was unlikely that he robbed a nonhuman predator of a meal. Finally, because he was not a vegetarian, his supper "spared" some other animal he might have purchased from a factory farm. If such an act of flesh eating is not wrong, then flesh eating is not always wrong, even in cultures where one has a choice. But did this act harm his character? Because I know him well, I know that it did not: by preventing waste without distaste, by taking responsibility for what he ate, his character was strengthened. He would not have become a better person had he eaten beans.

Many vegetarians admit that people who kill their own meat are better than those who delegate animal deaths to others, and some who kill their own meat refine their characters in surprising ways. I accompanied another friend, a hunter, one Christmas Day, into the woods where he ceremoniously lay an offering of seeds and nuts on each site where he had killed an animal that season. This yearly ritual of his own devising brought back no pheasant or rabbit; but it seemed to make him a better person. Some would say he would have been better yet if he hadn't shot anybody; but given that he had, his offerings seemed to improve him. A cynic would offer that he wished to conserve "game" for his use the next year, but in truth, he wanted to achieve a balance. His principle was that because he had taken from the forest, he would give back to it; because he had taken lives—as we all do, directly or indirectly, to survive—that he would help others to thrive.

The cloak of virtue seems to shorten the more we unravel it at its edges. What once appeared as a simple and sure solution to the problem of living turns out to be amorphous and ambiguous. Giving up meat may or may not improve us: we need the context to decide. Returning to meat may or may not ruin us: we need nuance to know.

Mean motives can lead to praiseworthy practices and to admirable actions; but character is not improved thereby. Vegetarians sometimes do commendable things, but harm themselves and/or others in the process. It is the spirit in which we do things which is important, whether we refuse or return to meat. What do we say about the vegetarian who does not want to offend his Jewish mother, and eats her chicken soup? How do we distinguish between *akrasia* or even sheer cowardice, and empathetic consideration, putting aside a selfish desire to be "better" in favor of a loving gesture? Some say love is more important than diet ("Better a mess of pottage with love than a stalled ox with hatred within.")[12] Others say flesh prepared with affection is better than vegetables prepared with anger. PETER said: "My wife and I have an imperfect relationship, and sometimes when I come home, she fixes my food. If there is disharmony in the relationship, if there is upset for both of us, I will not want to eat the food that she prepares. It's poison for me. And that to me is much more important than whether I'm eating chicken or broccoli."

If we shed blood for our dinners, our hands are not clean; but any vegetarian who finds her hands pristine needs to cultivate her own garden to get them honestly dirty; by growing one—by eating anything—we compete, taking food and/or space away from others. The road to hell may be paved with good intentions; but the road to heaven, if it is paved at all, is made with the same, and differs only with the addition of knowledge to good intent. Not all flaws are character flaws; there are flaws in the world as well, and one type of character flaw is not seeing what and where these are.

In *The Thee Generation*, Tom Regan sees the best people as those who ask, "What can I do for thee?" rather than "What can I do for me?" Concern for others, including nonhuman others, is central. Apart from "a shared sense of community, the self is seen to be an empty shell, the word 'I' the most impersonal of pronouns."[13] We do not become good by focusing inward on ourselves; we improve by focusing out upon the world, by valuing what is outside ourselves, and larger than ourselves. Vegetarianism out of a desire to aggrandize and inflate the self is no virtue.

Existentialist Jean Paul Sartre sees every human choice and action, no matter how private and personal, as if it were made for all persons. We do not literally legislate with our actions, but in being an example, we are also exemplar, shouting in effect, "This is what a human being ought to be!" Into what we make ourselves, we make humanity also, for what lives in us also lives in our species.

A world with humane people in it is better than a world without them, no matter what forces of evil may prevail, and it is a better world where we act naturally than where we try to do the "right" thing. One always fears that where ethics is needed to constrain us, dark motives will erupt or barriers restraining aggression will fail. Where a good will is lacking, law and logic may help, but those in need of law and logic are not the best people, even if they act in morally acceptable ways. Moral constraints are an interim solution as a check on our violence; but we need to change from within if the world is to improve. There is nothing more important to community than character.

In *Zen and the Art of Motorcycle Maintenance*, Pirsig wrote, "You want to know how to paint a perfect painting? It's easy. Make yourself perfect and then just paint naturally."[14] Although "perfect person" is an oxymoron, and although Pirsig was speaking of art, not ethics, there is also an art of living, *technê biou*, living well. Living well has nothing to do with the GNP or with accumulated economic wealth but with our real riches—the beauty of thought, attitude, and action of individual persons.

We sometimes ask of our vegetarianism: "What does it do for me?" but perhaps we should ask instead, "What do I do for it?" A vegetarian who acts out of compassion, for humans and nonhumans alike, contributes much to the world. Refusing to partake in violence may not stop its momentum, but it changes us. We become nonviolent. The actions we bring into the world will be nonviolent. In swimming upstream, we become strong. We may not have the satisfaction of seeing a large measure of harm which we have personally subtracted from the world, but we will have the satisfaction of knowing that we did not add to it. Schopenhauer said in *The Basis of Morality*, "Boundless compassion for all living things is the firmest and most certain guarantee of pure moral conduct."[15] The ethic of vegetarianism is an ethic of compassion; thus it is a virtue ethic, for we cannot do compassionate acts unless we are compassionate people. Hardening ourselves to suffering is bad for us, whether or not it spills out widely into the world, for if we are inured, we are already humans deeply injured, and that is enough.

People who eat flesh flagrantly and callously are not prototypes for what humans ought to be; but former vegetarians are not necessarily bad either. We cannot drive wedges into the flux of the world. There are no "sides" to take. To think there are is to use old, worn out metaphors of war. Vegetarians can be corrupted by their zeal for vegetarianism, and meat eaters by the appeal of meat.

We can still ask: Are vegetarians more virtuous? Are we more peaceful people? Do we commit fewer crimes? Are we more compassionate? Although my experience is anecdotal and needs qualifying, if I had to take my chances in a survival situation with twenty strangers, chosen at random, or with twenty vegetarian strangers, chosen at random, I'd take my chances with the vegetarians. I am aware that there may be among them misanthropes who hate people as much as they love other animals, and that I might well end up in the cooking pot; but fortunately, misanthropic vegetarians are rare. I am also aware of vegetarians who are food faddists and culture clones, swallowing their philosophies whole, like vitamin pills. These could be a problem, because they are too easily swayed; but I would think that those who would not eat lamb or veal would be less likely to want to eat me.

The question is whether there is any causal connection between vegetarianism and character. Are we vegetarian because we are good? Does our vegetarianism make us good, or better? It is not so simple. What logicians call "The Fallacy of the Common Cause" is to miss some third factor to which two things, apparently causally related, are actually related as effects. In the case of vegetarianism, that third factor may be knowledge. In the United States, at least, vegetarians are a relatively highly educated and informed group; so it may not be our characters, but our wider view of the world, which leads us both to our vegetarianism and to our "goodness." Therein lies my qualification, for a random assortment of vegetarians is likely to be a reflective lot. On the assumption that those who see widely are apt to feel deeply, I would choose the company of the random vegetarians.

Just as vegetarianism is not in itself a virtue, meat eating is not in itself a vice; but if we are vegetarian out of compassion, harmlessness, and love, then we are virtuous, not in virtue of our vegetarianism, but in virtue of those virtues which inspire (or even require) it. If we eat meat, we are not thereby cruel or corrupt; but if we eat it mockingly or malevolently, we are vicious, not in virtue of our meat eating, but in virtue of our vices. Only when we know the character of a vegetarian or of a flesh eater can we answer questions about vice and virtue—just as we cannot inquire into the spirituality of lapsos without examining their souls.

4

A Spiritual Pragmatist

*"The understanding cannot recognize
The soul, nor does the soul need other knowledge
To know itself, e'en as a shining light
Requires no light to make itself perceived."*
—Shankara, *Atma-Bodha*

Is what I am becoming "becoming" to me? Virtue has to do with what we are and are becoming; because it has to do with how we live, the virtuous life is dynamic. If virtue is a state of soul, then the soul is work in progress. A virtuous person is like an artist whose medium is character: virtuous people chisel away at it like sculptors. The shape which emerges is just and fair, temperate, compassionate, and courageous; what is cut away is cruelty and callousness, greed, envy, and pride.[1] Some, like Aristotle, conceive of virtue as an individualized mean between the extremes of deficiency and excess in character.

Sometimes we speak in terms of "spirit" instead of "character" or "virtue." If virtue is like shape, spirit is like color. In pursuing excellence, in letting the ideal live in my own being, I take on form; the aura around it, an emanation of my being, is my "soul." Spirit is the hue we wear, not the hue and cry we make about vice and virtue. If we are very, very good, we will be put into a prism for life. Achieving goodness is a matter of virtue or character. How we radiate that goodness to the world is a matter of spirit. Virtuous people are well-defined; spiritual people shine.

So we can ask: If we eat meat, can we be virtuous? Or we can ask: If we eat meat, can we be spiritual? The first is a question of ethics, the second a question of metaphysics. A moral philosopher can pronounce upon virtue and vice; a guru perhaps upon spirit. If we eat meat in a certain way and for certain reasons, we can both harm our character and dim our spirit; if we eat meat in other ways, and for other reasons, we may do neither.

What is it to be spiritual? People with spirit seem to be: non-violent; compassionate; at peace; empathetic; loving; concerned; open; holistic in thinking; sensitive; humble; gentle; healing; seekers of goodness and wisdom; self-possessed and calm. People lacking in spirit seem to be: ego-centric; self-absorbed; pretentious, caught up in things of the world; materialistic; pushy; one-sided; single-issue oriented; closed; full of hatred and anger; immune to the sufferings of others; misanthropic; striving for mastery and control; destructive and/or self-destructive. People full of soul seem suffused with light; people lacking soul seem dim and empty, deep wells of darkness.

The concepts "good," "virtue," and "spiritual" are easily tangled. One "radical vegetarian" claims: "The spiritual life demands a vegetarian diet," but later proclaims: "Not everyone was meant to be a vegetarian." Thus we conclude that not everyone was meant for the spiritual life. Still later he says: "Vegetarians are not a better sort of people."[2] Is this to say that they are not more good (virtuous) or more spiritual? Vegetarians may not be more good overall, and hence not better people; but if only vegetarians can live a spiritual life, on the assumption that living it makes us better than not, we are confused. Either no one lives the spiritual life at all, or vegetarians are better people.

Is it possible to prove that vegetarianism is necessary for the spiritual life? Certainly vegetarianism is not sufficient for it, for many vegetarians are the antithesis of the spiritual. But neither does it seem necessary; SIANNA is the most spiritual person I know, and she eats flesh. Thus vegetarianism seems neither necessary nor sufficient for the spiritual life. If it were both, then and only then, and only on the assumption that people living the spiritual life are better people, would it follow that vegetarians are better people.

Some might argue that we would always be *more* spiritual if we subsisted on plants . . . or on light. But subsisting on plants (or on light) "in the wrong spirit" would make no one spiritual: just as virtue is how we do, spirit is how we are. Because spirit is metaphysical, it is not measurable; because it is, literally, "out of this world," no tools of the world can gauge it. To ask who is more or less spiritual asks for more than who is more or less loving, healing, open, and so forth. These characteristics can be weighed, if not measured; but because spirit is what philosophers call a "supervenient" or "emergent" quality (in this case, how we *express* our virtue) we could add up all the qualities on the soul list and still not come up with spirit.

We can, however, find it by looking it in the face, that is, by looking into faces, from whence it shines. To find spirit, we need to go into the world and meet spiritual people. If virtue is striving, spirit is arriving: It is time to meet SIANNA.

SIANNA has been my friend for more than twenty years. She lives with a yellow cat and a little white dog by the sea, a bright burst of energy and wisdom in her little cottage, a match perpetually struck. Hers was the only interview I could not cut up. Listening to her is somewhat like hearing scripture which one does not dare quote out of context. I do not know who wrote our culture's sacred books, but I can vouch for the veracity and integrity of SIANNA.

As I transcribed our tape, I heard her lovely, lilting voice, as if a flower could speak, and the sound of my own soft weeping as background music for her speech. She asked me to read my list of questions; instead of answering them one by one, like the others, she said: "From the time I was quite young, I had a strong, intuitive, what you'd call 'spiritual life.' At the age of around ten, I began practicing yoga from an intuitive place. I never had contact with anyone who taught or showed or did yoga postures or meditations; but I began to do them spontaneously. And I questioned many of the patterns in my society right from a young age. I questioned the way human beings were working in the world. Being brought up Catholic and being very spiritual and a timid sort of person, I was even thrown out of my Christian Doctrine classes because of questions such as: If there are saints that have existed, why can't we all be saints? And if we are made in the spirit of God, then will we discover how to create life? There were many things I was questioning.

"By the time I was eleven-twelve, around that age, I began to really have a deep, inner pain inside my soul, my spirit, in regards to being a human being, and I *asked*, inside myself, for a direct experience of God so that I could continue in life and because I felt suicidal—not suicidal that I wanted to kill myself—but suicidal out of a sense of desperation that I felt that there was something very wrong in the culture and the society and in the life that I was living on this planet.

"And I made that request, and the day that I made that request, I had what is now called an "out of body experience." What happened is that I was taken into the light. And I looked down at my body that was laying in the bed at the time, and I— it looked just like a stone. And I realized: that's not who I *am*. I realized that I was a conscious being, aside from the body, and that the body was just one means of expression of my consciousness, and I was taken deeper and deeper into the light.

"I saw before me an extremely radiant being, and I took that, having been brought up Catholic, to be the Christ. And around me I was surrounded by numerous beings of light, and I was shown many things. I don't know if I was shown, or if it was just there, and I became aware of that; but I saw that all knowledge is just a field of electrical connections, and that at any time I could know anything simply by tapping into that field. And I saw that all humans are connected by a thread of light, so luminous that 'light' doesn't even begin to describe its essence. The love and the compassion that I felt radiating from the light to me was so profound that I began to beam that light and radiation and love back until I didn't know if it was coming from me or if it was coming to me. I was just one with this extreme power of light.

"I felt so accepted; I felt so accepting. I felt such peace, radiance, and at the same time, such vital energy, so alive that no earth experience has *ever* since then come *close* to that. I wanted to just continue on into the light, and I found myself, however, entering the mud-body that was mine—because to me, that's how it looked—just like a stone—like a piece of earth—and I found myself entering in, and I do not know whether I chose to come back or was sent back: I still don't know.

"But I found myself in the body, activating, and myself in the body again, and I woke up. And I was, as I say, I was around eleven or twelve or thirteen. I think it was around eleven-twelve; but at that time when I began, there was no one to speak to of this experience, and it was something so profound that I was wise enough not to try to talk to people who would not understand.

"What I did was I began to question everything within my Catholic religion. I started to study Buddhism; I started to study Hinduism. I went to the library and got various books on different religions, and began a study of a lot of different religions, trying to find that light within them and being discouraged when I read any *commentary* and encouraged when I read the *Bhagavad-Gita* or I read any of the texts of—quotes from—the Buddha or the Bible; I would go into an altered state, and I would get awareness about the human condition.

"It was around that time—actually, it was prior to that time—when actually I was about eight years old, that I had sensations that there was no need for me to eat any physical substance, that I could survive on light. I remember sitting on a stone in the back of my house, a big stone, and just putting my arms out to the light, and feeling that was the ultimate way to be fed. *After* the experience of being taken into the light, I was *convinced* that was all I needed for nourishment. However, I was incarnate, and I had all the physiological patterns of the family and the culture I was in, although I found myself not wanting to eat meat when my parents would push it on me; but it wasn't that I didn't want to eat meat; I didn't want to eat vegetables; I didn't want to eat anything.

"It all seemed awfully *gross*, and I felt more pain upon eating a vegetable than upon eating meat, certain types of meat, simply because I felt a closer connection with the life-force within the vegetables than I did with the animals, because of the ways in which the animals had been conditioned and treated: they has lost some of that essence within themselves.

"That was just my experience that I felt more aggravation eating certain substances. So I meditated on it, and what came to me was that everything I ate from then on I would ask that it would be like a blessing, that somehow, because I was incarnate—and although I didn't really want to be (I wanted to be in the light)—but since I was incarnate, I felt that there were higher forces that wanted me incarnate, and so being incarnate, that I would choose to bless everything that I ate—*everything* I ate, including the salt that I sprinkled on my food, that the salt was crystals, and the crystals, were—they had consciousness—and I was aware of the consciousness of the salt crystals even as I put them on my food, and aware that the salt my parents were using was not pure salt, but was salt that had been hurt. And I felt the pain of the crystals. So I began to bless everything, and so that when it entered into my body (and I use the word 'bless' because of my Catholic background)—but I would, you know, as a food came into me: Let me use it to bring the light and consciousness into the *human* condition. And that began the foundation of all— everything for years to come, whenever I would eat anything.

"And there were times when I was not so connected, when I got caught into the human drama of, you know, growing up, or relationships, or work, and I would kind of lose a conscious thread; but it was always there on some level. I would always return to it. When I was on my own, I got out of the house, my parents' house, then I began to eat vegetarian. It was just—it wasn't *even* something I thought about. I just—when I went shopping, I just tended to want to eat more light foods.

"The problem was I wasn't getting the nutrients I needed for my body. I've always been a little bit sickly; I have always had a delicate system, a highly sensitized system, and I'm aggravated (at least I have been growing up) by harsh emotions, intense energies, extreme mental energies. I was in universities; I was in a family where there was a lot of education, and the mental realm was very harsh on my system, because it felt very bullyish, very, very violent on a psychic level. And so I was constantly being badgered on the inner world, even though in those days I couldn't quite verbalize it. And my body was quite sickly because I was fighting off all these energies that seemed to me so cruel and coarse. And so when I was on my own, I started eating vegetarian. I was just drawn to it; it was just—light; it felt better.

"I was a strict vegetarian when I was in my early twenties for awhile—actually, I think it was my later teens—it's hard for me to remember—for about two years. Then I went back to lacto and ovo; I ate a couple of, you know, and egg every now and then. Oh—it's very hard for me to remember; I'd say another couple of years, a year, a *year*. At the beginning, there were some books out—oh, what's that Japanese tradition—macrobiotics—and so I became interested, and I started to feel that it seemed like an appropriate path.

"I also, at that time, was young, and had not developed fully my psychological self. I was swayed by fads at the time, and I felt that if more human beings ate vegetarian, that perhaps there would not be so much violence. I have since then come to realize that it's not what we eat; it's what we think, and our thinking *then* is a consequence of what we eat. So when that occurred to me, I started teaching classes because I realized—I started teaching classes because I was asked to teach classes.

"I was trained as an artist and people would come and talk to me about my artwork or about artwork or I would be teaching art classes in my home, or in other people's homes, or I'd offer them in halls, and people would start asking me about art, and whenever I talked about art, it seemed that it went into some kind of mystical trend, and people were fascinated. And so I was—more and more people began to ask me to teach classes and more and more people started coming to me for guidance—inner guidance, to connect with their own inner spirituality.

"And as a result of being taken into the light, or perhaps, even before—I am not sure—I have been what they call very 'clairvoyant.' I don't like the use of the word 'psychic'; I think I would prefer 'sensitive.' I am extremely sensitive on many realms. And as a result, people are aware of that in me, and sometimes not even aware that they are aware, will come to me for some kind of guidance. And I know that, and I feel that we are all one, and as long as one person is suffering, and one person isn't aware of who they are, and how spiritual they are, and how beautiful they are, then I suffer; they suffer; we all suffer. So out of that, I'm motivated to work with people who come to me, to the best of my ability.

"I was attacked brutally, and I was robbed one evening, and it was really my intuitive powers that saved my life, because the attacker was waiting for me at my doorstep, and so I intuited something, but I didn't know at the time. My rational mind was not in control, and my intuitive mind became very sharpened. And I crept behind the bushes in front of the apartment building I was living in which was—I'd never done that before—and because I did that, not knowing *why* I was doing it, I caught the man off-guard and he was not able to do any more damage than give me a good bump on the head and steal my money. And because I screamed, and miraculously, people came to my rescue, I was saved.

"I started eating meat after I was attacked; I began eating small amounts; my intuition told me I needed to eat meat. I felt that I was becoming too light and that I needed to ground myself, because I was incarnate, and I needed to work on the planet, and I had not learned to function as an ego. I was somehow ego-less, and it took me many years of going back and forth from vegetarianism back to meat, chicken, fish—it was—I followed my intuition.

"I look at food, especially the meats, and many vegetables, I look at that as medicine. And I found when I was called upon to do more and more consultations with people having to do with their spirituality and their inner realm, that I needed some form of—my particular metabolism and my particular blood type— and I do feel, Karuna,[3] that a lot has to do with our blood types, our heritage, that we have different blood types, and there are some blood types that need the proteins from the meat in order to function in the human incarnation—and others do not.

"And I feel that that's something that people can only know by going into deep meditation. And *unfortunately,* most people don't do that. And sometimes it changes, depending on those circumstances surrounding. And I would find that although I may be choosing to be in a vegetarian state, that if I had a lot of people coming to me who were pulling on—I don't mean 'pulling on'—that sounds very 'martyrdom' and I don't mean to sound that way—but if my energies became very involved with theirs, that in order to keep myself so I could actually *function*, in other words, walk, talk, answer the 'phone, make my bed etc., I would have to have some kind of animal protein so that I could even relate to these people without totally giving my—you know, totally losing my *own* life.

"So I use it as medicine. Another thing that has occurred in my life is that I've gotten very, very ill. Three times, I've gotten very, very ill with virus infections and in poisoning from chemicals in the environment where I literally have been bedridden. I have been very, very ill. And this—this last time which was about six years ago, where I could not walk for almost two years, except for maybe one day a week. I was crawling, and very—extremely ill. Fevers—high fevers—and chills and swollen glands caused me so much trouble that I didn't even know how to spell my name or remember my 'phone number—extreme illness. I found that I *craved* red meat and that I needed it periodically, and that I would actually feel better after I ate it; so I used it as medicine. And I continue to do so when I feel the need.

"And I bless the animals; I really bless the animals. *I bless everything I eat.* I just continue to pray that whatever I take into my body as a human being, that all of the life-force of the carrots, and the celery, and the potatoes, and the squashes, and the lovely raspberries and blueberries, and the wonderful spices of—oh—those wonderful energies of the little peppers and the parsleys, and the basil and all, including the salt (and now I do use a pure salt)—and all these wonderful energies that have such *consciousness*. A carrot has consciousness. It is *the* consciousness of the carrot. And there's nothing else in the universe that has the consciousness of a carrot. And there's nothing that has the consciousness of celery. Celery is celery, and it's magnificent in its pattern, in its growth, in its greenness. And when I take these foods into *my body, my body* is then incorporating these *wonderful* consciousnesses, these wonderful different patterns of creation, and to me it's a mystery, and it's a *great gift*.

"I don't feel *ever* that anything I take into my body, even when it's at some compulsive moments when you eat to stuff an emotion—even then, I feel such *gratitude* to all that's gone into making up the food that I take into my body, because I am filling myself with unique consciousnesses and bringing it into the human, and allowing these consciousnesses to integrate within the human, and praying that the human become so *awake* in the light that it rejoice in this human, in this incarnation, rather than taking this incarnation for granted—abusing the animals, abusing the plants, abusing the planet, abusing the soil, abusing itself—that we become instead an experience of rejoicing and of tremendous gratitude. So that's how I eat."

I remind SIANNA that she once told me, "I cringe whenever I eat a carrot. I love everything I eat." She replies: "I do. I especially love having a garden; but whenever I have a garden, and go out there to *pick* something that's alive, it is to me a mystical experience, it really is. I mean, a piece of lettuce that is filled with the life-force, and the fact that I take it into myself; it's *a holy* experience. I *don't* take lettuce for granted.

"I have also learned many *things* from the plants. When I was ill, very, very ill, I developed a fungal infection on my foot, and remember walking in the woods. And I was just quiet, walking with my cat, and all of a sudden, I was passing this incredibly beautiful big pine tree, and I stopped, and I was smelling it, and I put the pitch to my mouth and tasted it, and just reflected on the incredible taste of the pitch, and then as I did that, I felt that the pine tree was communicating with me, and the pine tree said, 'Take that pitch and put it on the fungus on your feet and they will be cured.' And I did. And it was cured. And so that was medicine. That was medicine, just as eating anything for me is medicine, medicine for the human condition until we can survive on light, because I do believe that we will someday survive on light. And we will not have to eat. We will go beyond this condition where we need to eat. And we will live on light. That's my personal—not belief, because I don't believe in belief, because then I have to defend them, and I'm not wise enough—but it's my personal *feeling.*

"What you're helping with is getting the human mind to stop making judgments and get into that state of mystery. It's a living moment. In other words, the minute we make a judgment about *anything*—eating meat, not eating meat, being a Christian, not being a Christian, being New Age, not being New Age, being pretty, not being pretty, being intelligent, not being intelligent—the minute we make a judgment about anything, we're in the—lower than the animal mind. Because the animal mind functions in synchronicity with the natural impulse, which is not detrimental to the whole: it functions intuitively, synchronistically with the nature around it, with the earth itself.

"But human beings—often what we do is function from our animal minds; but we don't function from the intuitive level we have because we use thought, and that is symbolic representation of a natural experience. Then what we do with our thoughts, we create a reality with our thoughts that's separate from the condition, the natural condition. So we create a world out of thought, with belief systems. This is right, and this is wrong; this is good, and this is bad; this is proper, this is improper; I'm good, you're bad; I'm right; you're wrong. See, because our thoughts are based from an animal consciousness which has to do with survival. But we separated it from the intuitive, synergistic relationship with nature. So then we begin to function according to the belief systems we've created, and as long as we *do* that, we're in violent opposition to our thoughts, to our self, because in order for thoughts to work *for* us, our thoughts have to be freed of judgment; they have to go to the realm where *thought* is natural and that's our higher self. That's where we are one mind, and everything we do is in relation to the well-being of the whole.

"We need to *think* that way first so that we will create cultures and societies and a way of being that will be in *accord* with our well-being as a whole, which will take *care* of our personal well-being. But most human beings function from the animal mind, which is not appropriate for human beings, because when we *do* that, we're functioning from judgment and lower thought and we end up destroying. It's our thoughts which destroy. Our thoughts are violence; our thoughts are the seeds of violence, are the core, the roots of our violence in the world—toward animals, toward nature, toward each other.

"So we've got to change our thoughts first, the way we think. We've got to stop the judgment, and start respecting everyone's particular, unique process, because some human beings need meat, and some human beings right now need vegetables. And instead of judging each other, we should just appreciate the difference, and offer it *all* to our higher self. We can create a more harmonious human experience on this planet—or on any planet where we might go—or any life station in space where we go."

I ask SIANNA whether she reverberates to the sufferings of confined animals. She says: "Well, the factory farmed animals are, well, to me, it's the same as factory farmed vegetables. It's horrendous. And whenever because of my financial situation or my physical situation where I am not able to get food that's organic, be they vegetables *or* animals, and they're not made with love—when someone feeds me food that's not made with love and it goes into my system, I have to be really conscious so that I bless that food more because I take it in. I am so sensitive to what goes into the food, whether it be the consciousness of the animals, the consciousness of the vegetables, the consciousness of the people who prepare it.

"It all affects me because I'm very much alive—not just in my physical body. I'm very much affected by the consciousness of whatever goes into that food. So *naturally* I'm drawn to food that is prepared with love, and food that is *grown* with respect and love. And it's hard to find, and I can't always get it. I choose to make most of my own food myself, grow it if I can, and when I can't, reflect upon before I eat anything. I do take time to reflect upon what I'm eating and I often ask forgiveness to the plants and to the animals for the way that we human beings have treated them.

"My personality has had a difficult time over the years trying to align itself with this sense of love and light inside my being, because my personality had many developmental flaws and I kept seeing these judgments inside my personality, feeling that some ways of living were right and some ways of living were wrong, and people who weren't spiritual should be spiritual. So I found myself doing the very thing I knew was inappropriate—making judgments.

"And I've come to this place where I can see that I'm aware that when human beings function from a place that is judgmental or critical or ignorant or abusive or violent, I'm able to separate the behavior from the being, and love the being, because it's just another factor of myself, and say that behavior—not that it's wrong, but it doesn't work. It causes pain or it causes separation or it causes violence or it causes hurt, and I can say eating food without consciousness is inappropriate; but I won't judge a person who is stuffing themselves with sirloin steaks, and that's all they eat, and so that person is *bad*. I'll say their behavior does not allow for them to feel the love and beauty that they are part of. And that causes me tremendous compassion. It's love and pain.

"And so there was a time when I was younger and I'd walk by a bar, and there'd be people coming out and they'd be just so full of poisonous energies, and I would just feel like I had to run to the other part of the street, so that I wouldn't be contaminated. Now I feel that I can walk right by them and wish them well, and see their behavior and have compassion for them for allowing themselves to behave in ways which keep them out of a sense of well-being for themselves, and for the *whole human race,* for the planet."

I ask SIANNA whether she has been speaking from an altered state and she says that she has not, that she is just sitting quietly with her cat. I tell her that I can't even look at a carrot the way I used to. She says: "Carrots are very sensitive. We have to lick them and tell them that we love them and then they're happy. I don't feel that cranberries are as sensitive; they don't mind our chomp-chomping into them as much; but carrots are so *sensitive.* Lick them a little and be kind of gentle with them, and tell them that we love them. I really feel when you tell them that—Oh, I wouldn't mind somebody eating me if they said they loved me. Go ahead; eat me. What a way to go! I really mean that. Yeah. Eat me. BUT LOVE ME FIRST."

I tell SIANNA that so many beautiful people are "in" my book, and that for me, so much is changed. She says: "The vegetarian world will never be the same." Then she continues: "On the sub-atomic level, we're all the same. On the subatomic level, we all reso-nate to the same dance. There is no difference between you and a cow or you or a table or a potato or a blueberry. We're all the same at the subatomic level."

I say to her: Maybe I should be eating my orange pencils in-stead of carrots. She says: "Well, you can't. Because at the atomic level in order to make yourself function within the particular con-figuration of your atomic pattern, you have to have things that reso-nate—but everything has consciousness. So I mean if we sat down, and I do feel that on some level we could just sit down and eat stone and get fully nourished, but that is—that's an ideal. It's only when a particular body is able to absorb the nutrients in a way that works at the atomic level. So, in other words, a lot of people function off ideals: Oh, we should just live off light, or we should just live off vegetables or we should just live off this or we should just live off that.

And those are all ideals; they are in the realm of thought. They become real when it works, when it's functional."

If the whole world is conscious, as SIANNA believes, does it matter what I eat, or only how I eat—as SIANNA believes? Do we get more "in touch" by making meat untouchable? SIANNA, reverberating with the pain of the world, both with animal suffering and with vegetable distress, seems to be connected. On a vegetarian diet, she felt light enough to float up and out of the world before her work in the world was through. She herself has suffered in staying. Is she *responsible* for the suffering of the animals whose bodies she ate in order to stay "grounded"? Does her soul bear a great stain? Thinking abstractly, it is easy to say that flesh eaters cannot be as spiritual, all other things being equal. But in the concrete, actual lives of people suggest otherwise.

5

Parameters and Plants

*"We don't eat living things. The thought is terrible
to us. You will think me foolish, but every tearing
off of a leaf would be a wound in my heart."*
— David Lindsay, *Voyage to Arcturus*

"Inside plants the same struggle rages.

Each leaf sweats.
Every root crawls down, confused."
—Richard Grossman, *The Animals*

If we do not eat animals, we must eat plants, or parts of plants; even if we could live on water, we would have to distill it to avoid taking microscopic life—and then where would they be? If we refuse to eat at all, we take our own lives, and the lives of those who dwell in and on us.

We need energy from outside ourselves if we are to live; even plants, who make our food and their own, need a star. We all live off the sun in one way or another. Plants are busy eating light, and animals are busy eating plants or other animals who have eaten plants.

If it seems worse to kill an animal than to kill a plant, it is because only animals protest. They kick and scream. They are too much like us: we identify. "Pesco-vegetarians," who call themselves "vegetarian" but who eat fish, must classify them as honorary members of the Plant Kingdom (or Queendom) because they do not scream. Their silence damns them.

Plants and fish are mute; but fish can get away. If plants could, would they? They tempt us with gifts so we will spare them, but not all plants sweeten the deal; the others we pull up by their roots. If you have no fruits—then up by your roots!

If plants are conscious, by what right do we kill them? Should we instead be fruitarians, taking only from the plant for life, and not life from the plant? If plants are less conscious than animals, do we have more of a right to kill them? Yet each time we eat anything, animal or vegetable, we kill bacteria in large numbers. We cannot live except by killing. Each inhale and exhale is at the expense of another's last breath.

The juice of fruits is not blood. If we can be well-nourished without shedding another's blood, ought we to eat only plants? Is it as bad to spill another's juice or sap, to skin it alive, to fling it, still respiring, into boiling broth or bubbling oil? We uproot plants, flay them and tear them and pierce them and eviscerate them—alive! I was once asked to imagine a shop with split-open plants hanging from hooks—a halved eggplant, a bisected turnip—with their insides exposed, impaled. Would such a shop be as grotesque as the butcher's? There is a blurry line, if there is a line at all, between animal and vegetable. Are the peels of vegetables like the skins of animals? Is a rind a hide? We skin vegetables alive, but animals, hopefully, only after they have died. What is the difference between the fuzz on the peach and the down on the chick—or on the caterpillar? The fur on a back and the fluff in a pod?

If we kill a being who protests, ours is an act of theft, for we steal from it a life it struggles to protect. If we take a fruit, it is given as a gift. "Here," says the plant, "take my offering and propagate my kind, but please spare me, and we shall offer more." If plants could be deeply wounded or psychologically distressed, if they could experience terror, and searing pain, then compassionate vegetarians would go hungry. But perceiving pain is of value only to a being who can try to escape it; so plants, who cannot get away, may not feel pain—even when taken whole. Immobile, they have no use for a sign which will not startle, a bell they cannot hear.

Even if they are aware, in their own ways, it is unlikely that they feel sharp sensations, for the capacity would do them no good: it would have no "survival value." Perhaps instead they have chemical ways of escaping, coping by becoming "high" on their own unabused substances—numbing rather than running. Even so, they have no nerves to fray, or brains to betray or dismay them.

Perhaps SIANNA feels the carrot's but not the cranberry's "pain" because pulling the root is closer to slaughtering than to harvesting. The cranberry may "bleed" but the root has more to lose. If we do not eat the stems, leaves, or fruits of plants, it is by their roots that we know them; but how much do we know?

Because the juice of fruits is not blood, and because we associate blood with life, we may think that in killing plants we have not taken their lives. KIVA, once a vegan, said: "I really liked the idea that there was no death involved in my diet, and that—wow!—the planet has made it possible for me to give myself sustenance without having to kill anything. That gave me a lot of pleasure. It seemed very simple, eating as low as I possibly could on the food chain." But because plants are alive, vegans do include death in their diets. Life is also associated with breath, and plants do breathe, not with the bellows of lungs, but with the tissues of their leaves.

Plants are alive; but do they have lives? If they have lives, do they experience them? If they can experience, do they have quality of life? Are they more content in sun than in shadow? Can they suffer? If they manufacture chemicals to discourage insects from eating them, are they not self-protective? If something is self-protective, does it not have a self to protect? Are plants selves? Do they have interests? If they have interests, can they be injured? A plant can be harmed, but can a plant be hurt?

It makes little sense to assure a plant a quick and painless death. We do not decapitate a vegetable before skinning it alive; we cannot cut off its head because it doesn't have one—or if like the Cheshire Cat it *is* one without a body to be severed from. So perhaps we are ahead of the game when we nourish our bodies with plants, even though some, like palms and artichokes, do have "hearts."

Plants are *planted*, non-ambulatory. They may have limbs, but not the kind for walking. They are not warm-blooded or cold-blooded; they are not blooded at all. But they do have sap; vital fluids flow in their stalks and stems. What seems stationary is full of activity within. But so is a stone. While not alive, its insides are dancing; its electrons are caroming in vast empty spaces to a choreography we did not invent and do not completely understand. Everything, whether organic or inorganic, is full of movement on some level.

The plant's universe may resemble a clam's universe, its protoplasm not taking in a large sweep of the world; but who knows the depth of its inner life? Some say plants perceive the deaths of other plants and animals; they may catch their breaths, even if their lives lack breadth. But are they individuals? There is a difference between "an individual thing" and "an individual." Fish use brightly colored flags and display to stand out—even though they cannot stand up —as individuals; but flowers, too, wave their bright temptations toward their real friends, not florists, but insects, and speak to them in colors they can understand—ultraviolet. So plants, too, can be singled out. Everything alive, it would seem, has identity.[1] Everything alive signals olfactorily, visually, audibly, or tactily (if not tactfully), "See me!" "Take me!" "Come to me!" "Flee from me!" "Spare me!"

Orchids mimic wasps who fertilize them, and the charade surpasses mere costume. The orchid not only dresses like a wasp, but is also shaped like one, and exudes the sex pheromones of the female ready for mating. Color, shape, scent, form, and size are coordinated perfectly in a *plant* to communicate with an *animal*.[2] Less dramatic plants provide meals to lure insects to their sex. Evolutionary theory cannot convince me that natural selection and mutation alone explain this. These are only "efficient" and "material" causes, to use Aristotle's terms, explaining the how and the what, but not the why and wherefore. Botanists wisely leave such questions to philosophers, but unwisely think only science provides real answers. My answer for why mimicry occurs is that the organisms involved are *involved* with each other. Plants no less than insects "know" how to seduce. They "know" what to wear and how to smell. Plante Fatale. Others "know" the way to an insect's heart is through its stomach.

Venus Flytraps and Pitcher Plants may have the same I.Q. as the average scallop; but each has identity. But do they have "personal" identity? It makes little sense to speak of the "personality" of a plant. A plant is individual, but has no individuality. One could contrive to cleverly switch my houseplants, and I would not notice (as I would if one switched my cats). My plants respond to light, but do not relate to me. We do not know each other. If a garden is an "it" and a gardener a "who," then what is a plant? Must everything we call a "who" be a person?

Chopping spinach with a cleaver years ago, in the presence of my two jade plants ("who" now "watch" me as I write), I suddenly saw myself performing a violent act. Plants I had tenderly tended now witnessed the untender surrender of those greens. "I would *never* do that to my jade plants," I thought, "even if they were delectably edible." I found myself treating some plants as strangers and others as friends. Perhaps as flesh eaters prefer anonymous meat, vegetarians need to eat anonymous plants, or at least not those they have known or fed for years. The longer we have fed a plant, perhaps, the less likely that we will want to be fed by it.

The jade plants are devoid of personality. They never greet me or thank me; but they do depend on me, for without my ministrations, they will wither. I would betray them if I withheld water. There is a relationship. Yet each year I harvest the fruits of a backyard organic garden. I take the fruit only, the bean, never the beanstalk, but "Jack," who plants them, does the "dirty work" for me at the end of the season when the stalks become compost. I could perhaps love the stalk—but the beans? Every one? We treat human corpses with respect; the corpses of animals we have loved are unthinkable, to most, as food, even if we are not vegetarian. Plants we have loved may be unthinkable as food; but are they corpses?

Grass seeds and maple pods fall into the black ornamental stones of our driveway. They germinate in an inhospitable place. Once they were poisoned; now they are pulled. I do the pulling to avoid the poisoning, and I apologize to every blade and seedling. I say to them, "You never could have survived here. This is a driveway. If I don't pull you up quickly and throw you away, someone else will do worse." Sometimes I plant a few.

When I speak of a plant I do not speak to, I still call it a "who." Is this what FRANK calls "over-empathy"? When I chop greens in front of my "pet" houseplants, do they scream? Are they upset? Who can they trust? Can we love plants for their own sakes? Can a plant have intrinsic value? Are they lovable? Do they love us in their own ways? Is each tree in the forest a self, and not just part of the woods? When we tap its sap, does it grow faint? Ought we to offer it juice afterward—or a piece of fruit?

We are told that plants are not sentient, that they turn to the light they cannot see or feel; differential rates of stem cell growth account neatly for the curve. But we could, in principle, offer a reductionistic, mechanistic theory of human movement as well, leaving consciousness out in the rain. We *know* we are conscious, even so. Do plants know they are conscious, in spite of the oversight of our science? Does one need eyes to see the light?

We believe we are justified in eating plants because they let us. It is not that they protest too little; it is that they do not protest at all. MARCIA said: "Plants are living things, too, and I'm aware of that when I pull the carrots. When I pulled the carrots out of the ground when I was a little kid, I would talk to them; I just talked to them and thanked them. When I pull up carrots, or when I'm eating plants, it just seems like a natural kind of partnership. The plant doesn't *ask* to be spared, and I feel like the plant grows its flesh and grows its fruit and so forth almost *expecting* that something is going to come and take that. And it just feels like part of a natural cycle. I think plants accept. I think that's part of the partnership. We're all in this together; you have to do these things respectfully. I'm aware of the carrot, and I'll thank it; but I think it's O.K. to pull up a carrot and eat it, because there's a partnership. In another era, our waste went back into the soil and made another carrot."

TONY agreed: "The plants accept the fact that they're here to serve, and we in turn will serve other things when we die. In macrobiotics, Ohsawa said never to take anything that doesn't wish to give itself at that point. When the time is right, the fruit will just fall off in your hand. If you grow the carrots, you've energized them. You've taken the seed, and given it your blessing. You're helping it do its thing. The plant understands its place. Things work a certain way here. The plant knows it's produced its fruit which will continue its children. The plant knows to produce fruit. How does it know this? It knows because of some force within; it seems simple; but when you think of it, how magical that this little seed—that all things are going to happen in this little seed.

"A plant doesn't have intellect, but we can communicate with it at some level. We can affect it, like when Jesus cursed the fig tree and it died. I was clearing a place to grow grapes, and to the cherry tree I said, 'If you don't produce, I have to take you down.' What happened was he wasn't producing cherries. 'I bring you food, and I bring you water, and now it's time that you gave something back and produce something. Otherwise, I have to take you down.' And the next spring, he was dead. So he was gone. We do influence plants. We can impart our energy on a level we don't really understand. We can have a communication with these things.

"I think you strike a rapport with houseplants. They respond; they flower; we can't ask any more than that. A plant responds to vibrations. Plants love happy environments, loving environments; they even like nice music. They love people who tend them lovingly. They respond in that manner.

"When I go out and clear some land, I know the trees are there, and have been there for a long time. I feel like an intruder when I have to take down a tree because I need that spot. I make my peace with the trees. I tell them I'll let their children grow—there, around, in other areas—that I will continue them, that I won't cut them all down. I say, 'I have to cut you down; but I'm going to let your children live, let them survive, so there will be others like you.' They grow in families. When you see trees, they're in families. You get a little grove of oak, of sumac—and it's wonderful. I have a great love for trees. When one is there a long time, and suddenly it comes down, as soon as it comes down, it throws a little one right at the bottom. They have such a mechanism for survival. From that spot, you'll see other trees come out.

"We don't hear pain from the plants. They're not as active. They don't have the same kind of feelings that a four-legged animal does, because when these animals are getting ready to be butchered, they know it. They don't want to die, and they protest and scream, just like a person being murdered. If people had to hear that screaming, most of them wouldn't eat meat."

FRANK said: "I had an instinctive feeling of wanting to eat things that were less closely related to me. I've always felt the more distantly related the thing was, that it was like inversely proportional to the inhibition against eating it. So a plant seemed very, very far removed as opposed to a cow or a bird. But the thing about plants is, at that age, kids would say, 'You shouldn't pull on that branch, because how would *you* feel?'

"Even from my scientific knowledge, I learned that a lot of plants thrive on having a little bit of trimming, and that it stimulates them to grow more; you cut the flowers to make more flowers. If something has one flower, you cut that off, and it sends up *two* shoots. It's like that Greek myth, the Hydra monster. You cut off one head, and it grows two back.

"So sometimes plants thrive on pruning; it's like they were designed to deal with damage from the weather, and in fact, their fruits are made to be enticing to animals as a mode of seed propagation. The fruit is *fragrant*; it has aromatic ethers and oils that attract animals to eat it, and it tastes good as a reward. And then the seeds are either spit out on the spot, or we eat the apple and then get to the core; it's stringy and unpleasant, so we throw it away, and we're doing the tree a favor. Or the seeds are encased in some resistant substance so they can go through the digestive system and come out the other end. That's a mode of seed dispersal. So eating plants or fruits or parts of plants didn't seem so bad because they were more like *designed* to be eaten—or at least parts of them.

"I even have trouble pulling up weeds. I have this house, and it terribly needs gardening. I see these beautiful plants struggling to reach the sun, and I feel sorry for them; but I've got to get over that. I think it's a psychological thing. It's over-empathy, a symbolic representation of something in my own life. Just as I don't want to be harvested cruelly or cut down in the prime of life, so I project that onto the plants."

Plants may be for eating—but not always for calories. Sometimes they are for philosophies—or for ecstasies. What they offer may not feed us, but free us from either physical or psychological pain. What they give instead of food may not nourish, but help us flourish. Plants, living on light, may offer enlightenment; spearmints and peppermints, en-light-en-mint. Basil, rue, rosemary, sassafras, or dill may awaken us as well. Secrets may be locked in the cells of plants; inside there may be cures—or visions.

TONY said: "Plants give us the softness. The plant produces peace. It gives you tranquillity, and the ability to see the real world of which it is a part. The real world is the one where we're connected to the earth and the universe. Some plants are called 'empathogens' because they render us empathic in the sense that we lose all anger and fear and become totally open to any responses around us without indoctrination. We can see clearly. We can see the earth; the connection comes back. The most common empathogen is called 'ecstasy.' It's made from essential oils that are aromatic, and can be made from sassafras; it can be made from calamus; it can be made from parsley, mint . . .

"Before we became so inundated with pollution, simple things like basil, parsley, and sage were once mind-altering. They were used to change moods. People knew the *power* of plants. In psycho-pharmacology, we have learned that moods are chemical; that's how they happen. When something goes out of whack chemically, the personality usually goes out of whack with it. In tribal lore, medicine men knew how to bring people back around by plants prescribed as ways of calming people down, or as ways of giving them more energy.

"Throughout history, the plants have been so much a part of us; but now we've been removed from plants, and that's where the danger lies. In the olden days, we were able to heal ourselves. Everyone had a garden for medicine. There was no household that didn't have a garden, because you needed a garden. There was always someone in the community who was able to use these plants for healing, for childbirth, for pain. These herbal remedies have been around for eons. They go back before time—just about. If we knew more about herbs, we wouldn't need doctors. We could keep our bodies in a better balance. Doctors have convinced us to go to these dying places, these white rooms in hospitals. I would much prefer to go out and lean against a tree, and wait for myself to die there. I know exactly the tree I would like.

"In Ayurvedic Medicine, simple basil is for the head chakra; they consider that it gives you clarity—along with gotu kola, calamus, and gingko. Now we call them 'smart drugs'; but they are basically models of these plants. Certain plants become allies for us to find things out, and if we approach them correctly, we can learn these things. But there must be the idea of wanting to know. That's what the daturas are about. They go back to ancient times; we find them in caves. Datura is a painkiller. Anyone who knows about herbs can go out into the woods and find plants to stop pain.

"Various foods cause various moods. In the Zen monasteries, the cook was the most important member of the community because his preparation of food would be what the others thought about; it would give them their moods. Beer was originally not like the beer we drink now. It had hops in it, but that was only one of the ingredients. Very little beer now contains any real amount of hops. Hops is something that really relaxes people. Hops is a third cousin to marijuana; they are related; they can actually be grafted one to the other. Sometimes they added a little henbane, and sometimes datura seeds so people could have visual experiences or prophesize. In one culture, if something was missing, or if someone was murdered, they would call upon the medicine man to induce a trance, usually with datura, to find out who the guilty culprit was. That was the promise of the plant.

"Plants have religious purposes. In the Native American Church—the peyote cult—they always said, 'The White Man goes into his church and talks about Jesus. We go into our church and talk *to* Jesus.' The priestess at Delphi had on a crown made of datura leaves. Our evolvement is due to plants. Without the plants we ingest, we could not get to other levels of consciousness. We used to ingest little mushrooms which contain psilocybin. These constituents allowed the consciousness of man to start evolving. That was the symbiotic relationship between man and vegetable. Man has always used the alkaloids to communicate with the gods."

How could such an alliance be symbiotic? Plants may raise our consciousness, give us truth, or philosophy, and a mystical connection, but how would *they* benefit? What is in them may be good for us, but what's in it for them? What good to the plant is our insight? If they "raise" us, will we then raise them? Perhaps what we see through them will save them if what we see is the preciousness of the natural world of which they are a part. If they tempt us with euphoria, perhaps they "want" us also to see the light; but they do not always give us bliss (at least in this life). Although they may allay our pains and sometimes soothe us, they sometimes kill us with their power. According to tradition, the Buddha was enlightened under a tree, but died poisoned by a plant.

We are not enlightened eating corpses; ingesting animal parts may give endurance, but not transcendence, the muscle, but not the mystical. While plants can draw us to the light, dead flesh is dark, taken from the body's secret, sunless inside. Because eating animals is associated with aggression and eating plants with peace, perhaps the ultimate wisdom from the plants is that we should eat them—and not animals—for the good of all.

If the fruits of our ethics make us sick, perhaps we should spit them out and try some other fare. Vegetarians spit out flesh, but not pulp. The abstemious vegan sprouts pithy truths to justify this, saying that fruits fall willingly; but she may sprout grains, beans, and seeds. Perhaps in the pith of each is also a truth, a compressed commentary on the soul-states of those who heap them on their plates. Who knows the right and wrong about eating plants? If sprouts could cry like the babies they are, would all vegans be fruitarians?

There may be splendor in the grass; but there is also the splendor of it. Vegetarians ought not to take vegetation for granted. Indeed, we ought to take our symbiotic covenants more seriously, for we no less than insects are here to serve plants—both at our meals and as our masters. Perhaps it is a sin akin to factory farming to render hybrids seedless and helpless, for it reverses ancient agreements: we are here to assist plants' propagation, not their sterilization.

We share DNA with plants; they are family members if we make the family circle wide enough. Most of us do not have children who become doctors; but plants can doctor us all. That beings who may feel no pain provide medication for our own is both irony and reason for gratitude. That metaphysical secrets may also be sealed in their cells is our "highest" reason to value them. If they "want" us to use them, it may be because the wiser we become, the more likely it will be that we will esteem them, as well as steam them. We ought to be more grateful to plants, even though this gratitude need not be expressed by sparing them. Indeed, it might be better expressed by sharing them. We can say, "Thank you!" even if we cannot hear them say, "You're welcome."

What should we eat? At a very young age, having just learned about photosynthesis, I wished that we all could be green, and live off light like plants do. Our genetic engineers may one day accomplish this, but for now as close as we come to living on light is eating those who do. So I eat meat: nut meat. And I drink milk: soy milk. I eat cheese: almond cheese. And I eat burgers made out of sunflower seeds. Eating fruits seems better than eating roots, but not much better; but eating roots seems much better than eating what moos— or crows—or bleats. Best seems to be taking small short lives, rather than long large ones. A lettuce of a season, destined to die at first frost, seems to have less to lose than a tree of long-standing. I would not topple a maple or an oak for my dinner, but I do eat bamboo shoots, and perhaps I need my roots in more ways than one.

By choosing to eat plants rather than animals, there is for me a feedback mechanism at work—seeing plants as nourishing, being nourished by them, becoming a gentler and more nourishing person, becoming more drawn to plant foods which I see as more and more nourishing, becoming more and more nourished by them.

Even though I am an animal, I am not made out of animals; I may be an "animal person" because I champion their rights; but I am really a "vegetable person" because I am made out of vegetables, even though I do not (yet!) fight for their rights.[3] Or is this only a half-truth? JOHN said: "In one of the Oz sequels, there are all these different characters who are animated and made out of different things, like the Scarecrow and so forth, and one of the nonhuman characters in Oz kind of pejoratively describes Dorothy and Toto as 'meat people.' 'You're made out of meat.' And that struck me, because I thought, 'It's true, isn't it?' He's saying, 'You are made out of meat, Dorothy. You creatures, you're all in this together. You're all meat people, and therefore not as good as I am.' I think that character was made out of candy. While I can eat a hamburger, and just think of it as 'stuff,' I am occasionally struck by this 'meat people' idea. In fact, it's true. It's all of us. We're just meat on the hoof."

If we are "meat people," it is because we are all made out of flesh—whether or not we eat it. We turn plants into meat, vegetables into animal. We cannot escape meat; we *are* "meat people." We may not begin with skins on our plates, but we all end up with it on our bones.

Raw, unadulterated flesh repels us, while raw, unadulterated fruit appeals to us; even raw, unadulterated roots and shoots are palatable to us. We do not dine on carrot "flesh" or avocado "flesh" because that without blood is not flesh. If flesh is muscle, then no vegetable has flesh: when we pull plants up by their roots, they do not pull back. If not protesting is the same as accepting, then plants accept.

In our culture, vegetarians, who eat grain, go against the grain, and hence must give reasons for what they do: the onus is on them, but not on those who conform to the norm of flesh. But like the ox whose neck is "conveniently" shaped to fit the yoke, the eater of the ox should shoulder the burden of proof (the yoke if not also the joke) for it is harder to justify meat than wheat.

What dies in pain dies in vain; but I do not believe that even the felled oak feels pain.[4] I may feel pain watching it fall; but the pain I feel is not its pain, but my own. My vegetarian credo is rooted in this:

Watch the fish die. Watch the cow die. Watch the sow die. Watch the lamb die. If you must eat flesh, eat flesh, but first watch the being die.

I do not eat flesh because in my mind's eye, I see billions of animals die. Because I do not like what I see, because what I see pains me, I do not eat what I cannot see die.

If I must eat plants, I shall watch plants die, and sometimes this pains me, but I do not tremble with their pain, perhaps because they themselves do not tremble with it.

I will not eat anything which makes me tremble deep inside envisioning it trembling in pain.

6

Fish out of Water

A fish out of water is a human out of air, out of atmosphere, wet and thick, at least compared to the thin vacuity of "outer space." Twenty miles up, and we're all fish out of water.

Fish, not fuzzy and warm, are less accessible to us than our stuffed toys. They have no arms to hug us or voices to greet us or to tell us where it hurts. They are like mobile slithering plants, sinuous and supple green things, as though they photosynthesized like the algae they eat, as though they were thick vines with eyes and hearts. We wouldn't wonder if we found them on stalks, ripe for the picking.

When we catch them, we don't tally up the yield in lives, but in pounds or tons, as though they were fodder, like alfalfa. Fish can't join us in the swim of our lives. They don't smile at us; they don't laugh. They can't take a joke. They are like vastly larger amoebae, reactive, conditionable, vaguely aware; but they don't have lives.

Their fry are spawned by the millions, more like individual germ cells than individual beings; how can the individual matter in such a system of reproductive roulette? They are as expendable in nature as they are in our eyes, valueless except as calories, or as trophies, and as instruments to make more of the same. Their lives are meaningless, even to themselves: What do they have to think about? What matters to them? They are cold and cold-hearted; they eat each other, sometimes their own young. Why should we care about their lives when they care so little about each other? Why should we care for those apparently not capable of caring at all?

It is as though they do not have nerves and spines, or organs like ours. They are space aliens, beyond our comprehension; they don't even breathe our air. That they, too, need oxygen is no more important than that fires do, or individual cells. We do not encounter these "others" on earth; we "fish" them out of their strangeness. There is no sympathy for them gasping out their lives on the banks of rivers and streams. Children are taught to catch them by running barbs through other living beings, laughing as they squirm, laughing as they drown. They are taught to tear the lips of fish, to tear out their mouths, and to see the activity of killing them as recreation or sport. As they lay dying, thrashing in an alien world, we abandon them to slow deaths. We don't identify.[1]

How do we distinguish their "white" flesh from red? Snow White and Rose Red? The White and Red Queens of Lewis Carroll? Are they symbols here? Red is vibrant, pulsing, throbbing with life-blood; white is ghost, dead, pure, perhaps something that never breathed at all. White as clouds, as shrouds, as foam on the sea; red as fire, as lava, as burning coals: too hot to touch, dangerous, inflammatory, potent. White is innocent, compliant, demure; red is lust and passion, uncontrollable, overwhelming.

How much of this symbolism lurks in our subconscious? If we were vegetarian, or call ourselves such, but eat fish, do we think of it as nut meat, as bleached seeds, not as pieces of animals who perceived, who once beheld the world with their eyes? The "flesh" of apple, of pear, of potato, of onion: white, safe. (Even when each is wrapped in red, we tend to peel them.) Beets are the "bloodiest" plant food I can imagine, sweet and ripe and dripping crimson; but red flesh drips blood, and blood (not borscht) is life.

Dead red flesh with breath almost still in it is disquieting, dis-taste-full, a dis-grace. And so we do not put this food back on our plates when we quit our vegetarianism. It is not rare steak that we choose, but usually white fish, cut up in very small pieces like a radish or a parsnip, safely tossed with vegetables in a stir-fry, masquerading as just another plant.

A Biologist's Story

FRANK said: "When I was in graduate school, I was going through one of my usual phases about feeling a little guilty about meat, and I had this very vivid dream. I went to school at Yale, in New Haven, which was in view of the ocean, and in my dream I was somehow walking near the ocean, and dolphins were communicat-ing. I was also working a little bit for the 'Save the Whale' movement at the time: this was 1977-1976. So, I was walking, in my dream I was walking, near the beach, and dolphins were surfacing several hun-dred feet offshore, and playfully jumping up through the air, and somehow they were beaming telepathic communication to me, and they were saying, 'Frank, you shouldn't feel guilty about eating meat because, you know, we're very intelligent and sentient creatures and we live in the ocean, and we eat fish. And you who walk upon the land—it's the normal order of things that you should eat the land creatures.' So I felt very comforted by that.

"Through all my vegetarianism, there's one big irony or contra-diction, which is that I never, ever, ever have any qualms about eating fish or shellfish. There's no intellectual justification for it: I just love fish. I always got teased that I was probably a whale in a past life or something. From the time I was a little kid, when all the other kids would go, 'EEE-YEW—fish!,' I loved fish. I loved shellfish. I loved any kind of raw clams, oysters, snails, whatever. When the grown-ups were having that kind of food, I didn't have any qualms about it. I didn't like the *bones* of fish; but when it was a fillet, I'd pick the meat off. But somehow the *bones* of fish seemed *purer*; they didn't have this obvious marrow; they didn't seem to have blood vessels running all through it, and I guess evolutionarily, it's one order removed. Fish and shellfish are lower vertebrates and invertebrates.

"I was one of those kids that if we went out with other families, all the kids would go, 'Oh! Fried chicken! Yum!' and they'd be sitting there like cannibals, munching on those little bones, those drumsticks, and I would be completely nauseated. I would have "The Fisherman's Platter' or 'The Captain's Plate.' And the other parents were resentful, because those dishes cost more. They were like $2.35 where the fried chicken was $0.95. 'Frank's parents spoil him,' they would say. But I would be there, 'Yum, scallops! Yum, shrimp! Little fish!' I loved it. And my birthday treat would be lobster which I now have an inhibition against eating because of their difficult life.

"I love lobster meat, but I now have a slight inhibition, because I know they have to go through this *incredibly* complex mating ritual, where the female has to have just molted, so she doesn't have a shell, and the male has to mate with her so carefully—incredible for this cannibalistic animal which eats it own young. They go through this incredibly *tender* mating ritual that rivals human mating.

"When we dissected a squid, I went out that night and had calamari. I couldn't stop thinking about having squid. I don't know; there are a lot of contradictions here. It's not a defensible position. I'm kind of an eclectic. I'll eat this; but I won't eat that. But I think squids and octopuses are cute and if I had to slaughter them, it would be hard. Even when I went fishing, I'd feel sorry for the fish. If I were in a survival situation, and I had to do it, I would do it; but if I have a choice, I want to be removed from the slaughtering process.

"I love Japanese food. When I lived in Japan, I lived in a fishing village, and I loved so-called 'raw' fish, which is a bad translation. In Japanese, it's not 'raw': it means 'clean' or 'pristine' or just 'uncooked.' But in English, the word 'raw' has many negative connotations, whereas the Japanese word for these things—and I don't even know how to translate it—it's just 'clean'; 'pristine'; 'unsullied'; 'untampered'; 'unpolluted.' I know there's a problem with seafood because of bio-concentration of mercury, and other problems in the water. Sometimes people say you shouldn't eat fish because you're getting all that stuff, especially with shellfish which are filter feeders. But my reaction to that is well, I'm just going to make sure that my immune system is strong; so I take herbs for my liver, and antioxidants, selenium, and things like that, to help counteract whatever heavy metals I'm ingesting.

"But my favorite fish in the world is salmon. I always long for fillet of salmon, craving it. Part of this may be knowing what a noble fish salmon is. I feel like I get some of the life energy from it. What is that—anadromous or catadromous? It goes through this thing of going up river and down river—I guess it's anadromous—to spawn. Now the salmon go through this incredible struggle to return where they came from—and that fierce energy! I like to eat fresher foods because I do think there is some kind of life-aura around it, as opposed to canned tuna. The longer the thing's been dead . . . I think it still has the protein, the amino acids, whatever, but I think our science may just be learning about energy and energy fields. Not to sound pseudo-scientific, but there may be something to that: the fresher a food is, maybe the better it is."

Marcia's Musings On Fish

"'Big fish eat little fish'; this was the kind of attitude I grew up with. It was just matter of fact; the wild animals eat other animals, and people eat the kinds of animals people eat. My father would go on a big fishing trip to Canada, and freeze fish, and that was our food for the winter. I do eat fish sometimes, yet it's always bothered me; fishing bothers me. I used to hero-worship my brother; I wanted to do everything he did. But I didn't like watching him fish or reeling them in or anything like that. I didn't like watching people fish—it did bother me.

"We'll eat fish or shellfood. Shellfood are even less aware than fish. I haven't had a hunk of fish for awhile. When we go up to the Cape, I'm more likely to have shellfish; but I might eat a piece of fish on the Cape, and then maybe a couple of times a year. I haven't eaten fish at home for some years. Oh, no; I'm sorry; we did have a barbecue where we had some fish kabobs; but we only do that if it's for company. If it's there, I might eat some of the barbecue.

"Every time I eat fish I wonder if maybe I shouldn't stop, and I always think: Maybe I'll get to that point. I'm always asking myself: Am I just rationalizing? Shouldn't I stop eating fish, too? And then I think: What would we eat on the Cape? You tell someone you eat fish because they don't know what to feed you; it's for convenience sake. It's convenient to eat fish once in awhile, to eat fish maybe six times a year. It does make me stop and think: Why do I do this? It makes me question: Why am I drawing the line here rather than somewhere else? I have qualms about it; we don't do it often. But I won't say, in principle, I won't eat it. There aren't any hard lines, that's the thing.

"If I could bond with *a* fish, I don't know that I could eat *any* fish. It would have to be a real bond there, and because so far, I don't experience it that way . . . But it is close enough that I wonder if I'm just keeping myself from experiencing them that way. Fish do have eyes; but their eyes are just different. Their eyes just seem different to me and their eyes are cold. There's a difference, for example, between a dolphin's look and a fish's look. A fish's look is more like a *reaction*—the unblinking eyes. Birds look at you and mammals do and dolphins do and I imagine whales do, although I have never looked a whale in the eye, I think, and seals do and things like that. But a fish's eye is sort of uncomprehending. I don't see a person in there, clearly at least.

"A fish's comprehension seems to be of a different sort. A cat relates to you; it *clearly* relates to you, even though it doesn't comprehend us in the way we do. Just look in a cat's eye, or even in a bird's eye. And I don't find that with fish. Maybe I'm insensitive to it. Sure, I know that fish can have 'personality'; some are lazy, and like to laze around, and some are darting here and there all the time; but they don't seem the same. They're reactive rather than responsive. They're definitely toward that end of things, more than the creatures I won't eat are. Their nervous systems aren't as developed, especially the shellfish and some of the mobile plants."

TONY said: "Fish are a whole other entity. Fish to me . . . I don't associate any sort of life, in terms of some sort of entity that I would want to communicate with. If I was extremely hungry, and there was no food, I would eat a pet fish. If there were no longer any vegetables left, I'm sure you'd find a way to catch that trout. You can't strike a rapport with clams; they can't look you in the eye. We can strike a rapport with a pet dog, or with a pet cow, with a fawn that might come into our yard. They have an anima or animus."

Peter's Partaking Of Fish

"Fishes are even more distant; but I don't know what goes on inside their consciousness. I don't know whether it's appropriate to be killing them or not. From a gut feeling, it doesn't feel too bad to kill a fish. I would feel much better about eating fish if I caught the fish myself. I don't have any ethical problem, and I don't have any problem experiencing the truth with eating fish. But getting it from the grocer, not knowing how the tuna was caught, or how it died, puts me at a distance. I regret that my life is alienated from reality to that extent.

"Now fish, I never consciously dropped from my diet. When I was at the ashram, there was probably a year or two when I didn't touch it. When I left the ashram, I would eat fish when I went out to restaurants. I don't remember when I decided to eat more fish. So I'd have to say I slowly came back into it; it came back into my life. In more recent years, there has been a bit more of a conscious decision in the sense that I'm not eating dairy anymore. I know the need that my body has for more powerful food; so I will have fish anywhere from once to five times a month, intentionally. Mostly it's when I go out to eat.

"I don't go out of my way to find unpolluted fish. I do consider that the redder, fleshier, fattier fishes tend to concentrate toxins more than others; but on the other hand, I don't like the mild, white fishes as much. I tend to eat mostly salmon and tuna; those are my favorite fishes. What I do eat, though, I eat in such small quantities that I'm not too concerned about the pollutants. I might eat at maximum a pound to two pounds of fish per month; it's probably less than that. So I am not too concerned about the pollutants. And I don't eat *canned* fish. I eat fish, usually raw, in Japanese restaurants. I wouldn't trust myself to do it; they're trained to deal with that.

"I do consider fish to be meat, and I do eat fish now, in the last few years, fairly regularly. My experience from a health standpoint is that a little bit of fish is very good for me; but when I eat too much fish, I will begin to get that stuffed, unclean feeling. At one point, and this was, I think, right before I went to the ashram, I remember I had fasted for three days. I have fasted three, four, or five days, and I broke the fast with raw fish. And it was the best way to break a fast I've ever done. It was the purest food I ever tasted. When you fast, you have a great sensitivity to that purity, and I remember trying to break fasts on grapes, on lettuce, on sprouts, and none of these were as effective as raw fish. It was *so* clean. It was great.

"I will notice, for instance, when I'm getting a little bit weak; my memory is not as sharp, things like that. I know that I need something that has a little more punch to it, and fish does supply that. Also if I want more sexual energy. Any meat will increase the sexual drive. I don't know if it's the testosterone, or just the protein; but it's clearly true. From a yin/yang point of view, it's yang energy, which you need as a man for sexual energy.

"If I were to retire from the world and lead a more monkish life, I would need less flesh. I wasn't thinking sexually, but just in terms of my involvement with the world; flesh supports me in that. It gives me the energy I need to live in the world, whereas if I were more secluded in the country, spending more time meditating, leading a more simple life, I probably wouldn't want any. Master Ni, when he visited a few months ago, said when we fixed him a really nice, simple macro meal, 'This is the food they ate in the Zen monasteries in Japan. You all should eat a little meat.' But sometimes I see it as an animal. The turkey I was carving up yesterday was a corpse; I had to kind of gulp to do it. The fish is cut up into tiny little pieces, and I don't see the whole thing."

Jonathan's Justification

"The line was probably getting pretty thin at certain points. I thought: Well, first of all, the fish, they've lived a good, natural life in the sea, and they are, I believe—their nervous system is not as evolved as a cow or other animal; so there's something about the suffering level I think isn't quite as bad. When they're pulled out of the water, I think they go pretty quickly.

"When I was in Nicaragua, and I had some fish, it was actually a bad experience. I felt there was something repulsive about this fish. The head was still on it; it was kind of like a whole fish. We ended up flying from Mexico to Nicaragua, and eating this lake fish—a whole fish. It looked disgusting. There was something about it, and suddenly my stomach started to turn, and I could not finish it. I did not end up getting ill, but one of my friends did. She got a belly ache out of it. At the time, it was unappetizing.

"I don't think I had any fish after that until 1986 when I went to Asia again, and Thailand, at which time it was appetizingly served, and I didn't get that feeling. Also, I had mussels and some types of fish flesh, too. I don't remember what types they were. In Thailand and Cambodia, you can get a lot of fresh seafood, and shrimp, particularly, were quite tasty and inexpensive. It was a fraction of the price here, and you'd have it in a stir-fry. I have to say that it wasn't out of necessity. I could have survived without it.

"Also in the back of my mind, as a nutritionist, I thought: This is a good source of protein. Something did shift; it was no longer disgusting to me. I was becoming more flexible, so I started to do it, a little fish, a little seafood. In Ecuador, where I was for four months, it's a pretty major part of the diet, especially on the coast. For instance, *ceviche*, which is a slightly cooked or even raw fish. They have a marinade and it's like the national diet in that part of the country. So there were moments like that.

"I never had an urge for fish, but it was kind of like: O.K., maybe I'll try this after I've already eaten it. After coming back from Central America, I actually did have some seafood going out to dinner which seemed a carry-over. I'd go to a restaurant with my father, and if there wasn't much alternative, I'd have some seafood dish. It's only been in restaurants, a few times after each trip. Then back to ovo-lacto.

"In Africa, either fresh or dried fish is used, and actually there were certain parts in Africa where I could justify it more as a nutritional necessity because there's no alternative for quality protein. There weren't any beans. There were situations that I'd be with people, and this is fairly recently—my last Africa trip—where I'd be in someone's home, and I would say, 'No meat.' And they would say, 'O.K. Is fish O.K.?' And I would say, 'Fish is O.K.' It made it easier to fit in and not be such an outcast or foreigner.

"In some African cultures, people just don't seem to feel that animals have feelings. I saw one disturbing episode. These were fisherpeople in Ghana, in a very simple village, and they'd hauled up a net full of fish, and among the fish was a type of eel not considered good eating, so they threw it on the sand, and these kids, little kids, started to come and were really just tormenting this poor eel, and flinging it around, stepping on it, and none of the adults said anything."

I asked JONATHAN whether he would choose to eat a free, wild fish from polluted waters, or an "organic" stressed fish from a crowded fish farm race-way. "I'd have to say, I'd go with the bred fish," he replied, adding, "I would hope that there were regulations for minimal humane conditions." When I asked him to suppose that there were not, he concluded, "Well, we'll just have to go back to beans!"

KIVA said: "I think a lot of people have selective humanity toward animals. They think if it's furry and has big brown eyes it's something you have to save; but if it's a chicken or a fish, that it's kind of ugly, and who cares? I had this dream I was sitting at a restaurant, and there was a conveyor belt, and on it were these big slabs of salmon and chicken, huge slabs on these big plates, and I really wanted a piece, and I was really ashamed, and I couldn't decide which one I wanted. 'Oh my God, I have to decide!' And I remember choosing the chicken, and taking a bite, and it was disgusting. I was eating this flesh, and I felt I should have eaten the salmon."

ROLF said: "My reasons for preferring fish to other kinds of animal flesh are not only moral but I think also to some extent nutritional; I think I'm more suspicious of animal foods that have been raised by man with all kinds of toxic chemicals. My initial reasons for not eating fish were that I thought that the seas were being over-fished, and that if I could live just as well without contributing to the depletion of the seas, I would feel better about that.

"I don't identify with fish, I don't think, as much as with mammals; the vegetarians I've known the longest time have always eaten fish, and called themselves 'vegetarians.' ELLY agreed: "As a vegetarian, I had eaten neurological low-life off and on for a while, like scallops. My vegetarianism is very much—*was*—based on a feeling of simpatico. I might not want to *hurt* another creature; I would not want to see any other creature tortured; but I couldn't necessarily *identify* with other creatures. I can't identify with certain insects; but I don't want to see them suffer. But I would sometimes, especially if I were at a restaurant where there was absolutely *nothing,* I would have something like scallops."

First we hook a fish; then we get hooked on fish. Fish become for former vegetarians the tofu of the sea. Rynn said: "I remember just recently I was selling my book at the Greenmarket, and this woman approached me, and told me she had read my books five or six years ago when she was in high school, and that they had persuaded her to become a vegetarian; but she had been feeling somewhat ener-vated recently, and she had taken to eating fish. And she was clutch-ing a bag of fish that she had just bought at the market. And I told her—I convinced her to take it back. I told her the dead flesh of an animal is not going to stimulate you at all. If you're feeling low, I said, I would rather resort to stimulants than to eat carrion. So she took it back, and I gave her the address of an apothecary shop; I recommended some good stimulants."

He confessed: "I even made up some excuses for her, and she said, 'That would be telling a lie.' I said, 'It's only a white lie.'" I told Rynn that inciting to white-lying did not sound like "moral purity" to me. "It's better to tell a white lie than to kill an animal," he said, forgetting that the fish in the bag were already dead. "You mean it's better to tell a white lie than to eat white fish!" I replied. We laughed; but Rynn's suggestion of substituting stimulants for shad or sole inspired me: ginseng instead of chicken wings; caffeine instead of calves, lean; goldenseal instead of golden fried eel; basil instead of braised veal; horseradish instead of horse with radish; marjoram instead of marinated ham. "I am, I am" going to get to fish—uppers instead of groupers.

We think that eating fish will revive us, as though with a transfusion; we think their deaths will replace the energy bled away in our hectic lives. But if we know the whole fish, as we sometimes do when we keep aquaria, would we then wish to eat any of the parts? Most of us enjoy flesh food to the extent that we see it not as flesh but as food; as far as good disguises go, fish neatly fit the bill, having no bills or beaks, or hands or feet, but only their eyes to distract us. When their white, bloodless flesh is filleted, our qualms go away; we find we have capitulated when they are decapitated: it is easier to eat an eviscerated fish—no ifs, ands, or guts about it.

According to taxonomists, fish belong to an order removed from our own. Thus we may think that because the order is removed, we can remove our reserve and order fish at the table we've reserved, as our waiter observes, "Your fish is my desire." As some would not eat anything which would try to get away, others try to get away with eating anything. Fish, unlike oysters or clams, do try to get away; so perhaps we do not get away with anything when we eat them. If we can drift-net back into eating fish after being vegetarian, we can drift away again—if we can find our way out of our rationalizations.

We draw our lines; sometimes fish are on the lines, and sometimes they are under them. When they are on the lines, we draw them in; when they are under them, we draw lines over their heads signifying that all which falls under them is "fair game." Such unfair games of demarcation are over the heads of fish in more ways than one. There may be little difference between a Venus Flytrap and a clam; but what about between a sea vegetable like kelp, and a mackerel? Fish are vertebrate animals with organs like our own. When they are transported, they suffer from motion sickness (although not from sea sickness in the sea) and vomit, which can foul the water in their tanks and kill them; [2] so we give them tranquilizers to calm them, not because we care about their moods, but because we want them for our food. Some say that if fish could scream, we would be more squeamish about catching them.

That we place fish "below" us shows in the way that many of us attain our vegetarianism. JONATHAN said: "It was a gradual process. First, I started eliminating what I thought were the grossest meats: hamburg, hot dogs, then beef, and then finally fish." And then "finally fish." What are we saying here? In some books advocating vegetarianism, for example, *Transition to Vegetarianism,* we are guided slowly, chapter by chapter, to meatlessness, eliminating first mammals, then birds, and then "finally" fish from our menus.[3] I confess once traveling this path of phases. There was something instinctive about it, seeing one kind of animal as a close relative, and another as a distant one—a mammal uncle, a second cousin hen, a salmon twice removed.

When PETER spoke of salmon and tuna as his "favorite fishes," he meant to eat, not to greet; but mine are those I greet. No matter how far "removed," I do see fish as relatives, perhaps because they can see me. My "favorite fishes" are those in my favorite lake, darting among patches of sun and shadow, their fins fringed with turquoise as I sit watching, looking into their water, as they look up at me, glowing like a land-fish in my multi-colored visor, my fin-flag, shielding me from the harsh midday glare.

When PETER faced the "truth about fish" he meant he could face the fact that they were killed for his meals; but the real truth about fish is that they are animals first, even if they are meals later. Tagore wrote: ". . . suddenly a big fish lept to the surface of the water and disappeared, displaying on its vanishing figure all the colors of the evening sky. It drew aside for a moment the multi-colored screen behind which there was a silent world full of the joy of life . . . Then suddenly the man at the helm exclaimed with a distinct note of regret, 'Ah, what a big fish!' It at once brought before his vision the picture of the fish caught and made ready for his supper. He could only look at the fish through his desire, and thus missed the whole truth of its existence." [4]

What is the truth about fish? Are they individuals, or just nearly identical, repeatable instances of Fishness? If matter individuates, as Aristotle argues, then each is individual, although perhaps not very individual. If the differences between them are less than the differences between "higher" mammals, then how different from each other are they? Tom Regan would say they are experiencing subjects of their own lives.[5] MARCIA finds them "uncomprehending"; but they are not so much uncomprehending as they are uncomprehending of us. (Given that I am that way much of the time myself, with fish I have much in common.) That fish are owners of their own lives is perhaps enough: that they will struggle against death seems reason enough to spare them.

If we eat fish, we may not notice a difference in the quality of our lives; but the fish would notice a difference in the quantity of theirs. Any being who can notice this, any being who can notice anything at all, is a being with some quality of life. Even if on a "scale" of things, fish are well below us, if they can suffer, do we really want them for our supper? If suffering is, as we are told, "the great leveler," then how can we make sense of "levels" of suffering?

7

Nature and Nuance

f life is "a flash in the pan," does it matter whether there is flesh in the pan? If we have a large vision, how do we see vegetarianism? The thriving of the fittest may be its great lesson; but in a natural system based on the surviving of them, does our choice remove us from fundamental truths? Does vegetarianism remove us from the natural world we say we cherish? If we are vegetarian, do we deny or devalue it, mock or diminish it? Do we set ourselves apart from it, or try to escape it? Do we transcend it? If we think "atomistically" about the individual animal, we may be moved by pity to try to save it; but if we think "holistically" about nature, and try to imitate it, must our compassion be swallowed whole, as so many others swallow each other?

Many of us become vegetarian because we love nature and do not wish to encourage activities which assail it; but how are we to value nature as far as diet is concerned? If imitation is the sincerest form of flattery, whom do we imitate? Should we become hunters? Foragers? Should we end agriculture? What do we eat—or whom? Is nature all about eating each other? ROLF said that "life lives off life"; but when we come face to face with life-taking, we may wish otherwise. "Thinking like a mountain"[1] means thinking about death as well as about life, although most vegetarians want to think about life only. Yet concern for individual animals is not nature's way. Thus imitating nature does not require vegetarianism; most people become vegetarians not because they love nature, but because they love animals.

A holistic perspective, nevertheless, yields a critique of modern meat. From this perspective, we see that nature is harmed less, for example, by subsistence hunting than by farming and that when we eat meat we are, collectively, responsible for much of the pollution which strangles it. The child born deformed because of agricultural pesticides is related to us; the mother cow who ate the sprayed fodder, and her calf, taken to the veal barn a day after birth, are related to us; the nitrates in our drinking water, the giardia in the streams, the depletion of ancient aquifers, now irrigating cattle feed, and the erosion of trampled soils are related to us; the poison 1080 in the bodies of wild animals, the coyotes snared or burned, the wolves and lions and eagles shot to protect the investors' "stock" are related to us—and the lives of millions of displaced wild horses and burros and antelope and elk. The deer dying in the hot sun, crucified on the ranchers' barbed wire, are related to us.

If we buy hamburger, the rainforest ranches are related to us; the lost fauna and flora and threatened indigenous peoples are related to us, and related to us are the birds who do not sing here in the spring because their winter homes there went up in smoke. Lady Bird, Lady Bird, fly from your home! Your forest has fallen, and your children have burned!

Meat eating is not an isolated act framed by our whims and hungers, but one which places us in relationship with human and nonhuman others. We are related not only to now-dead others (not as I-Thou but as I-It), but also enter into implicit contracts with those who slaughter and those who butcher, with truckers, wholesalers and retailers, and with everyone, including many children, who in witnessing our meals, see our mouths filled with dead flesh. We may even enter into relationship with physicians and with surgeons as a result of our decisions.

Some say meat eating is "a personal choice," but equivocate on the expression, sometimes using it to mean "one's own choice" or "no one's business but my own" and sometimes "beyond ethics" or "beyond rational debate"; but when we choose to eat flesh, what we eat is the business of who we eat as well as those who make it their business to purvey it to us. A steak may be an it; but a steer is a who. Thus if meat eating is a "personal choice" it is also a choice about who we are eating.

In this context, "personal" does not mean "wholly private" or "insulated." Even LINDA who said: "I think diets are really very personal," quickly added, "I mean, they *do* have social and political implications." Eating meat is not beyond ethics or rational debate. Matters of life and death are matters of ethics; eating involves life and death; so eating is a matter of ethics. We are both citizens of the world and animals in nature: our choices always go beyond us. There are few, if any, strictly "personal" decisions. How are we to rip ourselves out of the fabric of community? What we eat is not "out of this world" (even though it may sometimes taste that way). Whether we eat meat, give it up, or return to it, we involve others.

Ethics provides rules for other-oriented behavior—traditionally, rules for living in a human community. It is only recently that ethics has expanded to include the natural world,[2] probably because there is increasingly less of it relative to our burgeoning numbers, and value increases proportionally to what is rare. It once made sense not to invite nature into our circles, because there was so much more of it relative to us. We had to take care of ourselves; nature could take care of itself—and still will—although perhaps not in ways to our liking.

The voices in this chapter are not those of the ignorant, but of those who know as much about the wider consequences of meat production as any present vegetarian; yet the speakers now all eat meat. Just as we may take a lapsed vegetarian to vegetation, but can't make her live on it, we can remind her of her vegetarian philosophy, but can't make her live it. Some lapsos are reluctant flesh eaters; others are inured, but none deny the ideas by which they once lived. Why they no longer live them shows in their philosophies of nature. If we regard a plate, we see a notion; if we peer into a cupboard, we find a theory; if we inspect a larder, we discover a world view.

Do vegetarians live more harmoniously with nature? JONATHAN said: "Vegetarianism was definitely a way to get in tune with the natural world: human consciousness has the ability to feel a link to all life. I was developing the feeling that having consciousness means being more in tune with everything, the goal actually being a type of oneness."

Are flesh eaters somehow "out of tune"? Hunters profess to be "in tune" with nature by killing; vegetarians say they are "in tune" by not killing. For some, taking life is part of life, and connects them to it; for others, refusing to take life joins them to it. A hunter may help or hinder the creative processes of nature; a vegetarian may allow more wilderness to thrive by consuming less, but may still support monocultures, and their war on the wild. If a vegetarian values nature for its own sake, that is one thing, and if a hunter values nature for *his* own sake, that is another; but the hunter may value nature for its own sake, and the vegetarian may value her enjoyment of it.

Some say that predating goes against our nature, analogizing us to the vegetarian gorilla, rather than to our closer relative, the chimpanzee, who apparently kills for meat.[3] Others say that by being a predator we are part of the natural world. KIVA said: "I have more respect for people who go out and hunt. There are people who eat meat, and it never occurs to them that this is flesh." ROLF said: "I don't feel really judgmental even towards people who love hunting. It's something I've never done; it's not part of my family background. I have absolutely no desire to do it. But I think it is humanly quite an intelligible activity in light of our evolutionary history, and the cama-raderie and the excitement of the hunt. I'm re-reading Faulkner's "The Bear," and it makes some sense to me. I don't think it has much place in a world as crowded as ours, but certainly aboriginal hunting makes considerable sense."

JOHN said: "People who live above the Arctic Circle, and live there year 'round, do their own hunting and trapping, and live in cabins that don't have electricity, unless they have their own gener-ators. People further and further out are in subsistence situations where it is necessary for all of them that they hunt for their food. So of course they would shoot a caribou, and skin it and prepare it and eat it. Even when I was a vegetarian at my most ardent, I was able to say, 'Well, I can justify *that*, because if you're going to go the whole route and respect the creature you're killing—don't eat it unless you're prepared to do all that.' I certainly once bought into that argument which still holds some appeal to me, I must say."

Whether or not we kill it ourselves, some say it is better to eat a wild animal than a domesticated one. ROLF said: "I once ordered, I actually ordered, venison in a restaurant. I feel differently about venison simply because I think given the present ecology of the deer population, that it's probably best that they be shot, given that the predators are gone, and they haven't been cooped up like farm ani-mals. It just happened I didn't like it."

ELLY also liked the idea of eating something wild, and said: "My vegetarianism was based on a feeling of relatedness. I'd feel better if I was out wringing some little creature's neck—in a way. I would feel that I was living out my vegetarian ethics as a meat eater. I hate factory farming. For that reason alone, I'd rather go out, kill some wild thing, and eat it. Can you imagine me doing that? But I would feel that I was living in a more completely closed ethical circle if I was doing it for myself, if I took responsibility for all the actions leading up to it."

Ethics are compelling, but actions, telling. On New Year's Day, many years ago when out walking, I saw a trail of blood in the fresh snow and followed it. At trail's end, in a snowdrift, lay a Black Labrador, half-grown. I carried her home, and called ELLY, who arrived in a beat-up old station wagon for a trip to her favorite vet. The animal needed five hundred dollars worth of surgery, but was "salvageable." The two of us, both impoverished doctoral students at the time, decided to split the bill and save the dog; but notices I posted located the foundling's lost caregivers who paid the bill—and thanked us. I could not imagine ELLY "wringing some little thing's neck"—even if it were consonant with her world view. ELLY's heart is as tender as her mind is tough. She adopts strays, and ministers to the throwaways no one wants; it is to ELLY that one turns if an "animal problem" is thrown one's way. ELLY would never strangle anything.

Sometimes, like ELLY, we envision an ideal, and often we find these ideals in other cultures, perhaps because our own culture is bereft of them. NANCY said: "The American Indians who lived on this planet for thousands of years ate meat, and they never destroyed a thing." KIVA said: "In Native American cultures, they were aware they were taking a life, and the life was giving them life. If you acknowledge that fact, that there is death involved, it's more healthy that way."

VICKY said: "Once I explained my rationale for eating meat to a vegetarian housemate. I told him the Native Americans gave thanks to the spirit of the animal when they killed it, so I gave thanks when I ate it, too. He thought that was a poor excuse. I read Native American philosophy which denigrated the White man's ways: 'Everywhere he touches her, the earth is sore.' I wanted to be more like a Native American, part of the big circle, respecting Earth, respecting all creation, being responsible. Ironically, this led me to eating meat again."

ROLF said: "The attitude I respect the most towards the eating of flesh is the attitude that we sometimes find amongst the indigenous people. Rather than avoiding animal suffering, and trying to be pure, it is seen as an act of reverence. I don't do that myself, except sometimes at home, or occasionally I do it with good friends; I offer a prayer before eating. And I really like that attitude.[4] I even do toward the vegetables and the grains, and I pray, not so much to God, but to the beings themselves; but I don't think I've ever done this when I've eaten flesh."

Do these borrowings hallow our meals of meat? We usually do not witness the killing when an animal's spirit is said to be released: the spirit which may be present to a Native American or to a Pygmy is absent for us. So our prayers, in imitation of tribal ritual, lose meaning. Just as the animals to whom they are offered are long-dead, their spirits are long-gone: there is no longer anyone left to thank. One cannot abstract from Native American or other aboriginal forms out of context; ROLF was right, perhaps, to reserve his prayers for vegetation.

Ingenuous lapsos may borrow too generously from other cultures, but as vegetarians many held wide environmental views—often on a global scale. NANCY said: "It was a big consciousness, part of the awakening of consciousness, seeing the interrelatedness of man and the planet, and the interrelatedness of man and the other species." JONATHAN said: "It was a way of walking lightly. I was influenced by Rachael Carson's *Silent Spring*. I was very concerned with pesticides in the food—and in the environment." DAVID said: "It gets to a point where you want to step lightly, and you feel a calling not to consume so much. When you start seeing that life is dependent on other lives, you want to leave less traces." ROBBAN said: "I wanted to do the right thing for myself and the planet."

VICKY was vegetarian, in part, "because of the indirect discouragement of cattle ranching which replaces important rain forests with grazing land," and said, "I don't want the rain forest destroyed because of cattle ranching." KIVA, too, could not sanction "eating meat that's from mass production, that causes pain and suffering to thousands of cows, and depletes the ozone layer, and drops down the rain forest." ROLF said: "I think I feel less *parasitic* being a vegetarian, like I'm taking less from the earth which sustains us. The only point I've ever tried to get across in class is the environmental consequences of eating meat. Largely for reasons having to do with the health of the planet, I don't want to support the meat industry." KIVA said: "Even if you don't want to become a vegetarian, you can still be aware, and still try to do the best you possibly can in not harming the environment or other animals. If I eat chicken, it's free-range, and Happy Hen Eggs and dolphin-safe tuna fish."

If we refuse to do harm (*"primum non nocere"*) and practice *ahimsa* or non-maleficence, are we in harmony with a world in which so much is harmed? Is the way to harmoniousness harmlessness? ROLF said: "Living in harmony with nature, but also in society, may not be possible to do at the same time." TONY agreed: "I would like to live in that peaceful, benign, loving, existence, knowing that in extreme cases, that as the environment changes, we would have to change. If I lived in a pastoral society, there's no question that I would be a vegetarian. Vegetarianism goes along with harmonious living in a society; it's not a society based on dominance or domination."

One reason we cannot achieve harmony is because of how society works, but how does nature work? There is a large philosophical literature devoted to whether we can base an ethic *on* nature; certainly there are paradoxes if we try.[5] But sometimes seeing how nature works provides a context for understanding actions, even if it does not show us which actions are right or wrong. How we see meat eating depends on how we interpret the natural world. ROLF said: "How nature works, as a system, is not well-represented by an *ahimsa* approach. The natural order is as much involved with death and destruction as it is with creation, with beauty, and respect. Life lives off life; I don't think there's any way out of that. Agriculture is an 'unnatural' activity; but vegetarianism doesn't go 'against nature' given the present state of the world, because meat is so much more destructive of nature in its entirety.

"Many vegetarians are motivated primarily by concern with the sanctity of individual animal life; but my own commitment, more like Aldo Leopold's, is to the whole system, wanting to affirm *that* and live within its limitations. The Romantics saw the destructive potential in nature and struggled to accept it. They saw the 'awe-full-ness' of nature, and I think the word is really important. Nature is a powerfully destructive being as well as a creative being. The Indian tradition always saw that—the devouring Mother, Kali—and recognized that there cannot be birth without death. Destruction is part of life, and essential to it; but that doesn't mean trying to become as destructive as possible in emulation of nature."

ELLY said: "I see my relationship with the rest of the natural world in a fairly unsentimental way. For one thing, I don't see nature or the earth in a 'Mother Nature' way. That kind of Rousseauian thinking doesn't appeal to me at all. I don't find earthquakes, volcanoes, and floods nurturant images. So I don't romanticize them. The best way I could put this is that I feel myself to be a vulnerable being, and sense that vulnerability in all other beings. I think that's the basis of the strongest link that I feel to other creatures."

DAVID said: "The things we require to sustain ourselves cause suffering: we feed on each other. If it's the grains, or lettuce, or whatever, they sustain us, and they're also striving. They're striving, too. Things are a lot more complex than I used to think. We need to be respectful to our world and try to be sensitive to the fact that all beings are striving for happiness, and enjoying their lives, and I don't think that excludes even inanimate objects. In some way, I think we need to have respectful feelings towards them as well.

"It is said that Dogon, when he would go to the bridge and put his dipper in the water, would drink from it, and whatever was left, he would always pour *toward* him in respect to it. Once I heard that story, there was really something that was right about that. Even water that we don't see as infused with life has an aspect that's also striving. When he returned the water, whatever was left after drinking, he poured it toward him in respect for the water . . . It's a beautiful story, I think. So we look at inanimate objects suffused with something special. There is something special about all existence. It doesn't just go for animate objects."

Immersion in the life sciences may or may not teach us about the specialness of all life. FRANK said: "Not all animals are meant to have offspring. The way nature is, a lot of offspring are here for food. Every spore that comes off a powder puff mushroom—a puffball mushroom—if every one of those became a mushroom, the earth would be covered with mushrooms in a generation or two. Mother Nature is an impersonal goddess; she doesn't care about individuals at all. The Mother Nature Goddess just wants an endless profusion so that some will survive. It's a very impersonal thing.

"Guy Murchie, author of *Seven Mysteries of Life*, talks of recycling atoms. We're born of stars exploding. We *are* the universe, and all creatures are made out of the same stuff. That's the way of nature. It just churns and recycles the same atoms and molecules around and around and around, forming them into structures, and breaking them down again.

"There's life in us and on us—and living in us. It's a little bit disturbing at first to find out that our bodies are hosts for myriads of living creatures. In fact, our digestive systems wouldn't even work right if we didn't have these commensals. Even our cells—are they separate things? At least when I was in college, there was an evolutionary theory that mitochondria and chloroplasts were once like blue-green algae that just learned to live inside us. They were separate organisms that just banded together and entered our cells so that they could have a home, and in return, they'll do photosynthesis or energy management.

"The more cells you have banded together, the stronger the energy field becomes, until you reach the point of consciousness and self-consciousness and meta-consciousness. I used to think about it: where does consciousness come in? Maybe when there's enough density of cells, it just forms a field, just like if you wrap wires around a piece of steel and put current through it, it becomes an electro-magnet, whereas if you unwind it, stretch it out, it doesn't have that effect. It has a field, but it's too weak to do anything. So that's how I think of our brains—as these nerve cells wrapped around each other, generating a stronger field."

ROBBAN said: "I don't really believe that the matter-universe is all that important. I really think the whole issue of vegetarianism is kind of a moot point. It's all just a game anyway. Our body that we live in is just a physical shell. It doesn't have any reality of its own. The suffering that we go through or that animals go through is just part of this material thing that we're doing for whatever reason. The Aborigines speak of the animal or plant giving its life in service. The animal is offering its life to be of service, to become part of you, and it's all part of the circle of life. It's all part of the oneness of life.

"If I have a patient who comes in and they're sick, and they die, that's not the worst thing either. The purpose of life is not always to prolong life. We need to get a whole lot less attached to these things, including our ideas about vegetarianism and the way things *should* be. People interpret Eastern philosophy or the Bible as the be-all or the end-all when existence is what it is. Experience is not what we *think* about experience. We can sit there and *think* about experience all we want and that's not real. The only thing that's real is real experience. Have-tos and shoulds have done more harm to the soul and to the spirit of people than eating a steak will ever do."

Some former vegetarians wish to re-integrate into nature, while others have trouble seeing how that could be done, as if anything we do in the natural world is interference, unlike the activities of other animals who we see as fitting in. VICKY said: "There's a rule of etiquette when backpacking in the White Mountains National Park: 'Take only pictures, leave only footprints.' It tells us humans *don't belong*. We're only visiting nature; we're not supposed to influence it. It's an important rule in the woods, but I took that philosophy home with me. I didn't want to influence the earth *at all*—no slapping mosquitoes—but being part of the big circle means having an effect on the world. It means if a mosquito is annoying me, I'll kill it, with my hands, not with one of those purple bug-zappers.

"As a property owner for the first time in my life, I'm able to live out some ideals I've always had. I plan to make my one-acre property into a habitat all kinds of wildlife can live in, eat, drink, breed, and do their thing in. I feel that although we humans have invented the idea of property, what I really am here is a steward of this little plot of land. I'm not going to use insecticides. I'm going to plant native plants (that some call 'weeds'); I'm going to provide everything I can to give back to the creatures that live here what people are continuously taking away.

"I've read about 'gardening for wildlife' and 'native habitat gardening,' and plan to follow the advice. I've got a box of 'weed' seeds I collected last fall to plant in a 'wild' garden. I'm going to plant it so my neighbors see sunflowers and echinacea when they look over here. I also plan to plant fruit trees and berry bushes—not just for me, but for my creature neighbors, too. This is something I have looked forward to all my life. I'm sure the land will produce more than my husband and I can eat. We don't *need* meat now, and we'll need it even less next summer."

GAIL said: "I may become a homesteader. In my old age, I anticipate having cash-flow problems, and anticipate having to raise my food to make sure it's clean—or having to hunt it. Raising it would assure me of quality. I think I may have to learn to. It's not something I could do readily. I may *have* to do that to get good food. I think I have hunter genes, northern, Nordic, flesh-eating genes, I really do. Oh, God, I really do. I think there are many, many animal populations intended as a food source for other animal populations, and I feel they were evolved to *be* a food source. Evolution is sort of given; it has to supersede our cultural and philosophical conclusions about the immorality of eating meat, or of veganism. Veganism is a *cultural* development."

ELLY said: "I am extremely mammalian. I don't know what it is to be in touch with my 'animal nature,' because that seems almost like a contradiction. The animals simply *are*; so if I were to be in touch with my 'animal nature,' I would have to have an inchoate sense of myself as just one among many. The relationship would be a Taoist I-Thou: I wouldn't have to speak of it.

"I think the most troubling aspect of vegetarianism is that in one way I'm using my conception of myself as one among many to feel *closer* to the world I'm part of; but when I conceive of carnivorous animals killing—dogs, cats, and domesticated animals killing—I realize that what I am doing in an effort to feel closer to the world is actually very exclusive. It becomes an exclusively human kind of decision. As an angst-ridden, Kafka-esque Jew, I will never feel at one with the world; I realize that vegetarian or not, I will never feel at one with the world. There's too much inconsistency, too much horror; and yet on the level of vegetarianism, I think that's something I try to do, even though it's a self-contradicting effort, because by aspiring to vegetarianism, I'm aspiring to what I see as the *best* in human response, distinctively and uniquely human responsiveness. Vegetarianism is an exclusive choice not only because it's a uniquely human decision, but because it's a decision that's based on the availability of options. In a society where vegetation—a necessary variety of vegetation—isn't available, I can sanction meat eating."

Are humans "in" or "out" of nature? Vegetarian humans do not seem to me like natural animals, but rather like animals who, as part of their nature, learned to do something unnatural for their species. To justify eating meat by saying it is "natural" can mean either of two things: either it is part of our natural diet, as we evolved to be omnivores, or that flesh eating is a natural occurrence in nature. I take each to be a fact, but because we can no more wring values out of facts than blood out of bloodroot,[6] neither justifies flesh eating, although each explains it.

The way nature appears, it appears that vegetarians do not fit in; but behind appearance is law, and if the law behind the maw is evolution to complexity and high consciousness, if vegetarianism is a high consciousness, then vegetarians may be obeying a natural law. What vegetarians do is not rooted in hatred or horror of nature, or in saying "No!" to it, for vegetarians may express their love for its most complex creations by not eating them—just as meat eaters may express their love for nature by appreciating what they eat.

Vegetarians do not insult or spite nature by refusing to eat some parts of it. Choosing to eat less complex life forms is still a way of living in the world. Vegetarians are animals, too, and the vegetation they eat is part of nature. Mind, too, is as natural as matter; vegetarians merely make up their minds that animals matter. If vegetarians insisted on living on ideas or on thoughts which could not sustain them—now *that* would be unnatural! FRANK said: "Monkeys sit in trees eating bananas; they see a fat beetle walking down the branch; they grab it and shove it into their mouths as fast as they can. We're the clever monkey. If it moves, grab it." It is also natural to our species to "grab" ideas, and to many, vegetarianism is a good idea to grab. If in keeping with that idea, all that we keep around is plant food, then we do eat "whatever is around." If we are animals who can "eat anything," then any food is "natural" for us to eat.

At a high level of abstraction, nature is a gorgeous order, but one which shuffles energy as if individuals do not matter; at the level of tooth and claw, it is redder than we like to imagine.[7] Each being is who it is, but is also, ultimately, a meal for others. Because the compassion vegetarians may show to individual animals is not nature's way, we do not imitate nature by sparing them. A vegetarian may return a fish to its water, or save an insect drowning there, but forget that a fish might have needed that insect for its dinner, and that many smaller fish will be eaten by the fish we saved. The sympathy we feel for individual animals, and especially our desire not to eat them, may or may not be natural: we seem to be animals half in and half out of nature.

Nature looks best either from a great distance—from the perspective of ecosystems—or very close up, from the viewpoint of the microscope; but we live in the middle, where there is in addition to beautiful hue, the cry of things being killed and eaten. Nature in the middle runs better as a silent movie; but even its pictures can disturb. As animals, we are mired in nature; but we can also be inspired by it, for it is the order and not the slaughter in nature which moves us. From the point of view of those being killed and eaten, I want to say, with Edna St. Vincent Millay, "I know. But I do not approve."[8] But then who am I? And what do I know about the mysteries of life and evolution? As a vegetarian I know only that I am a being who thinks and chooses, and that because I think about food, therefore, I am not going to choose some of it.

8

Attitudes and Animals

*"Barnyard fowl, hogs, cattle, sheep, goats, draught horses are of the
productive nature of goods, and serve a useful, often a lucrative
end; therefore beauty is not readily imputed to them."*
—Thorstein Veblin, *The Theory of the Leisure Class*

*". . . the attitude toward animals, and their treatment, in twentieth
century American industrial meat production is literally sickening,
unethical, and a source of boundless bad luck for this society."*
—Gary Snyder, *The Practice of the Wild*

*"Mankind's true moral test, its fundamental test
(which lies deeply buried from view), consists of its attitude
towards those who are at its mercy: animals."*
—Milan Kundera, *The Unbearable Lightness of Being*

We raise many animals, but not many questions about the animals we are raising. We also hold many attitudes toward animals, but do not often question them, because then we would have to question ourselves, the ethos of our culture, and its traditions. Seldom scrutinized, our attitudes both lock us into our collective life and lock animals out of it—and out of our minds, for we think little about nonhumans, and as a result, little of them.

Many of our attitudes are rooted in our religions, especially in the Judeo-Christian traditions, which are themselves rooted in an agrarian way of life. From farming and the scriptures of farmers and pastoralists, we form our views. Sometimes we wonder at our behaviors when we catch ourselves acting oddly—putting out seed for finches and buntings while chickens roast in our ovens, feeding our guppies when we have other fish to fry.

GAIL said: "Being brought up Catholic was a horrible way to have a good relationship with animals. At least at the time period when I was being taught and lectured, we were told, very strictly, 'Animals *don't* go to Heaven; you really shouldn't get very attached to them. They were made for man to use; they have *no souls.*'

"When we were kids, we read these wonderful children's books like *Charlotte's Web.* In Catholicism and in Catholic school, these stories are ridiculed—at least at the time period I was going to Catholic school. You've got to watch out for getting too close to them; they have no souls; they're not God's creatures the way we are. They really just exist for civilization to use in whatever way it sees fit. They're meant to be *worked* by us. Very utilitarian. Very *cold.*

"And I'm horrified to think my family would put dogs and cats away. My parents and us kids, we got pretty blasé about it. We would put them away when they became inconvenient. I'm horrified to think of the *dear* animals we sent to be euthanized when people got tired of feeding them, rather than making more of an effort. Oh, it was terrible. Both my parents were: 'Well, it's time to take it over to the Humane Society now.' My brother and my sister and I would get together, and we'd say, 'My God, that was a *great* cat; we should have found some way; we should have tried harder. I wouldn't have minded spending the money now that I think about it. Just because it was getting a little irritating, no one was feeding them, or a vet said, 'This animal's going to need a hundred dollars worth of treatment,' and everyone said, 'Eh, let the vet put it down.'

"As a child, nowhere was there anything in my social structure wrong with that. The whole Catholic thing was it's a little sacrilegious to get too close to animals. People weren't talking about compassion to animals as they are now."

ROBBAN said: "I was raised Catholic, so I'm a Christian, obviously, and the Bible says God gave animals to be used. I don't see an animal as another person. If I had to kill *you* that would be another issue. I wouldn't advocate killing a person in order to eat it. I don't see an animal as another person—even my horse. They're wonderful animals, but they're still animals.

"I was raised in the midwest, in Ohio, on a farm. And to me, you could be friends with an animal and still eat it afterward. I had a pet cow; I had a pet calf. I had pet goats; I had pet sheep that would end up being dinner. And I got used to that concept very early on. It just didn't bother me. One day it was my pet, and the next day it was in my freezer. I got over it.

"From a philosophical or spiritual perspective, I feel God has put animals on the earth for our use, and that human beings are omnivores, and are intended to have some protein sources in our diet. We weren't intended to be completely vegetarian. You can tell by the teeth. And so that was never an issue for me; the animal issue was not the issue for me. It wasn't to avoid eating these poor animals that were raised for this purpose anyway.

"Blackie was a cute little calf, and Sparky was another one. It was a little black calf with a white star in the middle of its forehead, and he was so cute and so precious when he was little, and he grew up into a big animal, and was kind of dumb and stupid, actually, as he got older. One day he wasn't in the barn anymore, and I asked what happened to Sparky. I actually said this to my Mom. At that time, we had a big freezer, the kind that opens from the top; it opens like a chest. We were standing on the back porch, and she showed me where Sparky was, in all these nice packets of frozen meat in the freezer. There was a gulp, this was my friend. But then this was the purpose—this was why we had this cow to begin with. I had a lot of fun with him, but I didn't particularly miss him at that point.

"I had a goat named Snowflake. I don't think we ate her. I think she just went to the neighbors' after she got a little too big and out of control. She used to jump out of the stall. We had a barn and a few animals, mainly for our own use and enjoyment. I had horses when I was little. Seth. Horses are very intelligent animals. Queenie was my pony and Seth was my horse. They were my best friends growing up.

You can't develop that kind of attachment to a cow. It's like a dog. A dog is like a friend. I can't imagine eating my dog."

I remind ROBBAN that she called Sparky a "friend." She replied: "I did say that, didn't I? I definitely did not feel the *attachment* to the cow and the goat and the sheep. I never had the sense of attachment to them; but I could look deeply into my pony's or my horse's eyes, and just feel completely understood. My horse would do anything for me. He would put himself in a situation where he was in physical pain to please me. You don't get that kind of devotion from a cow. They just sit there and chew their cuds. In other cultures, they do eat dogs and horses. Culturally, I was raised to never eat a horse. It's not something that's expected. An animal like a cow is purposely bred and raised for that purpose."

We do not eat our dogs or horses, but sometimes we feed our horses to our dogs, from cans of horsemeat, or in other ways. A Buddhist vegetarian I knew called a veterinarian to come to her rural home to shoot her old horse rather than kill it with a lethal injection. She did not want the meat "to go to waste" but "to the dogs." Her dogs did feast on her horse who otherwise would have been a feast for maggots. Someone had to eat it—so why not her dogs? Would we feed one dog to another? If it rained cats and dogs, would we feed them to each other?

MARCIA's background is right out of "A Prairie Home Companion." Raised as a Protestant in a Scandinavian small town in rural North Dakota "where my father and the entire community was Norweigan," like ROBBAN, she also spent her childhood on a farm. She said: "On the farm we raised chickens and had some cattle. You have just enough cattle for your own use, basically. We just used them for milk. We had chickens for awhile. As far as farm animals go, ours had a good life. I still felt bad that the chickens were getting killed and so forth, and I always refused to watch. But it was just matter of fact. It did bother me, but I pretty much accepted it.

"When we lived on the farm, we ate primarily venison. My father would go hunting, and as soon as my brother got to be around nine, he would go hunting, too. We would get two deer, usually, per year; my Dad gets one and my brother one. My father and brother would actually do the butchering of the deer in one of the sheds; they would bring back their deer, and butcher it, and that was our meat for the year.

"We would make some of it into roasts, and then—and this was everybody's favorite—we would make what Scandinavians call '*spikechute*'—it's dried venison. You put it in brine, salt water, in crocks, and put it out on your porch. This is in the winter when it's very cold in North Dakota already. You put it out on your porch and you cover it. You let it sit there for I forget how long—some weeks. Then you take it out, and my parents would take out the clothesrack. In my parents' bedroom there was a radiator, the old kind of radiator, the Radiator Lions kind of radiator, and we put the clothesrack right next to the radiator in my parents' bedroom. Then you take these hunks of meat, tie a string through one end, and tie it up on the clothesrack in my parents' bedroom. And there it would dry for weeks and weeks. You'd wait until Dad said it was probably ready to start cutting some pieces. It's beef jerky—only it's venison jerky. It's dried venison, that's what it is.

"By the time we were in town, they'd take the deer, bring them home on top of the car, and then they would take them and hang them up in the basement. (We had an unfinished basement in our house.) They did the butchering there. While they were hanging up, before they actually started butchering them, and while they were hanging up, I'd go down there. I would start petting the deers' nostrils—I mean their nose—their snout. I'd pet the deer's head, and I'd cry and cry and cry. I'd look into their eyes, and then my father and brother would come and chase me upstairs because they did not want me there, because I was crying. I still continued to eat venison. I don't know how I reconciled it. I think it was partly that I hero-worshipped my brother, and wanted to do everything he did. So I wasn't going to get weepy."

FRANK, growing up thousands of miles away in an east coast,

suburban Jewish household, said: "I think in societies, or farm families, maybe one hundred or two hundred years ago, the cattle helped pull the hoe, and every once in a while they'd slaughter one, and have a meal. I think with that being a value, as the way of things, and you see everyone else doing it, this was a matter of fact, kind of frontier mentality, and it was just the way of things. 'I think this year we'll retire the cow, and eat it during the winter.'

"People like us who are not part of the agriculture system, have grown up with children's stories about the agriculture system. We've grown up with children's stories about the child that falls in love with the family cow, or *Charlotte's Web*, with the pig, and 'Can't we just keep this one as a pet?' 'You know, we've got to make a living; but if you're going to be responsible for it, and take care of it, then we won't slaughter it.' We've grown up with those children's stories that helped to form our over-sensitive values.

"I'm definitely over-empathetic because I read those little stories, or when I was younger, watched the movies. And I think it's quite possible that if people grow up with a different set of values, that's what you do. There are still people today who think that animals are separate from humans and that we're not all part of continuum. They say, 'Kill the chicken. *It's just an animal.* Who cares if it's cooped up?' Or like the veal thing. I think it's reprehensible. But the people who did it—it's like the concentration camp. Did they feel empathy for these people or were these people somehow subhumans in the minds of the soldiers? You're brain-washed. Whatever your training, you just go along with it. It's just part of the value system they grew up with; but it's a little shocking."

We grow up with attitudes, but sometimes we grow out of them. If this were not the case, there would be fewer vegetarians. Vegetarians may have to uproot themselves in order to live on roots, fruits, and shoots. What we learned at our parents' knees, we unlearn at universities, or in reflective living. Vegetarians, as a group, seem unafraid of change, and even of changes back again if they give up their vegetarianism. We may not be able to go home again but we can go back to meat again, eating it at home or elsewhere.

It is one thing to eat meat in ignorance and another to be an informed vegetarian; but what is it to be an informed former vegetarian? Some, like ELLY, know a little but not enough to hurt them. ELLY said: "I've actually read very few things on vegetarianism and ethical reasons for vegetarianism because I am so *appalled* by all of it. I have never read, for example, Peter Singer's stuff on factory farming. I'd *see* it; I'd look through the pages; but I didn't need to read them. They would just give me nightmares."

Some vegetarians are easily led like sheep; but unlike lambs sent off to slaughter, go back, like TONY, to eating lambs who are slaughtered. A little knowledge may be a dangerous thing, for it spoils our appetites; a little more knowledge can make us into vegetarians. Somewhere in between are our rationalizations. One rationalization for raising animals for food is called "The Logic of the Larder."[1] This argument convinced me for nearly half of my life: The animal would not have lived at all, if not grown for food, so given that it is better to have lived a short, good life than to have lived no life at all, we are justified in raising animals for food, for by eating them, we benefit, and by being born, they benefit. I once loved to eat steak; the steer who produced it loved to live. That he might have loved to live even longer was not a consideration, for if I were not going to eat him, he would not have lived or loved his life at all.

Traditionally, we established a relationship with animals in husbandry, only to betray it later; now we deny relationship so as not to betray it, but only to betray the animal. But what if the steer were given a glimpse, before birth, of his "short, good life." Would he have said "yes" or "no" to unanaesthetized castration, dehorning, and branding; to stressful shipping; to the feedlot; to drug-laced feed; to unnatural feed, perhaps fouled with feces, or mixed with cement dust or newspaper, with or without the print? Would he have said "yes" to drug injections and implants, to the prod and the stun gun?

Would other animals say "yes" to artificial insemination, assembly-line style, to the "rape rack," to forced pregnancies, to the theft of the young? Would they say "yes" to intense confinement, to crowding or to isolation, to boredom, to breathing foul air? Would they say "yes" to the destruction of their senses, or of body parts—to docked tails or ears, or severed beaks? Would they say "yes" to being nailed by their feet to the floor and force-fed with a hose until their livers "burst"? Would they say "yes" to the forced inhibition of all instinctive behavioral routines? To all sources of comfort? To denial of natural experience and the celebration of life? To one long funeral of sensation? Who would?

Food animals today live abysmal lives; how for the life of us do we live with this? We live off them, telling ourselves, perhaps, that "that's all they know; they can't feel deprived if they have nothing to miss." Perhaps, as omnivores, we have a natural right to eat flesh—but this flesh? Can we have a natural right to eat unnatural flesh?

Former vegetarians are not ignorant of the realities of the industrialization of meat. DAVID said: "A lot of the ways the animals are raised cause unnecessary pain—it does." Yet DAVID eats this meat. LINDA said: "It's not just that I'm hastening an animal's death, either. It's that these animals were bred artificially and had a completely unnatural life, solely for my use, and I do have a problem with that, even though I continue to be part of that. As a vegetarian, I thought, 'You're killing animals to eat, and I'm not.' That was before I worked for a dairy farmer and found out where milk comes from."

What LINDA, who calls herself "a farm wife," saw first hand, VICKY learned in school. She said: "I should mention that in a college ethics class I learned for the first time about milk-fed veal—how the baby cows are raised to be so weak that they can't stand up, just for the purpose of their meat being more tender when they get slaughtered. To this day, I have eaten no veal because of that knowledge, even though I used to like it. You may ask, 'What differentiates the baby cow from the adult cow?' I can hear those ghostly vegetarians behind my back accusing me of rationalizing. We learned about the cruel and unnecessary treatment of chickens. One time I saw a preview for a special news program about the chicken industry. The reporter said, 'After you see what we found out, you may never want to eat chicken again.' I purposely didn't watch it. I wanted to eat chickens again. When I order in a Chinese restaurant, I can't resist ordering Hunan Chicken."

JONATHAN said: "If I wanted to carry this to a logical conclusion about animal ethics, I couldn't deny there was a connection between milk and some slaughtered animals. The male cow has to die off: they can't give milk. You can romanticize around it by saying, 'Well, this is part of nature, and you don't have to waste.' You know you're sacrificing that male cow; but a lot boils down to how the milk was produced. Is it a factory farm or a small family cooperative?"

ROBBAN said: "I won't eat veal because of the way it's raised. I don't eat pork very often because I really don't like the animal, the vibration of the animal. I eat a lot of beef and chicken. We need to look at getting the hormones out of it, and getting the antibiotics out of it, and at more natural environments for these animals to grow in. The actual process of killing them is the least of the problem in terms of pain, because that happens so quickly that it's not painful.

"I wouldn't want an animal tortured. Absolutely not. That would be unspeakable. If an animal had to die a slow and painful death in order for me to enjoy the steak, I wouldn't do it. It's not right to cause suffering. If you have free-range chickens, if you have animals who are raised humanely, that's a totally different issue. Yours is a visualization in your mind, and it's not even close to the reality of the ways animals who are raised and slaughtered for food are killed. It's a very different process. It's like people with a fear of death have magnified what they conceive the process of death to be. I was raised on a farm. I know how these animals die. It's not painful. And if they're raised humanely, which most farmers do—"

An animal may not die a slow and painful death, but may live a slow and painful life. Even if most farmers are "humane," most animals are not raised by farmers, but by industrialists. According to Temple Grandin, a professor of Animal Science at Colorado State, in the 1960's when attitudes in agribusiness were influenced by Skinnerian behaviorism which denied feelings to animals, there were horrific abuses.[2] But now, thanks to her innovative "meat-packing" plant designs, which include curved, high-walled chutes leading cattle, peacefully and unaware, to the stun gun as they ascend "the stairway to Heaven," things are, literally and figuratively, looking up, for cows at least, on their way to meat their Maker. But because hers are *innovations*, we can deduce abuse in the system: Grandin herself has published documentation of it.[3]

What happens to a chicken when she loses her head? (We know what happens to her body.) Grandin admits that the slaughtering of chickens is still "particularly loathsome," but assures us that "eight seconds" after their throats are cut, their bodies are flooded with endorphins, so they don't die in pain. "Slaughter is more humane than nature,"[4] she says, but unnatural life must be balanced against unnatural death, no matter how "humane." How confined animals live before slaughter is not without pain, and even unconfined animals suffer. Grandin said of a mother cow's great cry after forced separation from her calf, "That's not a happy cow. That's one sad, unhappy, upset cow. She wants her baby. Bellowing for it, hunting for it . . . It's like grieving, mourning—"[5] And what of the feelings of the calf?

Is it better to treat animals like entities or like non-entities—as "protein machines" or as the invisible "disappeared"? Ironically, the better we treat farm animals, the more we enter into relationship with them, so that when we kill them, there is more of a bond to violate. If like chickens we "lose our heads" over animals, becoming familiar with them and giving them names—what then?

MICHAEL, who is English, shared: "In the *Financial Times* of London, which is a newspaper much more wonderful than it sounds, there was an article two weeks ago, three weeks ago, maybe, about meat eaters and vegetarians. And someone remembered being at an English farmhouse, and sitting down to dinner, which was lamb, and the farmer smacking his lips, saying to his assembled family, including the children, 'Elizabeth is really tender, isn't she?' It was definitely

'Elizabeth.' People are much more robust about this in the country."

Perhaps only in England would someone name a cow after a queen. When I was a child, also in the country, a friend (not named Mary) had a sheep named "Lambie Pie" who used to follow us around. Even as an avid meat eater then, I was mortified at the mortal lamb's last trip to the slaughterhouse. Although we did not eat Lambie Pie, she ended up as lamb in someone else's pie. And that was disconcerting enough—although I continued to eat lamp chops.

We may be more robust in the country, but we can also be more callous. A youngster at the Tyler County fair in Texas recently forced a hose into a pig's mouth and pumped water into it until it weighed enough to be judged.[6] The animal tipped the scale in its favor, but then slowly died. We can be sure that the animal both had a name and made one for its tormentor. My neighbors, who used to raise chickens and rabbits for food, killed and ate my friend's bunny who she boarded with them while away at summer camp, and shot their own abused dog after he began to terrorize children. (I still have the scar from Barney's bite, but I loved him anyway.) But when a tiny chick, to whom they gave an endearing name I have now forgotten, took sick, they brought him into their bedroom, and tried to tenderly nurse him back to health—not so much because they wanted a tender meal of him later, but because he was so pitiful. As a child I wondered, and now, forty years later, I still wonder why.

Baby chicks and rabbits make us think of Easter Bunnies and baskets of goodies; perhaps these associations save them—but not always. When traveling in the United States MICHAEL observed otherwise. He said: "Many, many years ago, traveling through California, on an off-road somewhere or another, just a little byway, I saw a sign outside what must have been a rabbit breeders. And the sign said: 'RABBITS FOR SALE.' Underneath 'RABBITS FOR SALE,' there were three words, one below another. And the first word on the first line was" 'PETS'— 'P-E-T-S'—i.e., rabbits as pets. And the next word under 'PETS' was 'BREEDERS,' so that after the rabbit is a pet, it becomes a breeder. And the third word under 'BREEDERS' was

'FRIERS'—thus completing The Three Ages of Rabbit."

I have read of market research conducted to see whether we were ready for "Bunny Burgers." (We weren't.) Although rabbits are already factory farmed liked chickens, furry bunnies arouse more sympathy than birds of a feather, perhaps because they resemble human babies more closely. We are concerned little with Chicken Little or with any other chicken, as Karen Davis, president of United Poultry Concerns would be quick to point out. We don't even give them food, she says, but rather "feed"[7]—so that we can feed on them later. Because we don't find them adorable, our attitude toward birds can be deplorable.

ROBBAN said: "Chickens are pretty sexless creatures, even if they do have a male and a female." TONY said: "Chickens don't bother me. I don't see any rapport with chickens whatsoever. They are creatures, but there's something about chickens after you raise them. They have their own little society, but it's not like four-legged creatures, like a goat or a cow. The difference for me is that the goat makes contact with me, and when I had goats here, I never used any for meat. I milked them. They used to follow you around like a dog, and they'd nuzzle you. In the morning, if you didn't get up in time to feed them, they'd make all sorts of noise. They were really nice creatures; they provided us with cheeses, and lots of milk, and they weren't that much work.

"If you've ever raised turkeys, God, you can't wait until they're out of your way! Turkeys are so dumb. They will sometimes look up in the air in a rainstorm and drown.[8] They are strange creatures to raise, believe me. A turkey is like something that doesn't do anything right. It's just something that eats, and gives you manure out the other end. Even chickens have more personality than turkeys."

In other words, chickens are more like *us*. Vegetarians, typically, see food animals as like us, and so refuse to eat them. TONY tried to "see animals [as] other than a meal on the table and see them as creatures who are inhabiting the earth with us." BARBARA said: "An animal was an object for consumption when I was not a vegetarian, and it became much more a sense of kindred spirits, not a sense that this is an object for my use. There was a real sense of: This is another life form, with its own soul and its own being." How are we to feel like "kindred spirits" with confined animals? The caged chicken or the rabbit in its hutch inspires only pity because it has no dignity. The hen or hare in the wild, wily and alert, brims with qualities we admire and with which we identify. Wild animals exude the power of competence and resilience, surviving under conditions we ourselves would not endure. We admire them for it.

TONY said: "When I take a walk and startle deer, they look at you, directly at you. I'll talk to them and say, 'Hey, it's O.K., just relax,' and they'll go back to eating. If I keep my vibrations in a tranquil place, they'll finish eating, look at you, and then they'll wander off." Of cows, their domesticated counterparts, Annie Dillard wrote: "They're a human product like rayon. They're like a field of shoes. They have cast iron shanks and tongues like foam insoles. You can't see through to their brains as you can with other animals; they have beef fat behind their eyes, beef stew."[9] Do we "keep our vibrations tranquil" for these?

We revere wild animals because we have not shackled or stupefied them. The unexpected sight of a wild animal is an occasion for awe; but how are we to respect those we expect, the standardized "stock" in yards or units? Sometimes we sentimentalize animals, both free and tame, creating what TONY calls a "Disney-like" aura around them. We are influenced by our comics as well as by our religions. But when we take animals out of our cartoons, the difference between natural and denatured is startling: the barnyard (or battery) turkey is only a caricature of its native counterpart, the "stalled ox" a shadow of its spry ancestor. Some find it harder to eat meat from a "real" animal than from its factory facsimile; perhaps that is why those who eat hamburger decry hunters who kill deer. Former vegetarians have the painful choice of capturing the free and eating them, or freeing the captured—by eating them.

9

Bloody Epiphanies

"It is plain that the law against the slaughter of animals is founded rather on vain superstition and womanish pity than on reason."
—Spinoza

"It is often said that if slaughter houses were made of glass, most people would be vegetarians."
—Jeffrey Moussaieff Masson, *When Elephants Weep*

People don't want to eat animals, but do want to eat meat. Ordinarily we do not find killing animals a delight, but only delight in eating those who were killed, abstracting our main course from its source, our dinner from the din at the abbatoir.

No one wants to hear about animal suffering during a meal, for that would ruin the enjoyment of it; but neither do we wish to hear about animal suffering afterward, for that would ruin the enjoyment of future meals. Postprandial desserts or cordials are called for, not unsweet revelations. How can we savor the unsavory? The one who kills "screaming life for food" is said to be "dead to mercy and compassion";[1] but most of us never hear the scream of the almost-dead, and hence cannot remember it when we are fed. Dead flesh is quiet; it cannot engage us in conversation; it cannot tell the story of itself. If it began to talk, and to tell us the truth, it might be we who would run screaming—from our plates.

TONY said: "I was present at the doing of a goat in. And that could convince me very easily that I wanted no part of this. Somebody gave me a goat that I didn't want. It was a young goat.' So I gave it to someone else, and that someone else said, 'I'll tell you what. I don't want the goat either, but we can have a party and we can feed a lot of people with that goat.' So I said, 'O.K.' He said, 'C'mon up here on Sunday morning, and we'll do the goat in.' So I did. I went up to this place, and I gave him the goat, and he took the goat to a place, and he conked it on the head with a sledgehammer. He thought the goat was out. Then he hung the goat up, and went to cut the goat's throat, and it's still making noise, so he had to conk him again, hard, with the sledgehammer, and he proceeded to cut his throat and bleed him. The sounds that creature made were like any other creature. It was like if you killed a person. It made the same kind of sound: a creature begging for its life. It knew its life was going to end there.

"So it stayed with me. I never forgot it. I took a taste of it; but I never really ate the flesh of that goat. I did it because I didn't want that elitist thing again. These people were all there, and they were going to enjoy it. So I grabbed a little piece and chomped on it. It didn't taste very good. Anyway, it was an unpleasant experience. So if the animal had to be slaughtered to give me my meat, any particular animal, then I certainly would not eat it. If you had to kill a cow over me, I wouldn't eat it. If they had to kill the cow for my meat, I would stop eating it. They've already killed the cow; he's already at the butcher's. So if I go up there and buy it . . . If I had to requisition it—no way."

PETER said: "In 1973, after graduating from St. John's, I went to Israel and lived three years on a kibbutz. I got to the kibbutz three days before the October war of 1973, by some coincidence of my karma. On that first night, we went into the chicken coops on the kibbutz, and we sent off ten thousand chickens to the army that night—in the dark, because we didn't want to get bombed while we were doing it. To feed the army, yes. The kibbutz raised chickens. And it was not only the most disgusting experience of my life, it also quite convinced me that eating food raised that way was an inappropriate thing to do. We took live chickens. We grabbed them by the legs. We threw them into crates, and they shat all over us while we were doing this. They were terrified. There were zillions of them in there, and that convinced me that something was wrong there. I don't know how clearly articulated that was for me twenty-odd years ago; but it was a substantial formative influence I went through during those years."

JONATHAN said: "I saw animals being slaughtered in Africa, and other places, and it's definitely not a pretty sight. They tend to treat animals badly. For instance, they'll take live chickens, tie their feet up, and hang them upside down on the side of a bush taxi, bumping for hours down the road. Goats are tied up on the roofs [of cars] in the hot sun. That was one reason I thought there was more suffering for these animals."

FRANK said: "When I did research in biochemistry as an undergraduate, I would go up to the slaughterhouse in New Haven and get these cow brains. Because I was studying a brain molecule, we would get cow brains from the slaughterhouse, bring them back, and do this whole processing to extract the molecule we were studying, the neurotubule in the brain cells. That was one of my jobs—to drive to the slaughterhouse and get the brains. I saw these cows being led down a ramp. They'd get a chain put around their legs, and they get hoisted up. They slit their throats. They wriggle wildly as they bleed to death. And then they hose them down. The whole place reeked. These guys were laughing, and wearing yellow raincoats, and there was blood flying all over the place. I thought to myself: 'God, if more people saw *this*, I think a lot of people would stop eating meat.'"

ROCKY asked: "How could people work in a slaughterhouse? Oh, God, what a miserable job! It must be degrading. It must make you jaundiced. How could you be so insensitive?" ROCKY enjoys barbecuing ribs on his backyard grill, but because he never sees the Adam whose ribs are taken, he is not bothered by it. "The other things you don't even see as animals. You don't see it as having four legs, or eyes or ears, or maybe you might have touched it or held it or seen it breathe. It's already a slab."

One of my Environmental Ethics students, as part of his final project, witnessed a cow slaughter in a near-by town. The proprietor of a local Chinese restaurant personally presided over one such killing weekly. (So much for the myth of rats in the chow mein—at least in this restaurant.) If we knew that the chef who prepared our beef Szechuan style had been there all the while the cow was bleeding and kicking, would we then feel related to the bovine on whom we dine? It is now only twice removed: when we order, we may shake hands with the hand which ordered it to be killed, and which shook hands with the marksman who shot it. Is this too close for comfort? We may leave a tip for service after drinking our tea, but when we leave, we pay for the flesh of *that cow*. Although most of my students were not vegetarians, they wanted to know the name of the restaurant so they could *avoid* going there. Our fortune cookies tell us we are kind—but are we? Or only "kind of"?

Meat comes from depersonalizing animals, just as war casualties come from de-personalizing humans. Likewise, what are normally considered nonpersons become persons in some circumstances. Prisoners of war, in otherwise lonely cells, have made friends with houseflies—as the perhaps equally lonely elderly make friends with baby carp swimming in tiny bowls. People who slaughter say they must distance themselves from those they kill—especially the "smalls"—baby animals.[2] When people distance themselves from others, the prohibitions against killing them weaken; violence against others, human and nonhuman alike, increases as we see others as *other*. One slaughterer, interviewed by one of my Animal Rights students, quit his job after mentally carving up people as he passed them on the street.

As we may distance ourselves from a lover we know will soon leave us, we distance ourselves from animals who leave the world because of us. Because we believe it is wrong to eat persons, we do not allow animals we intend to eat to become persons. When they do, like canines and felines and sometimes equines, we do not eat them. When pigs are substituted for dogs in medical laboratories, we do not protest as much (nor as much as they), for we cannot protest with a ham sandwich in our hands; but on our hands is the blood of an animal as sensitive as the dog we may love, and to whom we may feed the hambone. A pig was never "man's best friend." If cows were smaller and fluffier, would we eat them?

How do we make the transition between seeing animals and seeing them as meat? We put their lives out of our minds as we put their bodies into our mouths, forgetting that in those bodies were minds, and that they were once mindful of us, or of others like us, taking their lives. If they opened their mouths to protest, we did not hear them. When we say "grace" over their corpses, we close our eyes. In my house, we said a Scottish grace, not because we were Scottish, but because we ate meat three times a day. "Some can eat, but have no meat. Some have meat, but cannot eat. But we have meat, and we can eat, and so our God, we thank Thee." When we said that grace, we closed our eyes. We also close them to slaughter-houses, to brutality, to dying, and when we do confront it, we some-times laugh, not out of glee, but out of discomfort. We caricature animals and portray them as smiling accomplices in their own deaths.

As we close our eyes when we say grace, we close them to animal nature, forgetting that a natural animal is a graceful one, whether it is a wild turkey or boar or hen, and that we have robbed our food animals of their grace by confining them, making them slow and clumsy. By depriving them to make them tender, we render them less than alive, perhaps so that we will feel better about killing them later. They are not animals who become things; they were born as things ("production units");[3] when we do not see animals as real, there is no real transition from animals to meat.

We do not say when eating a turkey or a chicken, "Please pass me his thigh" or "Please pass me her breast." We do not say we are eating "a goose" but "goose"—something generic. If we were serving a goose, then we would have to serve a meal to her rather than have her served to us as a meal. ROLF ate "goose"—and also venison, but did not like it. Would he have liked the deer? If he had met her, she might have become en-deering. She might have had a name; he might have spoken to her; they might have become friends. Then perhaps she would have become a dear deer. But nameless beings whose flesh we eat are always "it." My hunter friend, who glibly calls former vegetarians "cured vegetarians," can only enjoy "anonymous meat."

When we cut off a piece of meat to eat, we also cut off its connection to the living animal; perhaps we can only cut it off in one sense if we have also cut it off in another. PETER said: "In fact, I see an animal as an 'it.' If the animal were actually presented in front of me, I'd be interested in him-or-her-ness; but in fact when a piece of flesh is put in front of me, I see it as belonging to 'it.' That creature. Kind of like an alligator taking a gazelle and just ripping into it. It doesn't think if it's male or female." ROLF said: "I render meat into an 'it.' I cut off the connection with a living being." TONY said: "I think of meat as food presentation of a pretty picture in a cookbook as opposed to the other aspects of it."

While many who bring home the bacon find the sight of a suckling pig on a spit, or one baking, disgusting, others are able to face who they will eat. In restaurants, some chose their fish or lobster which then arrives "prepared" at their tables, and while most of us do not choose our cows, children sometimes visit turkey farms to choose the Thanksgiving bird of honor much as they pick their own pumpkins for Halloween. Not all of us spend our lives denying, but it is an undeniable fact that we deny animals their lives.

Sometimes the revelation—often at a young age—that meat is from an animal leads us to vegetarianism; whether or not we remain vegetarian, such moments are epiphanal ones. KIVA experienced such an epiphany at age twelve. "One day, I was eating at a Chinese restaurant. I lifted the fork, and I said, "No! I don't want to eat this anymore!' I looked at my mother and said, 'I'm not eating anymore!' I was looking at the shrimp, and I thought, 'Wow! That's a little creature, and I don't want to eat it.'"

VICKY said: "As a child, Dr. Doolittle was one of my favorite guys. I wanted to become a zookeeper when I grew up, have lots of pets, and talk to the animals. Dr. Doolittle sings a song in which he describes how much he would love to eat all kinds of meat, '. . . and then I hear poor Gub-Gub squeal. Oh me, oh my, a reluctant vegetarian am I.' This is how I was first introduced into the concepts of vegetarianism (age five or so) and I remember thinking what an excellent idea it was not to eat animals and my mother said, 'Oh, no you don't! You eat whatever I put on the table!'"

ELLY said: "When I was seven, I remember the first moment I didn't want to eat meat anymore. My mother was putting a chicken in the oven, and all of a sudden, when she said 'chicken,' I connected it to those little birdies I would see skittering around—on TV mostly —and I said, 'That bird was *alive*,' and was very repelled by it. My mother said, 'Yes.' My mother, who is the master of unpersuasive explanations, went on to say, 'That bird lived in an Old Age Home. It was a very, very old bird, and *wanted* to die.' I remember thinking the equivalent of 'B.S.'"

The "Chicken Old Age Home" did not convince ELLY, although it was many years before she became a vegetarian. She said: "I remember the first time that I found out there was such a thing as a 'vegetarian.' I was probably around nine, out having lamb chops, and I said, 'I don't want to eat meat anymore!' I didn't like doing it; I didn't want to harm other animals. And my aunt said, 'Oh, you want to become a vegetarian!' And I remember saying, 'Oh, there are people who do this, and they have a name?'

"I remember the moment I made the decision when I was nineteen. I was out of college at this point. In college, I ate as much meat as I possibly could because I had never eaten good meat. I had promised myself I would become a vegetarian when I was seven; but I couldn't do that because my mother was such an appalling cook. I never knew that vegetables, when cooked, could still be green. They were always gray. I was culinarily deprived. My mother was a horrible, horrible cook. We had tuna casseroles two or three times a week, and those were the high point. I thought—I really thought—that cream of mushroom soup must be a kind of *crème brûlée* or something. It was the ultimate culinary cuisine at our house.

"I went to Wheaton when I was a kid. I never had things like pork chops. I used to slam as much of that stuff on my plate as I possibly could, always knowing I would stop when I was doing my own cooking. Back then you couldn't survive as a vegetarian with college cafeteria food. The salad bar? There *wasn't* a salad bar! Are you kidding? This was the sixties.

"Shortly after that, I left school, moved to another city, and was pretty much on my own. It was at this point that I *decided* to become a vegetarian. I remember going to a Friendly's restaurant back when they served steaks. I had this huge Porterhouse steak, which I thought was the greatest thing in the world, and I knew I was on the verge of making the transition. I looked down to my plate, and saw what I had always called 'juice.' It was red. And I said to my friend, 'That's not from blood, is it?' And he said, 'Yeah. It is.' And I said, 'I'm never eating it again.' And that was my epiphanal moment."

FRANK said: "When I was a little kid, age four, I was interested in dinosaurs. We went to the museum. We saw skeletons. I think somehow from that, when meat was served at the table, I saw a *carcass* that reminded me of death, and crematoriums and the holocaust—a whole chain of associations that were repulsive. They would bring a chicken to the table, and I would see a dead body.

"I was interested in anatomy and science at a very young age, and was looking through pictures. I wanted to know all the names of bones and everything. Then I realized that the same bones are in a cow. We're all the *same*. There's a commonality between us. So I guess at some inchoate level, I felt like I was eating one of my brethren.

"My parents were upset because I wouldn't eat meat. I started gagging at the sight of it. I would be physically nauseous. But the hypocritical or ironic thing was if it was *unrecognizable* as being meat, it didn't bother me. If it was Kosher bologna, or hot dogs, or hamburgers, it was so far removed from being meat that it didn't bother me. So it wasn't the flavor, or the smell, or the meat itself, but the sight of it being *on bones,* on a body. As long as it was this ethereal substance, manna, something that just appeared, it was O.K.

"Later I did all kinds of anatomy, and I realized looking at the human cadaver that it's just a piece of meat. I watched my teacher pull on a tendon, and animate the hand. I became a Buddhist after that for awhile. I didn't want that to be all there was. I wanted there to be something more. I loved studying anatomy, and looking at the body as a marvelous machine; but part of me, spiritually, felt a little freaked-out. I didn't *want* us to be just hunks of meat. I wanted to have a transcendent, spiritual part that was just *housed* in a body during this lifetime, and *continues,* and has some other existence. I stopped studying anatomy for awhile. I wanted to think about, learn about, the transcendental philosophies, as in Buddhism.

"Around 1982-83, I got fed up with eating gristle in meat products. I was eating those microwave kind of dinners, like Salisbury Steak, and I kept getting ones with gristle in it. That always repulsed me. Intellectually, I knew that in cave days, you just caught whatever you could; you didn't pick. When I used to see a piece of roast beef with a blood vessel in it, that was O.K. But as soon as there was some viscera, or the fasciae, somehow that was less O.K. Intellectually, that makes no sense. We evolved to eat and use all this stuff. But I guess I just personally didn't like to be reminded that it's a being similar to me.

"I'd be sitting down to this nice, yummy Salisbury steak, and I'm munching away at it, and I'd love the mushroom gravy, and then, all of a sudden, CLONK. There'd be this chunk of gristle. That was just the last straw; I didn't want that anymore. Again, it made no sense intellectually. So what? It's roughage: eat it. It's micropoly-glycerides, so what? The hydrochloric acid is going to break it down anyway. It's going to recombine the molecules. But I just didn't want it. It took my appetite away, and I said, 'That's it. I'm not eating it anymore.' And that's the last time I ever ate a mammal. I haven't purposely or knowingly eaten mammals since then, and I never intend to, unless I'm in a forest somewhere and have to survive."

The fact of life-taking "hits home" when we are confronted with the flesh of an animal "close to home." LINDA said: "This sort of thing came up at a potluck that I was at, and I had a real hard time with it as I was standing there. I didn't know any of the animals, because I hadn't met most of these people before, but suddenly I realized that they had all personally slaughtered and butchered the animals whose flesh we were eating. I was stunned for a few minutes. It was very immediate, especially when they got into this big discussion about how they kill pigs, and about what method is quickest, and gets it over with quicker for the pig—because they're actually quite concerned with not hurting the pig. They just wanted to kill it. And it's just a little too close to home. I found myself having more from the vegetable plates."

JOHN said: "This in-law of my wife's won a pig in a poker game, and kept the pig for awhile in the back yard. He used to feed the pig Twinkies, actually, if you want to get into weird diet. So we'd go out and see the pig when we'd come to visit. It had a name, and was a male, but I don't remember the name. Our daughter was very young at the time, saw this pig, and thought it was cute. One day, anyway, we arrived, and there were all kinds of pork dishes being served at the table, and my wife turns to me and says, 'I don't think I can eat this, because you realize—' and I was stupid. I hadn't made the connection yet.

"Now, perversely, this tests my vegetarian beliefs because part of me says, 'If I can eat this animal I *knew*, it's actually a better thing.' In other words, I *have* to eat this pig right now. So I did. I made the intellectual decision that if I could make an intellectual commitment to vegetarianism, I could also make this intellectual commitment to meat eating in the same sense. Because I had known him, I *had* to eat him. 'If I rejected this pig,' I was telling myself, 'you can't eat *any* meat.'"

Even vegetarian food is reputed to taste better when someone else prepares it. Perhaps this is because when we do not see the process, but only its final outcome, we are duly impressed and happy to be spared the work ourselves. But when the food was slaughtered, we would not have done the "dirty work" ourselves. Thus we prefer "processed" meat—as far away from the process of killing as possible. JOHN's poker-game pig was not a pig in poke, hidden from sight; he ate that pork with his eyes as open as his mouth.

KEN, a gourmet who went "on and off [vegetarianism] three or four times," said: "I think the final awakening came when I purchased a Smithfield's smoked ham in colonial Williamsburg. And while I was carving it up, I said, 'This is nothing but a pig. I like pigs. I don't want to eat them anymore. In fact, pigs aren't bothering me, cows aren't, chickens aren't.' So I stopped eating them." Others, too, confront what they do. ELLY said: "I couldn't separate the idea of animals as responsive beings from the idea of animals on my plate." KIVA agreed: "I can't separate the meat from the death of the animal. And it *is* an animal."

Perhaps if we saw the animal as a whole thing, we would also see it as a holy thing; but we are as alienated from animal life as we are from animal death. We know neither the animal, nor what was done to it, nor what we contribute to the world when we eat it. We know how to prepare it; if we "really know our veal," we know recipes for it, how to present it to the palate, but we do not know the veal calf. Nor would we want to, for then we may not want to eat it: at whom we would look with sadness, we could not cook with sauces.

Anthropologist Claude Lévi-Strauss said that animals are for thinking as well as for eating. I think animals are for thinking instead of for eating. I do not believe that meat eating is always wrong; yet I always find something wrong with it. I am vegetarian because of how I perceive meat—and how I conceive of it. One is aesthetic; the other, cognitive; neither is "ethical." I deduce neither from my revulsion nor from my inability to abstract cooked flesh from the living animal the conclusion that meat eating is immoral; but for me, it is both ugly and unthinkable.

Thus I am not, in the strict sense, an "ethical vegetarian" although I consider myself ethical and am a vegetarian. Yet there are moral overtones. Once when I thought of meat (which I loved) I associated it with vigor. I saw it in terms of what it could do for me. Now I see it from the point of view of what was done to another. Once my association was with life—my life. Now my association is with death—another's death. Thus my decision not to eat meat is based on altruism; what I don't want to suffer, I don't want for my supper.

Rynn goes further, and sees flesh eating as "animal murder." He said: "By proxy, you do kill the animal. Just because someone else has done it for you as a proxy doesn't absolve you from implication and guilt in the animal's death. Just as if you'd sent someone to commit an assassination, you may be even guiltier than the person who carries out the act. You do enter into the implication; you participate in the act, no matter how far removed, even if you do it at what seems to be a very safe remove from the actual act. You become a participant in it, just as when, let's say, you participate in the fruits of a bank robbery. Somehow someone is killed, say a guard is killed, and perhaps you have no direct participation in the act, but somehow the money comes into your keeping, and you realize that it's tainted money, that it's from a bank robbery. You become an accomplice." For Rynn, there is a flesh equivalent to "filthy lucre."

In the end, in our bloody revelations, we do not confront the divine, but the profane, not the sacred, but the horrid, not God, but food, animal food, far removed from manna from heaven, or from the primeval garden of fruit. We are enlightened not by a bite, but by opening the door to the abbatoir, and that vision of a butcher's un-original sin my stain our cheeks (if not also our souls) if we shed a tear or two now knowing what we know.

"Animals are not our tasters, nor we their kings";[4] but at the dinner table, we are tasters, not for animals, but of them. When dining on animals, we may feel like kings or queens, for if there is a piece of flesh before us, we may put ourselves before it and feel the grander; but if our travails are trivial, deserving only our smiles; if our lives are jokes, deserving only our laughter, then it must be laughter through our tears. If there is some BEYOND against which our pains and cries, no less real than theirs, are less than real, it does not make suffering go away; it only points away from it. Vegetarians take suffering at face value because in the faces of animals who suffer we see something of value.

Sometimes we say, "At first it bothered me, but I'm used to it now." Vivisectors say this—and slaughterers. And meat eaters say it, too, having come far from their childhood shock, and subsequent idealism, upon learning that the lamb chop was indeed chopped off the lamb. We become hardened; we become inured. But becoming accustomed to suffering neither diminishes it nor aggrandizes us or our worth. It only numbs us—a cruel irony given that it is not we but those who suffer who ought to be numb. If vegetarians sometimes seem self-sacrificing, it is because we care about the lives which others are sacrificing.

10

Thinking with the Body

"For the mind talks,
But the body knows."
—The Buddha, *Dhammapada*

Each one of us is one, but also many. The "one" who inhabits my body-community has her own ideas, but the many members of the community may have "ideas" of their own, especially about the nutrients they need to survive. There are more little creatures colonizing my body than my body's own cells: a lot of little lives depend on my philosophy. Unaware of my philosophy, and with none of their own, the work they do is not theoretical, but practical, not ideological, but biological. Yet they may have interests which clash with my own: who is to say that trillions of little needs weigh less than my single one, in this case, to perceive myself as nonviolent or spiritual by eschewing (not chewing) flesh?

"Holier-than-thou" is one thing—but holier than they? What if "they" clamor for more than the best vegetarian diet can offer them? Do I have a duty to my body? A moral obligation to its systems and its cells, to its symbionts, to its many opportunistic but invaluable helpers? If the spiritual path were flat and narrow, amply posted and obstacle-free, then the answers to such questions would be easy; but there is no way until our footsteps, guided by our choices, carve it out of possibility; and so the answer is not one, and the options, many.

Body Language

Pain is a great conversation-opener in the dialogue between the mind and the body. The body may not speak to us in sentences, but it speaks in symptoms and signs: when we hear them, we are listening to the body. After twenty years as an ovo-lacto vegetarian, NANCY's subconscious broke through, besieging her with messages. "You ignore your messages, and they scream louder and louder. You can only ignore it a certain amount of time. *If I don't let my body have what it needs, I'm not the person I want to be.*

"For me, meat is when I need it. When I eat flesh, I feel better. Physically. It takes away some of the physical symptoms so I feel better emotionally and spiritually. Everyone has to eat what's good for them. We change. I'm not the same person I was twenty years ago. I feel better on this diet. Eating fish and chicken gets away for me a certain amount of depression I fought all my life because of the tryptophan, and I think that's what my body was craving.

"I started to crave meat to the point where it entered my dreams. I would dream of eating chicken, fish. It would be all-encompassing. I fought it and I fought it . . . but my body was teaching me I would feel better the other way. Do I eat a diet which makes me feel worse because I can't do as much? When your body is saying 'Yes!' and you're saying 'No!' you are consciously making a decision to keep yourself in the dark.

"I love grains; I love beans; I love tofu. I love the smells; I love the textures. When I cook for myself with fish and chicken, I don't feel the same way. I just *do* it. I'm not into it. It's not a creative thing. In catering, I've never taken any job where people request animal protein. I'm a vegetarian caterer because I don't want to prepare flesh. I won't even make fish or chicken in a catering thing. I'll only do vegetarian catering because I don't really want to eat meat. I just do it because I'm so restricted in my eating. I don't have any choice. If you can't eat wheat, and you can't eat corn, and you can't eat a lot of grains, what do you eat? I can't eat seitan—it would kill me. I can't eat tempeh—it kills me because of the mold. I have the fish, or I have intense pain.

"My body keeps craving [flesh]; I eat it only when my body says, 'This is what you need.' Then I feel better; I have more energy; I definitely feel better. People who are vegetarian might need to go back to eating meat occasionally. I don't think any diet is for the rest of your life because you're not the same: you're an evolving creature. I once felt that no one should take the life of an animal, and I felt that if I could go through this life without causing the death of any creature, that is what I would like to attain; but sometimes, physically, it's not possible."

Eating For Three

"I feel like I'm in AA. 'My name is LINDA, and I eat hamburger. I've been eating ground cow meat.' I didn't drift into it; I dove. I got pregnant, and God, I wanted hamburgers! I still do. I craved that instant full-protein thing, and I would eat it, and feel wonderful. I had awful morning sickness, and when I started eating hamburgers, it was like, 'Oh, I love these!' It was awful. I really felt bad about it. Here I was after twenty years just devouring hamburgers. I was ashamed to tell anyone.

"I had a really hard time with just vegetable protein. I've had a really hard time keeping myself healthy enough to sustain myself, and the baby I'm still feeding from myself, and the one I was carrying. I couldn't feed three. I couldn't get through that time when I was pregnant and breast-feeding. *I couldn't feed three people just on a vegetarian diet.* I just couldn't do it.

"I tried my darndest. I was sucking down Yellow Dock tincture like it was going out of style. Yellow Dock is a weed, and you grind it up and soak it, and, you know, tincture implies alcohol. It's supposed to be a very good source of iron. And I was taking pre-natal vitamins. I was eating black beans, and garbanzo beans, and dark leafy greens. My husband's a vegetable farmer, so we eat huge quantities of vegetables all the time. I just walk out into the field with a lettuce knife and 'go hunting.' That's what we call it.

"I would eat as much protein stuff as I could. You wouldn't believe the diet you have to be on to be able to do it. I had to eat so *much*. It was just so much easier to have a piece of chicken once in awhile, or a beef dish, but only with the beef thoroughly disguised, and once a week, a hamburger. It's still a craving. I eat it between two slices of whole wheat bread—no sprouts—but between two slices of whole wheat bread. I feel better when I eat it.

"When you get right down to it, you really have to eat in such a way that you can function properly. Some people think they can only do that on a whale blubber diet, for instance. It's not for me to judge that—except when macrobiotic people force me to go on a no-protein, no-calcium diet when I visit them and I'm pregnant. Then I get a little irritable. In the wintertime, these particular macrobiotic people don't eat greens. I nearly fainted when I spent the weekend with them, and they didn't feed me properly. I just about fainted in their house. Ordinarily, it wouldn't bother me, but I view it as like fasting.

"They could have had some seaweed handy; that would have helped. They underfed me. They could have fed me perfectly well, especially just for a weekend, if they had just thought about it. What does a pregnant woman need? Three things spring to mind: calcium, iron, and protein. You can get that in a macrobiotic diet if you think about it." Two people sat down to a plate of grain that weekend, one sitting in the chair, and the other sitting inside the sitter. "One of them was kicking pretty hard: 'Let me have some more food!'" Just as we are sometimes "of two minds" about something, it would seem that we can sometimes be "of two bodies."

First The Egg, Then The Chicken

With her actions, KIVA answered the old conundrum, not about ultimate origins, but about the step she would take to end her teenage years as a vegetarian. After eight years as a vegan, she said: "It started with eggs. I woke up and had a big craving for eggs, and I kept avoiding it, and finally I went to a restaurant, and had a big omelet, and I felt great.

"When I went to school, they used me as a kind of experiment. The teacher was basically saying that everyone has to eat in the way that makes them feel the best,[1] and she wasn't an advocate for one specific diet. She said, 'Everything's an experiment,' and so she would tell us to experiment, and that it is not really a big moral issue. I told her how it made me feel energetic, and so I became like a specimen. They would ask if I had eaten eggs again, and how I *felt*. Everyone was saying, "Kiva, you should try chicken," and I was saying, "No! I will never eat chicken again!' I just kind of eased into it. It started with eggs, and then—

"I didn't want to make the leap to eating chicken. One day I came home and my mother was preparing chicken for herself. The fact that she had made it . . . the fact that it was organic . . . I knew it was free range . . . I decided to have a bite, and I ended up eating a whole piece, and I felt like I had an injection of some kind of energy. I felt almost *too* energetic, almost like I had caffeine.

"I didn't eat it again for awhile, but the teacher was saying, "Listen to yourself, and realize that if you *feel* good, you can *do* a lot more good than if you don't feel good. Whatever you eat, if you're doing good things with it, you're taking that good along with you." *I started listening to my body*. Occasionally, I would have this incredible craving where no matter how many soybeans or [how much] tofu I ate, it wasn't enough. So I started to listen to it, and every once in a while, I would eat a tuna fish sandwich or chicken, and I would feel much better.

"There are certain times when I *crave* animal protein, and then I'll eat it, and then don't want it for a long time. Sometimes, I'll eat it, and it will be like I'm not getting as much as I did the last time: maybe I shouldn't eat it for awhile. There's a definite craving. Usually I become preoccupied with it, and if you ignore it—You have a craving for cheese, and then you eat soy cheese, and your body says, 'It tastes like cheese . . . It kind of feels like cheese . . .' But your body says,

'WAIT! It's NOT cheese!' You can eat five packages of soy cheese and still want regular cheese. I just learned that if you're craving it, just eat it, and it's over."

When bodies express needs, the mind hears their rumblings as grumblings. When the body's need becomes desire, and desire, obsession, then perhaps the best way to heed the body is to feed it what it wants. Only if meat eating were a sin could we say that the best way to be saved is not to give in, but to get over it.

Bio-Logic

Rynn, predictably, finds fault with the body's logic. He said: "In cases of extreme illness, one could hardly deny a person his request for meat; but I think it's largely a psychological belief. I don't think it's organic; I think it's psychological. The mind is a very powerful organ, and can control all of the vital processes. We can't underestimate the self-hypnotic powers of the mind. It's a form of psychosomatic suggestion. It's more a craving than an addiction; but perhaps there are some addictive properties to flesh as there are to nicotine; perhaps there are some addictive chemicals. I don't deny that meat eaters could *feel* better. Yes; I don't deny that."

Is a craving a feeling—or an idea? Is it the body's urging—or the mind's surging? When the body acts as though it has a mind of its own, we may not know "who" to believe. Sometimes what we want to believe is belied by how our bodies want to live; the flow of our ideas is interrupted by its language of lethargy or malaise, its chidings of chills or fevers, its diversion of dis-ease.

We have ideas, and we have cravings, and we have ideas about our cravings—and sometimes, if we are philosophers, we have cravings for ideas. What should we believe? What kind of thing is hunger, and what kind of thing is what anthropologist Marvin Harris calls the "hunger for meat"? Can the body crave anything the mind does not know of? When former vegetarians say their bodies "crave" meat, do they mean their bodies crave hamburgers—or the nutrients therein? Can our cellular "machinery" crave objects it cannot conceptualize? How can we know that what we desire is what the body needs? Can we silence our selves long enough to listen to our cells?

The mind does not know everything, and the mind is not the only thing that knows. Yet the mind is not a thing at all, and the body's knowing is not the same as the mind's. The business and the talent of the mind is interpretation, and the body's, feeling. The body knows when it wants sex, food, or sleep—and when it's time to die. It communicates *clearly* about its needs and its hungers, and about the release or relief it requires from privation or tension—and from life itself. It is my body which knows I am cold: I need no thermometer to tell me. My body knows when it is tired: I need no clock to show me. My body has a mind of its own, usually minding its own business until it needs me to direct it toward equilibrium.

The body does not speak the mind's language, but one of its own: with its somatic syntax, it may threaten us with illness when denied what the mind "has no stomach for." We may be repulsed at the thought of eating flesh, or we may experience a repulsion which is neither deduction nor induction, but a visceral conclusion—thinking with the body.

Just as some foods "agree" with us, body and mind may agree with each other—or the body may disagree with the mind's idea of what to feed it. Can a vegetarian hear the body's clamoring for flesh over the din of the mind's idea of what to have for dinner? Where we once felt repelled at the thought of meat, we may later relish our hamburger (with or without the relish). What happened? Did the body change its mind? Did the mind remind the body of a good idea? Is the return to meat the mind's idea—or the body's?

KIVA heard her body, but did not *act* until she had word from the mind. "I didn't act on my cravings until I had reasons. I had enough signs to listen to those cravings; but I think it was more, 'This will help the way you feel physically.' If I hadn't had all the intellectual background, all the different views and philosophies saying meat is helpful—I read an analysis of people who need meat, and everything about it was me, just like describing me to a 'T'—cold hands, cold feet, tendency to have poor posture, aches, often cold. There are a lot of medical models I've been exposed to, and they all pointed in the direction that I should be eating animal protein—the Chinese medical model saying that there are certain people who are hot and dry, or cold and damp, and they were saying I'm a cold and damp personality, and that foods like chicken would warm my body. I would benefit from eating warming and drying foods like chicken.

"I felt I needed some kind of spark. Someone told me it was like a spark of fire in the spleen. It can dry things out and give you energy. So I started with feelings, and I needed the reasons to push it. Three years ago, if you said I'd eat chicken again, I wouldn't agree. I think it gives a real vitality. I have that craving, and eat meat, and feel like I'm getting a burst of energy." KIVA was caught between two philosophies—veganism and Chinese medicine; but in the end, her mind attended to her body.

Bodies and Beliefs

Our food choices create us both literally and figuratively (and create our figures, literally) for as food remakes our bodies, cell by cell, our choices make our selves, idea by idea. When a body does not care for our instructions for its feeding, do we listen to the noises it makes, or to our beliefs about what these mean? We do not live on ideas, even if we live for them: in addition to our philosophies, we need calories. From what should these come? The mind, a known trickster, may addict the body, getting it hooked on what it thinks is good for it; but the mind's thirst for ideas may leave the body parched and dry. Then the body may behave in ways the mind does not think well of, becoming ill on a diet the well-intentioned intellect insists should keep it healthy.

ROBBAN said: "Too often patients come to me and they're following a diet because of a certain belief system. Either they've become vegetarian because they can't think of animals being killed, or for spiritual reasons, or for religions reasons—and they're *sick*. I'm trying to get them better, and I can't convince them that they really need to alter their diet, because it's not right for their metabolic type. I think everyone has their own path spiritually, and also physically, people require different diets. You really need to tune into the wisdom of your body, and what you feel is right for your own body, and to be eating not according to some external code of ethics or rules about eating. It may be exactly the wrong diet.

"I have patients and I know they're eating the wrong diet for philosophical reasons. I say, 'If you want your health to suffer for this philosophical or moral reason, that's your choice. You've got to make the choice. What is important is the way you feel, and how in balance you are with your diet, not some external principle that says you have to do this or you shouldn't do that.'"

DAVID said: "When I was in California, I had a friend who was really into macrobiotics, and he felt increasingly ill; but he really believed in Ohsawa,[2] and so he would get up in the morning and say, 'I feel strong!' Yet on his macrobiotic diet, he felt increasingly ill, and it got to a point where he just had to acknowledge that this was not right for him."

JONATHAN told of a friend "who couldn't hack the raw foods diet she was on for about a year." He said: "Ultimately, she'd have to give in to her cravings, and she'd go on binges of eating crackers and brown rice—and these were whole wheat crackers, too. She conceded to me, tearfully, that she wasn't cut out for the really spiritually pure diet, and she had to go back to some cooked foods. It was a sad thing to see, because clearly it wasn't necessary to be on this raw foods diet for your spiritual development; it showed a down side of having a very strict diet that can cause a lot of pressure on people."

This we could call "pressure on the non-cooker." JONATHAN told of another raw foodist who was "very proud" when her menses ceased while on this diet: she believed that it was a sign that she was "pure." JONATHAN commented: "That's an example of taking a philosophy to explain what's going on as a positive nutritional development when it's really a negative one." A raw foods diet may be " a good cleansing diet," he said—but not in this way.

Our beliefs about what is good for us may in fact be bad for us. A participant in a raw foods retreat at the home of Viktoras Kulvinskas shared an image of a circle of raw foodists huddling around a quartz heater in Woodstock, Connecticut in early autumn, shivering in their sweaters, teeth chattering, while he, an ovo-lacto vegetarian, was comfortable in shirt sleeves. Some long-time raw foodists are thriving; but here it was clear that these bodies, shivering and shaking, were speaking: they were requesting something to warm them up— more calories, or something hot to thaw them. What *they* needed was relief—not belief.

AVA (from Australia) who grew weak and ill after a decade as a vegetarian, wrote to me that "it took awhile to get unbrainwashed about what is healthy." She said: "I slowly got weaker, but I did not realize it until I went to my first Chinese doctor, and realized what bad shape I was in." AVA now believes in eating meat, and after thirteen years of it, calls herself "vital and healthy and as spiritual as ever." For what the body longs, the mind may say, 'Wrong!' knowing the context in which it is embedded; but when ideas conspire against the heart's desire, the body may sicken, deprived of what makes us sick at heart. Ultimately, the sickness at heart may become sickness unto death if the mind silences the body altogether.

Bodies Of Evidence

Visceral reactions to meat are various: sometimes the body insists on it, and sometimes insists that we desist from it. ROCKY said: "I had hankerings for the stuff. When I was just getting involved with being a vegetarian, I visited a friend of mine in California who was definitely a vegetarian. I was staying at his house in Los Angeles, and when he was working during the day, I would go around the corner to Popeye's and get some fried chicken—and hide the bones. I remember he made some cream of wheat with sliced apples in it. Oh, God! I didn't want this! I wanted *real* food!"

FRANK said: "When I was at Yale, the dining halls were on strike and I lived in the International Dorm because I loved all different cultures and languages. The Indian students were really nice, and fed me, because I loved Indian food. They were so happy to find an American who loved Indian food that they would invite me to their vegetarian meals. They were Hindus, so they were real vegetarians and vegans. And I loved the food. I loved learning about it; I loved the spiciness. And then an hour later, I'd go across the street and get a tuna grinder. I couldn't give it up. I didn't *feel* right unless I had some kind of animal protein."

Bodies can also reject—and violently expel—what they once handled well. ROCKY said: "I did try meat again one time as a vegetarian. I went to visit a friend of mine at school, in New Hampshire, and he cooked a steak. We had steak there, and I got sick. I threw up. My stomach couldn't handle it. I vomited. No doubt about it."

Sometimes bodies reject flesh even when the mind is on the meat's side. Rynn said: "I converted a lady friend of mine to vegetarianism, and when we broke up, after going together for a number of years, she formed a new liaison with a carnivore, and she tried to convert back to carnivorism. She found she couldn't, because her body rejected the meat. When she would take some meat, she would vomit. So her body had developed a defense mechanism against flesh eating. Probably the body's natural revulsion came into play, and she began having vomiting reflexes even when she was drinking a soup that was laced with beef stock, as it often is in vegetable soup. Her body would immediately reject it, and she'd have to run to the bathroom. She tried to adjust to a carnivorous diet to please her new boyfriend, and found that she couldn't. She still can't have flesh in any form, even in the form of a broth."

Bodies can show other symptoms when we eat meat: even though its sensual attraction is for many undeniable, its residue in the body may be undesirable. TONY said: "I knew the feeling of the wonderfully tasting meat, but how later you just sat there, food-drugged, sitting in your chair like a boa-constrictor, digesting your meal. I didn't like that feeling. I was able to distinguish between those feelings and what I preferred to feel—that I could move at any time, rather than having to sit there and digest my meal. Eating vegetarian, you never felt stuffed. You didn't interfere with your movement; you never had the feeling that you couldn't bend down because your stomach was full. I like always feeling light and mobile."

LEONARD agreed: "I don't like that feeling of a rock sitting in my stomach. You eat meat, and two or three hours later it's sitting like a *rock*; it's sitting like a stone in your stomach. It doesn't set as well as it did; it's not a good feeling to have something not digest in your body; it's a disagreeable feeling."

The body can tell us we need to eat meat—or that we need to "meat" its needs in some other way. When Marvin Harris insists on a universal preference for meat among tribal peoples ("Virtually every band or village studied by anthropologists expressed a special esteem for animal flesh")[3] and insists that primates prefer the insects which infest the fruit to the fruit itself, spitting out the pulp, and eating the bugs,[4] he may misconstrue the "body of evidence," for they may not hunger for meat, per se, but for variety, desiring what is rare in their daily fare. Just because meat contains what we need does not mean that we need to eat meat. If chimps devour grubs or young gazelles, it may be because bean burritos do not grow on their trees, and if tribal peoples universally esteem meat, it may be because, as something rare, it becomes a measure of value, like money. Thus the "hunger" for meat may be another kind of greed altogether.

Body To Body

A not so well-kept "secret" among vegetarians is that we smell better than "carnivores." With no shreds of rotting meat lurking in the crevasses between our teeth, or taking sluggish trips through the byways of our bodies, we exude an aroma more like the clover and alfalfa breath of Bossie the cow than the fumes of Fido who dined on the remains of Bossie. But is this true—or is it a sub-culture's myth—a belief about the body?

JONATHAN said: "Until recently, I would not want to kiss a woman who was a meat eater, and that was just another kind of gut feeling. It would have been pretty repulsive to kiss a woman who was a meat eater in the early half of my vegetarian life. While now it's my preference to date only vegetarian women, I'm not quite as disgusted by the idea the she was eating meat."

PETER said: "As a chiropractor, I'm in physical proximity with a large variety of people, a wide range of people. I can feel not only the meat, but the bad food in their system: that's very obvious to me. *I know when people eat meat.* The body's cleanliness is very measurable. It's physiological—not just in the gut and the intestines, but in the breath and body odor."

Rynn said: "To a vegan, the bodily exhalations of carnivores would be quite offensive. When Westerners travel to Japan and India, their body odors are quite apparent to the natives and they consider Westerners to be very foul-smelling. I think that Madison Avenue is so successful at purveying deodorants and perfumes because the bodily secretions of carnivores are so repugnant, even to each other, that they have to be masked by perfumes and deodorants."

Rynn disagrees with former vegetarians like PETER, who professes that meat eating enhances male sexuality, and with ROBBAN who says, as a physician, "For men, vegetarianism is *very* unhealthy. They get thin; they get very wan-looking, very effeminate. Cholesterol does get converted into testosterone, you know. Men should eat meat." Rynn says: "Male sexuality does not depend on the consumption of carrion, of dead flesh. I think it would undermine sexuality. The most virile and vigorously sexual societies have been largely vegetarian, for example, India during the time when the *Kama Sutra* was composed, and the erotic statuary of Khajuraho, in which people were participating in the most exquisite sexual poses. Many of the poses that the statuary illustrate are scenes from *Kama Sutra*, positions from the *Kama Sutra*. They were highly erotic and uninhibited in their expression of eroticism. If anything, flesh eating is a barrier to pleasure. It's repugnant; the body odors given off by non-vegetarians are quite repellent and it's hard to imagine carnivores entwined as sinuously as they are in the erotic figures of Khajuraho.

"Because of my commitment to animal rights, and because I'm something of a spiritual and ethical vegetarian, women don't expect me to be a Don Juan or a Cassanova; they expect me to have a very meager appetite for sex. I'm put off by the prospect of becoming intimate with a flesh eating female. I've had a relationship in the past with a flesh eating female, and became violently ill. I guess in a way, I was ingesting the cells of animals."

ELLY, speaking of the "vile molecular emanations" from a "stinky vegan" female she's known, disagrees with the folk wisdom among vegetarians. "I could stink before and I could stink now; I thought that was a less vain way of saying I smelled good before, and I smell good now. I have experienced vegan exhalations—the vile molecular dispersions of a vegan body—and they weren't pleasant. This whole 'My body's sweeter than your body' is nothing more than 'I have a ten inch one.' It's a come-on. That's what it seems like to me. The people I have loved the most have not been vegetarian. There was no aesthetic problem, like they had blood on their lips. I can be very fond of non-vegetarians."

I confess that I am drawn to bodies made of almonds and soy, of avocados and yams, of quinoa and corn, of kasha and kale. I am drawn to other people, too, the gentle and striving kinds, even when their bodies are made of hens and trout, of calves and lambs and sows; but I am not drawn to these bodies. This is a fact about me, and pronounces nothing about the worth or attractiveness of flesh eaters: it is only that I am not attracted to them. Perhaps I am thinking with my body; maybe my body will change its mind—although it hasn't yet. What Rynn calls "exhalations of the crypt" may be true, or may be myth; perhaps it is best to leave such questions open and continue to be surprised when vegans express their surprise that omnivores, members of the dietary rank and file, and not rank and vile.[5] One vegan who falls in love regularly with non-vegetarian women always exclaims to his amazement that their bodies are "clean"; others may be amazed to learn that those with sweet bodies may have sour dispositions!

Is the "clean vegan" a fiction or a fact about metabolism? PETER said it is the inefficient digestion of an unnatural diet which is responsible for omnivore odor. "We didn't evolve to use so much protein and fat: we can generalize that vegetarians have cleaner bodies." Dyspeptic vegans and omnivores with stomachs of steel may be exceptions which prove the rule—but perhaps we should just wait and sniff.

The Dilemma Of Dualism

In the East, we have chakras; in the West, Descartes. The Chinese use one word for both "mind" and "heart"; but Westerners split us into mind and body. Instead of seven centers of power, top to toe, we console ourselves with our two poles. Vegetarians, who dislike Descartes' dualism which denies minds to the bodies of animals, seem unwittingly to resurrect it with their vocabularies: the language of "body" and "mind" is irresistible. But must we be mired in his metaphysics to talk in these terms? Must we agree with our antihero?

Experientially, we know what we mean when we talk this way, even if we do not know what it is to know, who *we* are, or what it means to mean. What we mean, our language has no room for: that we are beings who express ourselves sometimes mentally and sometimes physically. It is we who think and feel; it is not a mind thinking, and a body feeling. There is no thing inside any thing, because mind and body are not what we are but how we are. We can no more separate mental from physical than thought from thinker or breath from breather. When we say we are "thinking with the body" or our "bodies have minds of their own," we mean that we are aware of what we sense without interpreting it.

If dualism is not dead, then it ought to be; the division of the person into separate entities is a Western *convention*. From Plato we inherited the notion that the body is insensate clay, animated by *psyche,* and from Descartes, the notion of the ghost in the machine. Judeo-Christian God breathes life into dust, and reclaims it afterward. The soul, higher and better, eventually leaves this world for something "on high" and better.

Thus when we talk of minds and bodies, we tend to see them as separate things, like the forces of good and evil, or cowboys and Indians, the mind dressed in white for easy recognition, and always winning in the end, for "the better and the stronger," at least in westerns and in Western philosophy, must always prevail. We could have listened instead to Aristotle who although making mind most valuable, sees it and the body as indis-soul-uable. The body is neither inert clay nor a machine without a power source, but is itself a striving thing. When former vegetarians say they "hear their body's wisdom," they speak not like Platonists or Cartesians, but like Aristotleans.

PETER spoke this way when he said: "It is up to us to pay attention to the signs and symptoms of the critter, and act accordingly." PETER, in fact, sees the body "as something like a plant. Would you say a plant *wants* something?" For Aristotle, even plants have souls—and goals—although they do not know or have conscious desires. When I see my spider plant's leaf tips turning brown, I know that it needs water whether it "wants" it or not. I cannot feel its "pain"; but when my body has needs, it tells me eloquently—and directly. If my body is like a plant, it is a very clever one, and my relationship to it is very intimate.

ROLF uses the expression "the epistemology of the body" to describe phenomena such as micromovements giving us away when we are lying. If we deny the body such power, we devalue it; if we deny it its own kind of intelligence, we are less apt to hear its wisdom. ROLF, a professional dancer, said that when he does improvisation, "the thinking has to come right out of the body; it comes from the motion of the body itself. If you try to anticipate, you won't be ready. You can't calculate or have ideas about what you want to do."

We can be informed by feeling as well as by reason: we can see or we can see as. We speak as though the mind is knower, and body known, but each knows in a different way. It sometimes seems that the mind knows what the body shows—and vice versa—as though they shared a party line; but it is we who know, sometimes in one way, and sometimes in another. As there is more to meat than meets the eye, there is more to me than what I call "I" if I think I *am* my mind. Philosophers have argued that everything is in the mind, including the body, and that everything is in the body, including the mind. But it is best to say that both body and mind are us (and not in us) and that we express ourselves in these two ways.

When the philosophy of vegetarianism is challenged, it is usually challenged not by another philosophy but by the demands of the body. Sometimes ideas we cannot digest may be of what we need to ingest if we are to be healthy. Even when the body tells us to eat dirt, it is informing us of its condition. When the body says, "No!" to what the mind tries to dish out to it, or when the body craves what the mind denies it, we *feel* something is wrong with what we *think* is good for us.

We may ask: What is biological and what is psychological? But if we are beings who express ourselves both mentally and physically, we do not live in separate pockets of our being. Because the ways we express ourselves are different, it is convenient, within the confines of our language, to speak of the "mental" and the "physical"; but separating them is misleading, because we can feel with our thoughts and think with our feelings. Our language functions to ease conversation, not to end confusion. If we are beings who express ourselves both mentally and physically, then who are we? If it is we, and not the mind or the body that knows, what is this self that knows? Ultimately, this is a mystery, unknowable and ineffable.

11

Meat as Medicine

"Good medicine has often a bitter smack."
—Japanese Proverb

There are many bitter pills we swallow: rejection, promises broken, the thwarting of desire; loss of love, lack of love, loss or lack of independence; futile attachment, guilt and shame; the dissolution of dreams; scattered wealth or shattered health; direction denied, or meaning demeaned. For an avowed vegetarian whose ill health may be cured by swallowing well-timed capsules of meat, the choice may be as traumatic; but while the thought of meat may first lead to revulsion, it may then lead to compulsion to take the bitter pill, and surrender for something better—a cure.

Bitter pills sometimes bring about sweet recoveries, and happily, most pills need not be taken for long. We may use them to re-establish equilibrium or to re-capture the zest we lost (although not necessarily because of our vegetarianism). Sometimes we get well without injections or interventions, but sometimes we must give in. What we once saw as an abomination, we may now see as salvation; what we once saw as hateful, or even as harmful, we now see as helpful. And indeed it may be: going to the butcher's may replace going to the doctor's—an irony given that the first surgeons *were* the butchers—literally.

We may not need meat to stay healthy; but even vegetarians get sick. We may then blame our diets as the cause; but whatever the cause, the cure may be diet. Just as a meatless regime once cured some ills, and may have prevented others, adding meat as medicine may assuage what ails us now. Some physicians, like ROBBAN, insist that for a small subset of the population, vegetarianism may be ill-advised, and that for some, it may be "suicide." In this case, the avowed vegetarian must swallow the bitter pill for life—or at least until her metabolism changes.

Not everyone agrees with ROBBAN. JONATHAN (who has an M.A. in nutrition) finds it "ridiculous" and "absurd" that someone may need high intakes of cholesterol or animal protein, although he later admitted that there could be the exceptional or "bizarre" individual. Theories about health and nutrition are rife with admissions that what is missing is a strict science. Vegan physicians, and even omnivorous ones, like DAVID, tell us, "vegetarianism is better for your health," and that vegetarians have fewer cancers, less osteoporosis, less heart disease, and more stamina.

But is every vegetarian who eats a perfect diet perfectly healthy? And what about vegans whose diets are abominations? At conferences, after hearing the typical rousing lecture on vegetarianism, one is tempted to conclude that vegans are immortal. At the end of one such lecture, an audience member raised his hand and asked, "What *do* vegetarians die of, anyway?" We die of death like everyone else, and we get sick with disease like everyone else.

Sometimes we get sick because of what GAIL calls "sloppy vegetarianism"—eating sweets instead of sprouts, white bread instead of black beans, pasta instead of kasha, salted chips instead of salads, fast food and sloe gin—all vegetarian. We may wine and dine (and even smoke!) and like one physician I know, substitute the parmesan for the veal, and butter our bread until we thicken unto death.

GAIL was right to warn us: "I see young people going vegetarian; but they keep going to McDonalds and they just eat the French fries and the Coke. I can see them doing a lot of damage, and I always want to tell them, 'Just being a vegetarian doesn't do it. You're growing. It's better to have that junky protein than nothing.' It's scary what they're doing to themselves. It's a big responsibility when you go vegetarian, to study, and to learn the discipline of taking care of your body by substituting healthy foods."

On refined foods, we are not well-fed, even if we avoid eating animals long-dead. A vegetarian diet is not necessarily a healthful diet, and a diet which includes a modest amount of meat may be better than a diet which is incomplete. This is why some, like MAR-CIA, believe that where variety is lacking, as it is in some tribal societies, flesh foods may be needed to ensure health. "I think it is a little simple-minded if we don't realize that there are places—like some of the African countries and so forth—where meat eating is really necessary for people."

In this country, one can be a vegan, and partake only in eggless and dairyless cookies and cakes. Health food stores now offer the industry-sanctioned equivalent of Oreos. LEONARD, who owns such a store, says, "Start from scratch!" but few vegetarians do. KIVA said: "There are so many people in my generation who eat pasta and soda and that's all. You can't just take what you eat normally, and subtract meat. You have to add a lot of foods—bean based proteins—and a lot more vegetables."

If health declines as a result of a junk diet, or on a careful diet, for other reasons, then for some, like those who suffer from candida or from other infections, a vegetarian diet may not be as effective as an omnivorous one for curing them. It may at first be inconceivable for a long-time vegetarian like NANCY to do this; but as necessity mothers invention, illness mothers intervention, sometimes in ways we consider drastic or extreme.

Health is not of the body alone; it is we who are ill or well. Can we be healthy eating something we are sick at the thought of? Can we be healthy if what we see and smell at our dinners makes us feel like sinners? If we nourish our spirits, our bodies may be sick; and if we nourish our bodies, our spirits may be sick. Sometimes we are faced with nourishing one or the other; so in either case we feel sick. But to use meat as medicine is not to value it for itself. Philosophers distinguish extrinsic from intrinsic value, what is useful from what is good in itself. If a vegetarian uses meat as medicine, it is as though she chose root canal work for a toothache, or a mastectomy for breast cancer. Such interventions are justified only as means, not as ends in themselves, so what we mean when say that meat is medicine is that it can be used to achieve the end of health. Stories like ELLY's and BARBARA's show us how sad this choice can be, but that it need not imply a change of philosophy.

Intestinal Fortitude

After twenty-four years as a vegetarian, ELLY began eating all types of meat. "I'm not one of those body-phobic, self-conscious, nutrition-oriented vegetarians: that always turned me off because it was so narcissistic. My vegetarianism was always outer-directed. And it would have bored me to do all this balancing and mixing. When I really turned was after I got *extremely* sick with colitis-like symptoms, and was told over and over—and resisted for quite awhile —that the only thing [for it] was occasionally eating some form of meat."

ELLY has been eating meat "no more than twice a week" for a year. "Usually poultry; but I've run the gamut of my four-legged friends. Pig . . . Cow . . . What else is there? The first animal I *didn't* want to eat was the first animal I returned to: I cooked some fried chicken. I've always loved it. I'm not someone who stopped eating meat because I didn't like it; as matter of fact, I *hated* vegetables when I became a vegetarian. I loathed them, and never had a salad. I didn't have a salad for the first six years of my vegetarianism. I *hated* vegetables. I wasn't equivocal about it.

"My intestinal activity calmed down. What they think now, after a year of testing and specialists, is that I was hit with this incredible bacterial infection which I never really recovered from. My intestines just went into overdrive, and they've since calmed down. They're far from calm; but they're much better. I don't feel great emotionally; but I felt I had little choice. I was resigned to it. I never felt guilty; I never felt badly; I didn't feel it was a moral lapse. I felt it was a physical necessity—which it was.

"I suppose quite a few people who eat meat do feel it's a physical necessity; but I think that's a secondary explanation. I think they eat it because they like it. I still feel a distance from most meat eaters. I feel a sense of kinship with people who don't eat meat because they want to contribute somehow to the relief of suffering of animals. I feel no kinship with people whose primary reason is health. I suppose I could say the same thing about myself: my primary reason for eating meat is health. Is that narcissistic?

"I still feel I'm the same person. I don't think I've undergone any volcanic, phenomenological change. I have a feeling within a week or two I'm going back to a fairly purist vegetarianism. That's what my heart wants. I'm much better. I hope I will return to it when my intestines are a little bit more under control. I feel a sense of sorrow that this was necessary for me."

Barbara's "Betrayal"

Twenty years ago, BARBARA cooked two meals at home—vegetarian for herself and "something like Beefaroni" for her husband. A few years later, they ate vegetarian together; but now BARBARA again cooks two meals at home—vegetarian for her husband, and something else for herself—in a classic case of what is called "chiastic inversion."[1] The reason for the role reversal started with a visit to a Buddhist acupuncturist . . .

"Last November, I started seeing an acupuncturist, and interestingly enough, the acupuncturist is a vegetarian. He's Vietnamese—a former Buddhist monk. Walking into his office is like walking into a small, very simple temple. He has a altar with a Buddha there, and beautiful offerings and candles. It's a very simple practice. You walk in, and there's a cardboard table, a curtain and a bed—and that's it. I'm very drawn to him—very impressed with him. He's a very humble person, and I trust him implicitly; I have a tremendous respect for him.

"He is third generation in his family doing herbs and acupuncture. His English is not very good, but I know he was an abbot in a monastery in Viet Nam, and he's been training at this since he was ten years old. I'd guess him to be my age—mid-forties. Primarily he does pulse reading. Within a month, he started telling me I needed to eat meat. I resisted for several months, just boiling chicken bones and using the broth. He said, 'It's not enough. You need red meat. You need liver.' He sees it as part of medicine, as part of healing.

"My problems started years ago when I was very heavy and eating lots of meat. For about twenty years, I'd had developing problems with chronic pain on my right side, and it's gotten to the point where it's just painful to sit. I went through the whole gamut of traditional medicine, none of which helped. I started using chiropractic and massage a couple of years ago—and no benefits there. He's the first person to give me at least a sense of what's going on, which is not having a regular period since I was fifteen. I didn't tell him I didn't have my period, because I never would have thought to connect it. He knew right away, just by reading my pulse, that my circulation was very bad on my right side. What's been going on for more than twenty years is not having a regular menstrual cycle which has led to toxins staying in my body, and affecting my nervous system and circulation.

"My regular doctors told me years ago to start eating meat, and I never did; but here is someone who is a Buddhist and a vegetarian saying I need to eat meat, and I really trust him. I trust he's not someone coming from the conventional anti-vegetarian place. Where he's coming from has an impact on my own approach to it. I finally broke down about a year ago. I have an image of myself in tears at the thought of eating meat, and disgusted that I had to do something that goes against my philosophy of life.

"My first meal was probably the equivalent of an ounce of

chicken. I prepared it myself; I baked it. I got little chicken wings: I haven't yet done a whole chicken. I eat as little as can. I got chicken wings the first time because there's just a little meat on there: you're not seeing a whole animal. That was the closest I could come to it. The idea of baking that in my own oven was hard for me—the smell of it, and everything about it. I remember first the smell and then sitting down to a meal of those baked little chicken wings on my plate; I can feel my stomach turn just talking about it. I felt very resistant. This isn't fair! I don't want to do this! There were a lot of emotions that came up.

"I still cook two different meals at home. I had liver tonight, and he had a pasta dish, so it's the reverse. We're back to doing two meals separately. I eat liver. I eat ground beef and chicken: we're up to legs. I can't wait to join my husband again! His [food] looks so good! I can't wait to be vegetarian again. Absolutely, this is only temporary. 'A few more months,' [the doctor] says, 'a few more months'; but 'a few more months' always turns out to be different from my concept of 'a few more months.' So I'm not sure how long this is going to be. The thing that keeps me hanging on is the feeling that this is only temporary.

"I feel very uncomfortable; I feel very guilty. It's like breaking a trust; it feels like a betrayal for me. But this man changed my life! I thought I'd never get it back! It's been so long . . . At least this helps cleanse me. I've been boiling herbs as well, sometimes at night for five hours, so it's hard to say if it's the change in diet, or the herbs, or both. I hope it's just a matter of a month, and we can let go of this."

Eating animals again, both ELLY and BARBARA technically cease to be vegetarian, although each holds fast to a vegetarian philosophy. When BARBARA says she "can't wait" to be a vegetarian again, we feel she still is, and what she means is that she can't wait to eat that way again. When ELLY, who believes she "never really left," says vegetarianism is what her hearts wants, we believe her: twenty years of commitment have made these women who they are. Are they "former vegetarians"—or vegetarians on vacation? Omnivores—or vegetarians on sick leave?

A Bittersweet Tale

GAIL, in contrast, eats vegetarian (or not) for reasons of health only. Her story neatly illustrates the Hindu proverb: "When sugar can kill, why feed poison?" She said: "A macrobiotic chef in my store started creating a lot of interest. I carry around some terrible memories of my Mom's cancer, because I took care of her intensely before she died. I would worry about female cancers. The macrobiotic chef told me that animal foods are associated with female problems and cancers. She told all the customers that a panacea for female problems is to stop eating flesh foods. I went almost vegan. Macrobiotic I went.

"They use a lot of malted grain syrups—they do. And it was so easy. No one emphasized to me that sweets were going to make a problem. The chef made a lot of pastry and did a lot of sweet baking; she used a lot of fruit in her baking— lots and lots of dried fruit. She didn't eat any animal foods at all. She didn't eat much protein at all. I got into this thinking I was going to get away from all those scary female cancers I was seeing all around me; but all of a sudden, I got bad yeast infections that lasted a long time and were real uncomfortable. I started waking up in the middle of the night, and being unable to go back to sleep.

"I was diagnosed and put on a candida diet. A candida diet is high-protein, but the doctor told me, 'You can continue to be vegetarian. Beans are your protein, but no more of the starch.' And I felt better; so I continued this until I got the candida out of my system—about four years later. Then I went back to eating sweeteners. Sweets were easy to grab—and lots of starches. Two years later, here I am still eating a heavily starchy diet with plenty of sweets, and here I am all of a sudden feeling so drowsy in the afternoon that you'd have to call it 'passing out.' Really—just incapacitating drowsiness in the afternoons. It was scary. I didn't know what was going on. I kept improving my diet and eating better quality foods.

"Then I looked at Dr. Atkins' *New Diet Revolution*. It had a chapter on insulin reactionism. When people eat too many sweets, they start to oversecrete insulin which makes you feel hungry, which makes you eat more, and these people were eating themselves up to huge weights because they ate too many sweets—too many *concentrated* sweets. Dr. Atkins explained that when you get into this kind of insulin trouble, your body gets used to secreting too much insulin because of all the sweets and starches. He helped people reset the insulin setting they created in their bodies—their over-insulinism— by having them eat extremely high protein meals with no starch and no sweeteners. He said you can re-train your body's insulin secretion patterns that way.

"That clicked with me: I got the feeling that was my problem. It was a combination of being too sloppy, too starchy, eating too many sweets, and losing track a little of tofu and tempeh. So for two years, I did what he said in the book. He said: *'You need flesh'* He didn't say a *thing* about tofu and tempeh! He said it's got to be *flesh*. I found that meat was easy to get in my store, and I started eating meat from the store.

"For about one and three quarter years, my breakfast was meat, steamed vegetables, and either butter or flax seed oil, and my lunch was the same. My dinner was a little bit of meat or tofu and tempeh, and steamed vegetables, and for dessert, was a piece of toast. I did this for one and three quarter years. I didn't go to any doctors. I *fixed* myself. I felt so good, and had so much energy! A lot of little naggy health problems got corrected. I felt *terrific*!

"I'm not saying this is the way a healthy person should start to eat, but I had to re-balance myself because I got real sloppy in that last vegetarian era. I was a sloppy vegetarian: I ate starch for breakfast, starch for dinner, sweets all day long. I just got myself sick. I had this mantra in front of me, remembering the macrobiotic chef saying, 'Flesh food will give you female cancers; flesh foods will give you female cancers; they're the cancer creators.'

"Now the fad is high-carbs, fat-free. I think the pendulum is starting to swing back and we're on the cusp. There are a few brilliant doctors telling people there are healthy fats you *need:* Dr. Ronald Hoffman is the best.[2] Also a master nutritionist who was a vegetarian for a long time is telling people you need a certain amount: he now eats fish. I think there are different body types, different metabolisms; I think I may be one of the body types that was designed to utilize meat. I think there are people with body types that don't so much need it; some people may be O.K. *never* eating meat.

"Just lately, I'm eating a lot less meat. I will keep checking in and seeing how I feel. I feel like I'm pretty tuned in to my health, and if I felt like meat was going to give me the energy that I needed, I'd use it once in a while for that. I consider meat eating a corrective balance restorer. I would tell a vegan to experiment from time to time to see if it has a corrective effect on health problems."

NANCY was the antithesis of a "sloppy vegetarian," offering nutrition classes at her health food store, and practicing what she preached; but she also developed candida. As her former range of options dwindled, she had to make choices within a shrinking frame —choices consistent with her other values. She said: "If I didn't have allergies, and if I didn't have candida, I'd be very happy on a vegetarian diet. If you're doing it right, I still believe wholeheartedly in that diet. If you're doing it right, that's great. My major goal is to get rid of the symptoms I have. You do what you have to do to feel better."

NANCY will return to her vegetarianism as soon as she recovers from candida. "If someone came up with a whole new way of keeping it in check, I would very easily; but I'm not willing to go through the pain. It isn't worth it to pump myself up with a toxic drug—which it would have to be—because the only thing that will get rid of it is Benadryl, and it's so intense, it's not worth that. On a planetary scale, it's even more evil—the drug industry. And I don't want to do that to my body. You can't discount one part of the body to compensate for the other: you have to keep them all in balance. That's very hard when the picture changes."

FRANK, a biology teacher, agrees with GAIL that "a lot of problems are caused by too much carbohydrates. Mother Nature created a bell curve: some people can eat chocolate and live to be ninety, and other people can just look at a piece of bread and get fat. We're all somewhere on this bell curve: there's no one diet for everybody. We live in a culture that's been manipulated because carbohydrates are cheap to manufacture and easy to store, and we're just having sugar shoved down our throats. The average person is so ignorant of nutrition that it makes me want to throw my hands up.

"I think vegetarianism is a fad. I think it's a controlled form of anorexia sometimes: I think there's a lot of anorexia that's masking as vegetarianism. I think people do it and then get health problems because they're not getting nourished. The average person who says, 'I'm going to be vegetarian because it's wrong to kill' is missing the boat. Some of them get wonderful benefits from it; but a lot of them get out of whack because it's too much carbohydrate. I don't think we're meant to eat just grains. We're not browser animals. We have sharp teeth for ripping stuff as well as molars for grinding."

INGRID's experience as a young college student illustrates what FRANK suggests—that vegetarianism is sometimes a form of anorexia. INGRID ate "no flesh, but lots of sugar." She developed an eating disorder—fasting, bingeing, and bulimia—which "went out of control" and turned into what she called "self-starvation." Finally, she heard her body say, "Take something in and nourish yourself." She broke her flesh fast with cold cuts, and now eats "organic chicken, lamb, beef stews, and soups." She said: "I listen to how it feels in my body" and called her return to meat from anorexia "re-balancing."

From Down Under

While some wish to return to vegetarianism after "re-balancing," others know they will never go back. Beginning in her mid-twenties, AVA embarked on a decade of vegetarianism, but believes she shipwrecked because of it. She said: "I see no great benefits to following a vegetarian diet. I realized after a lot of study that I had hurt my health." AVA now sees vegetarians as "spacey and weaker, and more prone to PMS and depression." Convinced by "the six thousand year old system of Chinese medicine" that she must eat meat, she is now "grounded again, and at fifty-three, very healthy."

AVA worries about other vegetarians. "In Australia, people who are vegetarian eat a lot of salad and raw food. This causes the health to deteriorate ever faster. It is important to eat organic meat and a lot of fish. My ratio of meat to steamed vegetables is high. My husband, a doctor, has had the same experience, and eats a lot more meat than I do: he says he cannot produce as much work without it. We are both in excellent health after recovering from chronic fatigue (him) and cervical cancer (me). We had no Western treatment. I run a health clinic in Australia, and I have seen no really healthy vegetarians. Most people don't know what to look for or blame other things for their bad health."

A Physician's Prescription

Our bodies speak to us most eloquently through illness and disease—diagnosing and doctoring us, describing what ails us. A body can embody a prescription for a litany of needs: if we ignore them, we may be sorry that we did not take heed. Once enthusiastic about macrobiotics, ROBBAN said: "Initially, I felt a little clearer; however, after several months, I started to get very sick. It was winter by that time, and I'm not usually susceptible to colds and sore throats; but I started having shaking chills, and I felt like I was running a very high fever without other symptoms of a cold. I wasn't congested or anything, but just these shaking chills and ached all over, like I had a bad virus.

"It got to the point where I was sitting in my office with my coat on, shaking. So I called a friend from the Kushi Institute,[3] and she said, 'Go get a big piece of steak, and cook it, and eat it.' She was also before that a metabolic technician with Kelley,[4] so she had both perspectives. As soon as she heard my symptoms, she said, 'You're a parasympathetic dominant; you shouldn't be off meat. Parasympathetic dominants need to eat meat.' And I said, 'O.K. I mean, I feel really bad going off the diet here . . .' I went out and ate it, and the chill cleared instantly—I mean, *within ten minutes.* I was free of the feeling, and it never came back again. So no way am I ever going off meat again!

"That was years ago: the steak was great! When I ate that first steak, it was the best thing I ever tasted. I went to the restaurant next door because I was at my office, and ordered grilled steak. It felt so *right.* I remember it feeling very good, very right in my body. I was really tuning into my body, not concepts of the way I thought the world should be. Talk about control! We think we're going to dictate to God what our bodies function best on! I really doubt there's a God out there that would create people to require meat, and then say, 'But you have to be vegetarian to be spiritually enlightened.' That doesn't click with me.

"I really *wanted* to be a sympathetic dominant. I really *wanted* to eat this wonderful vegetarian diet, and yet my body . . . That's what I feel: even eating a *small* amount of carbohydrate, whether it's brown rice or some junk food, makes me feel tired and logy and foggy. That's just the way my body is. I've gone to Omega [Institute] and felt like a space cadet the whole time I was there because of the food. I was just down at Omega in the Caribbean, and I couldn't even *eat* their food! I had to go out to other restaurants. I was getting airy-fairy and out of it. It was ridiculous. They even had eggs there; they did have eggs for breakfast, which was my saving grace.

"Now could I get along on an ovo-lacto vegetarian diet? I probably could, but I feel best, to tell you the truth, on the Atkins diet—meat, chicken, eggs, heavy cream, and a few vegetables. Seriously, when I eat that way, I have tons of energy—like I can work all day and all night. That's the difference in metabolic type. In other words, we don't have to say, 'I'm right; no, you're right. No, I'm right. No, you're right.' You know what I mean.

"There are certain people, myself, for instance, who will run a very low cholesterol when they're off animal products. Your body *needs* cholesterol: it needs it to make steroid hormones. The liver is supposed to make them; but there are select individuals who will run a real low cholesterol. I've seen a lot of infertility in macrobiotic people whose livers don't make enough cholesterol, and they drop their estrogen and testosterone levels.

"If your cholesterol drops below 140, you can actually see the increase of certain diseases—depression, suicide, accidental death due to lack of concentration or spaciness. You start seeing increases of liver cancer. Lowering cholesterol too far is definitely dangerous to your health. Most people can make cholesterol with their livers just fine; but there are probably some people who cannot—probably a subset of the population, in which case they need to get it from some sort of dietary source. Since drinking milk or eating eggs doesn't involve killing an animal, I would tell them to at least eat dairy and eggs.

"I think it's really metabolic type; you're obviously a different metabolic type than I am. Some people do best on a low-fat, low-protein diet, and lots of complex carbs and lots of fiber, and other people you can't get well until you put them on low-carb diets. There are three types that are primarily vegetarian, and three types that need more meat. Theoretically, there are people who are breatharians, who don't do well on *any* food; they do their best just on energy—light. That's getting a little far out, so we won't talk about that.

"Basically, if you boil it all down, it's three types—a sympathetic dominant, a parasympathetic dominant, and a mixed type. You can change at different times in your life from one to the other. Kelley had an elaborate system of blood chemistry analysis, urinalysis, and a questionnaire by which he could identify what the metabolic type was. Then he would recommend a diet based on that.

"Kelley's work makes the best sense of anything I've ever seen. People who are sympathetic dominant—their adrenal glands are really strong, and their nervous system is really strong, but their digestion is very weak. Those are people who develop cancer if they eat the

Standard American Diet because they have a weak pancreas. In this particular metabolic type, they do better with vegetarian diets. In the parasympathetic dominant, they have a really strong digestion, so they can handle meat. They can digest it very easily; but they tend not to develop as much cancer because they have a strong pancreas. But there are instances of people who go on a vegetarian diet and develop cancer: those are the people who are parasympathetic dominant. Probably seventy per cent of the population is sympathetic dominant, and probably thirty per cent are parasympathetic dominant. I may be off on these percentages; I'm just guessing. Eighty per cent of my patients are parasympathetic dominant.

"I have patients that if they look at a carbohydrate, their cholesterol and triglycerides skyrocket. And they're at serious risk of dying of heart disease if they don't follow Atkins' diet. If they follow a vegetarian diet, it would literally be suicidal.

"A forty-one year old psychologist came to me, and he had been eating the American Heart Association diet for heart disease which is semi low-fat, supposedly—fish, chicken, vegetables, and grains. And he felt *terrible*. He felt really tired—wasn't feeling very well at all. He started having chest pains, and went to the cardiologist, and they found a blocked artery, and so he underwent an angioplasty—which failed. He continued to have angina after that, and he had very high triglycerides and a very high cholesterol. The cholesterol when I saw him was about 350, and the triglycerides were about 800—and that was on Lopid which they had given him to try to lower his blood fats. When he went on the low-carb diet, the so-called 'Atkins Diet,' all of those blood parameters fell into the normal range. He also felt better—felt more energetic. He was able to do more. He didn't want to undergo bypass surgery: he wanted to do it in a more natural way.

"There is no one answer. You've got to look at every individual. I can get away with eating carbs; I may not feel as well, but I can get away with it. I will eat carbs; if someone serves vegetarian, I'll eat it. I won't feel as well, but I won't make a big deal of it. I didn't insist that Omega serve me a steak. When we went out in the evening, I ate something different from what was being served there. I eat some type of animal protein every day. I usually have eggs for breakfast and I have steak or chicken or fish for lunch and dinner. Sometimes I have two steaks in one day. My philosophy is to individualize, to be moderate in all things. Two steaks a day is moderate for *me*."

ROBBAN will not go back to vegetarianism "unless my metabolic type changes. I don't want to feel lousy. I like feeling good, thank you. I don't think God would have created parasympathetic dominants if He didn't mean us to eat meat. I know I have too much to accomplish in my life. I know what I'm doing, and I know what my purpose for being here is. If I don't fulfill that purpose, it would be really tragic." ROBBAN's reviving on a diet on which most of us would not be thriving gives new meaning to the Biblical adage: "Physician, heal *thyself*."[5]

Jonathan's Rejoinder

"I don't believe it for a moment, not for one second, that someone *needs* to have high-fat, high-cholesterol in their diet. That someone might even die if they don't have animal products in their diets is patently absurd. For those people, they have not been eating a balanced vegetarian diet, and that's why they're getting sick; it has nothing to do with diet per se. *Obviously,* they're not eating a balanced diet, whether it's for psychological reasons or lack of knowledge; but I challenge anyone to give me scientific reasons why some people cannot withhold animal products from their diet and be healthy. In terms of scientific knowledge, I don't see any theory to explain that. Ridiculous. Absurd. I challenge them to come up with evidence.

"The most conservative nutritional organization in the world is the American Dietetic Association. In 1988, they published a policy statement in which they finally admitted that you can be completely healthy on a vegetarian diet, or on a vegan diet as long as you supplement with B12. There's no known reason why you can't be optimally healthy on a vegetarian diet. That's a *consensus view* that took decades of convincing the ADA. In former days, they flat-out said, 'No. You *can't* be healthy on a vegetarian diet.' They equated it with a crank diet, with a fad diet. It took years for them to have review committees and they finally said, 'Look, the evidence is overwhelming.' This is looking at hundreds of studies. *There's no evidence that a healthy person can't remain healthy on a vegetarian diet.*

"It's a whole different category if they have liver disease. There's always the one bizarre individual, I guess. If they have some sort of disease condition, they may require some other food in their diet: that's a whole different situation. You have to be careful with anecdotal evidence. One person can't make cholesterol. Does that mean everyone should be eating a lot of cholesterol just in case?" As if he heard MICHAEL say, "With the speed at which I burn up food with my highly inefficient metabolism, I would be grazing like a giraffe all day if I didn't eat fish and chicken," he continued: "Some people might jump to the wrong conclusion: it's an easy explanation. They'll say, 'Well, my metabolism is different. That's why I have to eat meat.'

"It's *easier* for certain people to get more of some nutrients on an omnivore diet. If you're eating red meat, it's *easier* to absorb zinc and iron. It may be more *difficult* to get certain nutrients on a vegan diet, but it's possible. Ideally, if people are eating with the knowledge of how to do this, they can be healthy. There's always the individual out there who has particular needs that are going to be more easily met if they have red meat in their diet." [6]

We could call this a matter of "meat-abolism." One such individual is a friend of MICHAEL's in England who has a kidney problem which requires him to eat two pounds of meat a day, for his damaged kidneys secrete protein so quickly, he cannot replenish it with vegetarian sources. Such a case is not "bizarre," and may require the sufferer to prepare those whose suffering he once tried to spare.

"New nutritional information comes out every day; people have to find their own way," said JONATHAN, who agrees that some people cannot "thrive" on a vegetarian diet, but who thinks the number is much smaller than ROBBAN believes it is. She is a physician who sees the sick; he is a nutritionist who counsels the well; so for JONATHAN the unhealthy may well appear to be exceptional.

AVA thought vegetarianism made her sick; JONATHAN would say an inadequate vegetarian diet made her sick; ROBBAN might say she was the wrong metabolic type to be a vegetarian; but as some try meat to cure their ills, others try vegetarianism to prevent them, fearing that they will sicken on flesh—whether or not they sicken of it—contracting a contagion like CJD from a cow infected with BSE, or an immunodeficiency disease from one infected with BIV, or trichinosis from pork, or salmonella from poultry "products." Others fear rBGH despite the assurance of those who profit from it.

Health risks, however remote, make meat unthinkable, untouchable, and ultimately, untasteable, for many; and for many, the thought of feeding on animals fed on medicinals to fend off their own diseases—hog cholera, sheep rot, or cattle plague—is off-putting.[7] Plant eating is seen as prophylactic. When one considers the bio-accumulation of toxins in animal tissues, vegetarianism as preventive medicine becomes a living issue.

If we compare a careful vegetarian diet with the Standard American Diet, we have a winner; but this does not so much show that vegetarianism is the best diet as it suggests that the Standard American Diet is the worst. If we compare a careful vegetarian diet to one to which we add an ounce of organic meat every week, or even daily, the diet is no longer vegetarian, but perhaps no less good, and certainly much better than the S.A.D. So showing that a vegetarian diet is better than the S.A.D. accomplishes very little, for it shows neither that a vegetarian diet is better than the same diet to which a small amount of flesh is added, nor that vegetarianism is the best diet.

If we compare the S.A.D. with the worst possible meatless diet, one I can hardly bear to dignify with the name "vegetarian" (for it need contain neither vegetables nor anything vital) the winner will be the S.A.D. Thus if our only criterion for evaluating vegetarianism were bodily health, then the choice is not between eating meat, or not, but between eating well and eating ill, and hence between being well and being ill. Adding or subtracting meat is not itself the issue,[8] although when vegetarians compare their good diets to the poor ones of omnivores, they make it seem so. But the real issue for many vegetarians goes beyond bodily health. Thus we can still argue that vegetarianism is our best choice, even if we cannot show it is our best diet.

If there are sympathetic dominants and parasympathetic dominants, then I must be an empathetic dominant, for, so far, my fellow feelings for my fellow beings have prevented me from making medicine out of them. If health and nutrition is our only reason for vegetarianism, then it makes sense to experiment with meat; but if we are vegans whose reasons are spiritual or ethical, then the doctor's telling us to try a little tenderloin may be tantamount to telling the God-fearing to devil-worship now and then. The best diet balances health of body against wealth of spirit. When all else has been tried, and only meat proves true, then we may have a duty to our spirits to get our bodies well.

12

Convenience and Conscience

"A dinner!
How horrible!
I am to be made the pretext for killing all those wretched
animals, and birds, and fish! Thank you for nothing."
—George Bernard Shaw

"Don't talk with your mouth full, " we are told, but not "Don't talk with your mouth empty." Yet vegetarians sometimes need to talk about why their mouths are empty while other mouths are full. In a manner of speaking—is it impolite to be "right"? Must etiquette edge out ethics and morals move over for manners? How are we to balance personal idealism and social obligation? Are there occasions when we must be silent and just grin and eat it? If a prospective employer offers medallions of veal, do we conceal our ideals? Or should we speak out against what others take in, even when our conclusions might be taken as intrusions?

How do we get away with getting away from meat? In a violent culture, a pacifist protests; in a carnivorous culture, a vegetarian resists. If omnivores offer meat, we could hide it under the potatoes as we did the peas when we were children; but then we couldn't eat the potatoes. More peas, please. We could arrive with our own picnic basket (as some orthodox Jews do with their own dishes) but we might mortify the hostess by eating our live produce instead of the dead roast she produces. We could say, simply, "I'm on a diet," and if pressed, "What kind?" reply, "Vegetarian." We could mention cholesterol or heart disease; but what do we say to, "But a little bit (or bite) never hurt anyone"? Having never been a particularly polite person (more of a pest than a good guest) as the black sheep I might reply, "Only the lamb"—or chicken or pig or cow.

To "I've been slaving all day over this recipe—just try it" we could say, "No—you and the others eat it; this way there will be more for those who will most enjoy it." We could remember an urgent errand and return in time for tea. ("No cream, please.") We could coax the cat or dog to our feet and surreptitiously drop tidbits. When passed the platter running over with juices, we could say, "I'll pass on that" and pass the platter on. If asked why, we could say it wouldn't be right to make others lose their appetites and promise to fill them in later when their stomachs are no longer filled with meat. We could make a big fuss over the potatoes or the peas and ask for recipes. What else would appease? We could arrive in our "Love Animals, Don't Eat Them" tee shirt, or my favorite, " I Think; Therefore I Am A Vegetarian."

Is it rude or crude to refuse their food? I admire near vegetarians who are flexible; I'm just not that way myself; but I do wish to be a peaceful person, one who does not make a scene. (At table, vegetarians should be seen refusing meat, but not heard protesting it.) We could say, "I'm not as hungry as I thought I was, but the salad looks delicious," hoping that rumbling stomachs won't give us away, and resist the temptation to check the dressing for traces of Parmesan cheese. We could say that our reasons are "personal" and that we'll explain when we know them better; but if we are eating with family who know us all too well, they may fear we have a rare disease. Then we can say, no, we are just eating in a way which makes disease rare. We could say, "I'm sure you will understand: I haven't touched the stuff in more than twenty years. It's hard to say what might happen." If our hostess feared we might be sick, she might feel less heartsick. Better to stick to our convictions than to have her chicken stick in our throats.

Is it in bad taste to refuse what would taste bad? If someone refuses broccoli or beets, lima beans or spinach, or even dessert, no one makes quite the fuss that is made when someone refuses meat. It cannot be because meat is more expensive: my organic vegetables and fruits cost more than hamburger and probably more than steak. Meat is a symbol in our culture of the best we have to offer. It is no accident that we say we "present" it at the table, for flesh proffered is offered as a gift. (Even felines who bring carrion home to their human companions understand this.) Thus it is a greater insult to refuse what is perceived to have the greater value.

Omnivores cannot fathom the vegetarian's aversion to what they most prize, any more than the cat can understand our revulsion at the dead rodent. Fried chicken is more savory than unbuttered corn—so why not indulge? Why not *live* a little? The vegetarian might wonder why, when Chicken Little had to die; but it is best not to talk when our minds are full of this idea. The simple appetite of the vegetarian confuses those who take pleasure in rich foods: Poor deprived souls! Vegetarians may make gourmets or gourmands feel foolish or guilty for enjoying their meals, just as teetotalers may make connoisseurs uncomfortable savoring their fine wines alone; but as long as we don't whine about it, we haven't wronged anyone.

Complicity loves company; but since ethics weighs more heavily than etiquette and morals more than manners, if it is not immoral to be impolite, then vegetarians are within their rights. Yet many vegetarians choose accommodation over consternation and acquiescence over politesse. Some claim that compassion for people present outweighs compassion for animals absent (or present only as corpses). The choice is not always a simple one, for it is not easy to balance the happiness of hosts over the worthiness of ideals. What matters the most? If conscience comes before complaisance, we should not cave in under social pressure. There would not have been a Socrates or a Christ if virtue required that we never upset anyone. *"Ad astra per aspera."* ("To the stars through difficulties.")

Vegetarians encounter their difficulties in starlight or in moonlight, in sunlight or in candlelight, when they eat in restaurants; attend breakfast, lunch or dinner parties; or return as prodigals to traditional family meals. Some give in and give up, and others do not; but all have their reasons.

Restaurant Reviews

JOHN broke his vegetarianism in a restaurant all alone, under no social pressure to conform; but while not conforming, he found himself performing—for ghosts. "The first time was a big, juicy hamburger in a restaurant, out in the world. Here I was, in a rapidly deteriorating marriage and in a situation where another friendship with a vegetarian was also deteriorating, suddenly cut adrift. In these circumstances, it became possible to entertain all sorts of morbid thoughts—including eating meat.

"It was a token of my then manic-depressive condition. God dammit! I'm going to eat meat! I'll show you! Or else I'll show the world! It was an act of aggressive self-assertion and depression at that point;[1] but I was also amused by myself at the same time, that it was possible for me to sit there and regard myself as a performer in my own play. WOW! Here's a dramatic moment that I've scripted for myself: Man faces burger all alone at lonely lunch counter—and who was laughing? Who gave a damn? But we set up these little psycho-dramas for ourselves. Two relationships with two vegetarians were deteriorating. They won't know it, but this will really bother them!" At this dinner theater, JOHN was on stage, in front of people who did not even know they were the audience.

As film critic, JOHN eats not between meals, but between movies. As a result, he has developed a between-shows philosophy—"to go." "Maybe being the film critic has done me in as far as meat eating goes. If I'm the film critic, I'm not just going to subject myself to the higher end; it's necessary for me to subject myself to the mainstream. It's necessary for me to see 'Tales from the Crypt: Demon Night' and it's necessary for me to find a basis in which to discern which horror film is better than which horror film, and which shoot 'em up chase cars movie is better than which shoot 'em up chase cars movie. I want to be able to place it all in some perspective. So that's the philosophy I'm applying here—the desire to remain part of the mainstream as much as I can without polluting my mind too much. I've had people say, 'I don't know how you can sit there and watch some of the movies you see,' and believe me, there are times when the thought does cross my mind. So it goes with meat. There are times when I'm eating a piece of meat and hit gristle and think, 'Man! This is why I can't stand eating meat!' And then part of me will say, 'But you're eating it right now!' And I'll say, 'Well, don't tell anybody.'

"It was much more being part of the world, a little older and a little wiser. I was the professional reviewer and therefore having to eat between movies. There's a tendency to eat on the run, and then, what's available. Unfortunately, if you're seeking vegetarian options, you're going to be eating a lot of pizza or a fairly limited strain of Chinese. It's like Bill Clinton's politics: You set a lofty goal for yourself, and then the real world intrudes, and you make all these compromises. What you end up with is 'biting off more than you can chew.' If you want some variety in your diet, and you're eating out a lot, it's a matter of thinking, 'I've had enough cheese. It's time to order out for lunch. Well, they do make a great steamed burger down the road.'

"Although the philosophical thrust of vegetarianism continues to make sense to me, here's what it boils down to: If there was a world in which there were as many vegetarian options—not even as many —if there was a fifth of the options relative to meat eating, I would probably be a vegetarian ninety-nine per cent of the time or even one hundred per cent of the time. It's really the convenience thing; it's unfortunate, but true. It would be an excellent world if more of us had more vegetarian options, but how are we going to get more vegetarian options unless more people are vegetarian? So of course it's a 'Catch 22.' The way the world works and the way we work within it is such that it's a matter of energy more than anything else. When I have more time and energy to devote to this essentially philosophical idea which I think vegetarianism is—

"I find vegetarianism quite admirable and here's where I chastise myself for kowtowing to convenience. There's a part of me that's appalled at myself, 'Oh, you've built an entire life on convenience, you fool!' I think it's possible to read it that way."

ROCKY also found eating out inconvenient. He said: "When I worked, I was working in a factory during the day which was no problem, because I could always get something to eat; but when I was on the night shift for a year, it was very difficult to find that kind of food. I had to prepare food ahead of time because I would have lunch at five o'clock in the morning, and it made things more difficult in that respect. And then after I started losing my friends, I started drifting back toward eating meat again. It was easier sharing with friends—just more convenient, I guess."

Like JOHN, who was "cut adrift" from other vegetarians, ROCKY had no support from friends; and like JOHN, he broke his vegetarianism in a restaurant—but with an omnivorous companion. He said: "When I was a vegetarian, I used to get into little arguments with my friends, calling them 'meatheads' and stuff like that. They thought I was weird; they thought they were losing me, actually. I went out for breakfast one morning with a friend of mine; he ordered an egg breakfast, and he had sausage on the plate. I tried some of the sausage, and it was good. I remember later on he remarked that he had broken my streak of vegetarianism over a sausage. A little harmless thing . . . I remember the restaurant, the booth I sat in even.

"I wish I had continued my vegetarianism; but it sort of rubbed off. Frankly, I would be more vegetarian if I had more support. If I had a relationship with a vegetarian, that would be a big influence on me: I'd go back to a vegetarian diet if I was sharing it with someone. I just basically eat meat out of convenience, more than anything else."

NANCY had support; but illness made eating out inconvenient for her. Boxed in by food sensitivities and allergies, she seldom eats in restaurants; but like JOHN, she wishes there were more options. She said: "Part of it is a natural foods industry that doesn't really address other dietary issues besides dairy and animal products. I've been fighting this in my industry for years. Only in the last five or six years has the industry accepted that people do have allergies.

"I would like to go out to eat once in awhile, and very often it's pasta. But if you can't eat a lot of grains—what do you eat? If you're starved—if you're really hungry? Salad is fine, but sometimes you need the protein. I can eat tofu, but you can't always get tofu. I can't eat cooked tomatoes. If I can get plain broiled fish and rice, I'm not going to get a headache. If I eat the vegetarian meal, there's a chance there's flour in it; they use tamari that has wheat in it. There isn't really a choice at that point.

"If they would just use wheat-free tamari, I would eat the stir-fries very happily; but it's not there. Yes; you can tell them to do it without; but I can get that at home and if I'm out, it's a special occasion and I want to eat something that's not boring. Brown rice and steamed vegetables all the time loses its glamour. If you're out, you're treating yourself, and it's just not worth the compromise."

Sometimes a restaurant meal of meat is the last meat a patron ever tastes, not because of death by food poisoning, but because the desire for meat dies there. MICHAEL said: "About two years ago, we went to a health food store in Florida. It's a large, excellent organic food store with a restaurant attached, and in the restaurant, as in the store itself, in fact, they sell organically raised meat. And we each had an organic hamburger.

"The sense, interestingly, was of a very horrible, overstuffed feeling at the end of it. Part of the reason we stopped eating red meat—stopped absolutely 'dead'—was the thought of what it's fed on—what one is eating indirectly—the hormones, the brains of other animals, possibly diseased. These cows came from pastures where the water flows from a natural spring and there is no pesticide in the pasture. They are fed otherwise in the winter on organic grains and so on and so forth. It's third party inspected. It's believable: that wasn't the point. Putting aside the possibility that people might cheat, which would apply to everything that one buys, or one does, regrettably, putting that aside, we thought, 'My goodness, this is the place to try eating meat again'—and I had no desire to repeat the experience afterward."

KEN, a former restauranteur, is a (former) former vegetarian who calls himself a "vegan wannabee," eating dairy "out of convenience more than desire." A culinary genius who calculates that between his vegetarian restaurant and consulting for colleges and food services, that four hundred thousand vegetarian meals have been served because of him, KEN says he has saved twenty thousand chickens. Yet even he tried flesh at a Japanese restaurant. He said: "I tried fish once ten years ago—at that time, maybe out of dietary boredom. I went out to dinner with my wife and a couple of friends, and I tried sautéed shrimp and scallops and a shrimp dumpling—and they all tasted terrible. I felt bad about eating them, and never did again. I didn't enjoy the food; I think it would have been rough if it tasted really good.

"I have nothing against the taste of meat. If someone is barbecuing meat, it smells good; but it's nothing I'd want to eat. It smells good because it was something I was accustomed to. That's why I refer to some of my favorite dishes as 'cuisine mirage' where I mimic the flavors and textures of food I grew up with. We never have hamburger. We have grills that have never seen a hamburger; they've seen veggie burgers. I learned to cook as a gourmet chef. I don't see anything wrong with the flavor; I just don't like the source. I like animals; I respect them." Like father, like—daughter. This Thanksgiving, eating "out" at Grandma's house, KEN's seven year old announced, presented with the turkey: "I don't want to eat that; it's just a poor bird."

A Taste For The Past

Like KEN, LEONARD feels a nostalgia for the foods of his youth; but instead of reinventing them as KEN does, he "samples" or "tastes" them on occasion. He said: "It became a matter of sentiment. You recall about what you might have had some years ago, when you were a child, and that caught your fancy, and if you liked it, and happened to run across it, and it was available—Working around the store, if you have a cook that prepares one or two meat items, then there it is sitting in front of you, and it doesn't get sold, so what do you do with it? You can't eat it all, so you taste a little bit of it.

"I roasted a chicken here at the store because I was the only cook here at the time. So I roasted a chicken. So what do you do with it? There's little pieces you don't use, so you taste this and you taste that, and you taste a little more, and you taste a little more. It also happened with some organic beef. It happened with some organic hamburger—excellent fresh meat which was going to be frozen—very high-priced prime beef with exquisite flavor—so you tasted a little bit of it. It's just a taste. It's just a memory of days gone by.

"There was some Polish kielbasa that I was ordering for two or three of my customers. I thought they would like it and maybe I could taste a little bit of it myself and bring back old times—just for old time's sake. So I ordered some, which was about six weeks ago when I had a portion of it—and not since. So that's probably the last time I had meat—to report on it, to report to some customers, merely because it's here. Maybe to sample it.

"And sometimes I give meat to the dog. I'll give her a fresh meat, frozen—freshly thawed-out meat—so in order not to give her the whole pound (and this is very seldom, maybe once every six months) I just taste it, a little bit of it, a couple of tablespoons full. But of late, the dog hasn't gotten any. In the last three or four months, the dog has maybe had meat once or twice, and I think of those once or twice I didn't have any at all. If I eat meat or dairy, it's not planned; it might be something on the spur of the moment. I never bring it home. It's something that brings you back to your childhood; it's not something you're going to continue. O.K. Now I'm set for another ten years."

TONY also ate meat because of reminiscence and childhood memories. He said: "My mother couldn't understand why at her famous Sunday Italian meal I would no longer eat her meatballs—

and this was tantamount to heresy. My mother was loving and understanding, and her thing was to indulge with giving food all the time, as a show of affection. Of course, at this point, that's not what I wanted."

Years later, a more mellow son returned. "At my parents' house, they were cooking a lamb; it was a leg of lamb. It was family thing: I just went along with it. I found at that point that certain things were no longer important. The lamb was delicious. It was Sunday dinner and it was reminiscent of childhood with all the smells that go along with that, being raised in a household where, on a Sunday, the whole house was filled with wonderful aromas. Your mother, or maybe your grandmother, starts cooking at about five in the morning. If it was cooked in my environment, the smells repulsed me; I hadn't cooked meat for so long in that environment; but if it was someone else's environment, it didn't repulse me.

"Meat's a cultural thing, and you feel the comfort of that culture, and because as a child your mother was preparing all these wonderful meals, it's hard to give that aspect of it up. It's like denying your family, or denying the pleasures of your youth. Later on, you get to a different understanding and you realize they wanted to do the best by you and they did, because you were able to go to another way of doing it where you felt less disturbance to yourself and to the environment."

All In The Family

As one of a "baker's dozen," BARBARA did not see much of her family after becoming a vegetarian—although there was a lot of family to see. She said, "I'm from a large family; I'm one of thirteen children. I was the only vegetarian; there was a lot of teasing. I've been in situations where I'd go to a wake or family event, and maybe once or twice a year in kind of delicate situations [I would eat meat]. Actually, I stopped going home for the holidays: vegetarianism was part of it. Around the time I made the change, going back for family things was hard; going back to visit is still a challenge. I've just learned to pack my own food; I just take my own food with me, and when I do, I make different recipes to share."

As an adult, BARBARA made that choice; as a child, VICKY was given no choice, and to this day, eats what is on the family table. She said: "When I go to my Mom's and she serves it, I eat it. I was brought up in a family which brought the Protestant work ethic to the dinner table: 'It is your job to eat whatever is on this plate; so just do it, and don't complain. If you don't eat everything, you don't get dessert.' Food aversions were treated like flaws to be overcome, except when my parents had the same dislike (I never had to eat Brussels sprouts; but as it turns out, I *like* them.)

"Also, allergic symptoms were responded to with denial. I was allergic to cow products as an infant, and had to be fed soy milk to avoid getting sick. The doctor and my parents both aspired to help me 'get used to' cow milk, and I was forced to drink it as soon as it stopped making me sick. It doesn't make me sick now; but having learned what I've learned about allergies, I'm certainly not going to force my kids to eat things they are allergic to! So the point is, if I had wanted to become a vegetarian *prior* to college, I would have had to face a lot of torment. My family expected me to eat whatever they put on the table, and I did, rather than cause a storm."

After years of living on her own as a vegetarian on the West Coast, GAIL returned to the east to live with her family, and found them all (including her once-vegetarian father) now eating meat. She said: "When I came back from California in 1978, my father was eating meat again. Meat was being eaten in the store because good meats were starting to be produced; they were when I came back to live with my family again and manage my father's business. These things were being served in our house. My father had begun to eat meat and my brother lived in the house and ate lots of meat, and so did my aunt, and so we prepared it together.

"We were making hot dogs and burgers at home. We were making natural, antibiotic-free, hormone-free, hot dogs and burgers from Shiloh Farms at home. It would be quickie hot dishes—probably something that in the cold weather was appetizing. At first, I only wanted a little. At first it was odd. And then gradually I'd be hungry, and it would be there, and it would smell good, and it would be easy. And gradually I ate more and more.

"When I created my own household in 1982 with a boyfriend, we went vegetarian. The temptation to eat meat was gone. It felt good for me as we cooked together. We worked hard at making really nutritious food. Vegetarianism satisfied me again. He was a cook, and he got excited about cooking the stuff. I went back into vegetarianism again and stayed with it through the eighties."

Like GAIL, JONATHAN created his own vegetarian "family" for support. He said: "I've always tried to live with people who were vegetarian, always living in group situations in all-vegetarian households. My priority was to find at least one person who was going to be vegetarian. My friend and I kind of set the rules for the kitchen: No meat allowed. There were a couple of other people that weren't full-time vegetarians, but they went along with that rule. And basically since then, I've always tried to live with people who were vegetarians. The vast majority of my friends were vegetarians, so we'd have vegetarian dinner parties; we'd go shopping at natural foods stores; so it was an integrated part of my life.

"My parents didn't really argue that much. In the end, I changed them more than they ever changed me." Although JONATHAN admits that "one of the reasons people revert is because of social pressure," he held his ground at family gatherings. On Thanksgiving, he refused the turkey "because you're more rebellious. This is a serious issue. When I first became a vegetarian, I was staking my ground here: this was a principled fight. If I wanted to please everyone, in terms of good etiquette, it would be the right thing to do; but this is where we made our decision. It's a deeper level than etiquette."

On holidays with his family, PETER did differently. He said: "I wouldn't eat meat just out of a casual desire. I ate meat because my family was having it for Thanksgiving and Christmas and I didn't want to be a grinch about *that*. So that's the only reason I had it. I allow my children to experiment with all sorts of foods. It's pretty free, and part of that is that the energy of childhood is very different from the energy of an adult. To put it in macrobiotic terms, they're much more yang. That's appropriate. It would be inappropriate for me to try to make them more yin and deny them meat. I'm not one to impose my will on my children. If they want to experiment in that way and if that's working for their bodies to eat in that way—My kids don't like brown rice anymore; they don't like tofu. They don't want to eat the way we eat. It's not my job to control what happens in my children's lives. I consider tons of red meat injurious, but hamburger now and then—I don't have a problem with that. I think it's probably even good for them.

"I try more and more in my life to let other people do whatever it is they need to do. Occasionally, I feel bad when I eat the turkey, which is the only land flesh that I tend to eat. I don't feel quite right doing that; I don't really want to be eating turkey. But because it's Thanksgiving, and people are eating it—that's why I'll eat it. I don't have to; but this year it was a decision not to make it more difficult for everyone else: that's really why I did it."

When NANCY's Jewish mother offered her chicken, she'd say, "'Oh, God, how gross! No way!' Very typical type of reaction. They didn't like the way I ate, well, too bad." DAVID's initial reaction was similar, but then he changed. He said: "I had a support group in California; but when I left, it was very, very difficult to be a vegetarian because no one else was. My mother was a Jewish mother and cooking was meaningful to her. I would come home and say I couldn't eat anything she was cooking. She was oriented toward cooking meat, or non-vegetarian stuff, and it would just drive her crazy. I was thinking how stupid that was, now that I look back on it. I acted without considering the human relationship to my mother who I really loved and cared about, and I was hurtful toward her."

Going home again can baffle those who stayed behind and did not change. JOHN said: "Going to visit my folks in New Jersey, they'd say, 'Well, you don't eat meat, right?' So they'd go out of their way to make some God-awful concoction and it would be, 'Now you're making something you don't know how to cook, and it's terrible, and I have to sit here and eat it.' I tried to say, 'Ma, don't go out of your way; make whatever you want to make, and just put it down in front of me, and I swear I'll eat it, and I won't complain. And if I don't eat it, don't take it personally.' It would really depend on what mood I was in that day more than anything else. So I guess what I'm realizing is, oh, they just don't get it. I still don't eat meat often enough, so that when I visit my parents, they'll say, 'Are you eating meat now, or what?'"

The "or what" can be a problem even to the most accommodating. JOHN showed the limit of familial loyalty—at least with respect to food. He said: "A relative of my wife's, an in-law of hers, used to eat lard. 'Well, I grew up on a farm, and sometimes I'd sit down and eat a stick of lard, a half a pound of lard.' LARD! And I'm nodding because what was there to say to this guy? He was beyond the pale. He was the Heinrich Himmler of vegetarians." Lard, anyone? Sometimes what is offered is as bad. JOHN continued: "I won't eat veal; but I was just having a conversation with a fellow who was bemoaning the fact that his mother forced him into eating veal the other night—and he's no vegetarian by any stretch of the imagination. But she was saying this was all she had, and she had slaved over it all day, and he kept saying, 'But, Ma, veal?' Somehow veal was crossing a line for him, and I found that fascinating. And sure, it's crossing a line for me. Gosh, I haven't had the stuff in twenty years because the level of cruelty there seems so enormous."

Like PETER, JOHN does, however, eat turkey at family gatherings. "The most recent time was Thanksgiving and here's TURKEY, and oh, gosh, that sure looks inviting, and I used to particularly like turkey on Thanksgiving, and well, what harm would it do? And yes, once I had done that, then it was like, 'Who am I kidding? Am I just kidding myself? Is this just a pose I'm affecting somehow?' I spent a lot of time testing my own smugness level. Once I got there, it seemed like it wasn't such a sin. I was able to convince myself I hadn't committed a mortal sin, or perhaps even a venial one. It was a matter of perspective."

The Welcome Guest

Some vegetarians are the epitome of good manners. ROLF said: "If someone invites me to dinner, I will eat what they serve. I feel it's a little accusative or socially rude [to refuse] so there have been a few occasions in the last few years when I have actually eaten some meat. It doesn't bother me at all physically; it's just a kind of social courtesy. It's a decision not to offend or to set myself apart. I usually don't eat much. I'll just eat a little piece; but I don't feel like making an issue, 'I'm a vegetarian,' you know.

"Fowl I've had on Thanksgiving or Christmas when I'm invited to somebody's house, and once when I went to a restaurant [on a holiday] with friends where they were serving goose and that's all they served. I've eaten beef maybe once at a wedding reception. I don't experience conflict when I occasionally eat meat at somebody's home. In a restaurant, I'm not offending anyone by not ordering meat; but if someone invites me over to dinner, I don't want my friends to feel as though they have to cook some sort of special meal for me, so I'll try to accommodate myself to what the circumstances are.

"If I thought my not eating meat when a guest in other people's homes would influence them to live in a similar way, I would probably do it; but I fear making my behavior an accusation. If I could do it as an example without it also being an accusation, I'd be pretty comfortable with that."

Rynn takes exception to ROLF's accommodation. He said: "Some people are vegetarian at home but at dinner parties, they don't want to inconvenience the hostess. Privately, they're vegetarians, but they don't have the courage of their convictions when they go to dinner parties. They don't want to offend the hostess, so they repress their vegetarianism for that evening. I think that's really a sign of moral cowardice.[2] I think that what you should do is not so much consider the feelings of the hostess as the animal who has given up its life and who has been tortured in the slaughterhouse. To me, that's a higher consideration. You have to weigh the pain [of the hostess] against the ultimate inconvenience to the animal who is slaughtered for the food the hostess is serving. It is one thing to commit a breach of etiquette; it's another to commit the moral breach of killing another creature. It's unfortunate that one has to ruffle the feelings of one's host or hostess; but it's better than to commit animal murder."

Like ROLF, TONY preferred to be a polite guest. He said: "I changed environments when I moved to Connecticut. If you remember, twenty years ago, there was nothing here. And the food I was used to in New York [City] I didn't have. In the beginning, I went with goat's milk, and we did a lot of our own stuff. Then I split up with my macrobiotic wife and all of a sudden I realized—for myself, that is—that there's a danger of being elitist in vegetarianism. So I found that if someone is going to present something—and it's an unusual occurrence—that I would go along with it, and if it was meat, I would eat it. And I would look at it as something that would benefit my body at that moment, and I would think healthfully about it. What started to happen is that I became elitist because I was with poorer people, and I didn't like the feeling of placing myself as an outcast in terms of food and causing problems if I was going there and going to eat: 'And what are we going to feed the vegetarian?' I started to feel very elitist; that's when it started to change for me."

LEONARD varied his approach. He said: "Somebody would invite me over, and I would have a meal of whatever was on the table. I never really started meat again; I didn't even drift into it: little things happened. Somebody would invite me over, and not being an avowed vegetarian, I would have a meal of whatever was on the table. It wasn't all the time; most of the time I'd say, 'I'm sorry, but I don't eat meat'; but occasionally, I would accept it. If they have other food there, I don't eat the meat. I just say, 'No, thanks.'"

GAIL had more trouble "just saying no." She said: "I admit if it's sitting in front of me, I'm going to eat it. I'm a little bit pragmatic.

If I'm at somebody's house, rather than offend them, I'll eat the Purdue chicken; rather than make waves and cause embarrassment or cause people to make fun of me, I might just be quiet and eat the Purdue chicken at a gathering."

LINDA would *never* let anyone walk over her: she was a hardhat construction worker who held her own among tough men. She said: "I used to run forty miles a week and I didn't own a car for years and years. I worked construction on a vegetarian diet. I was a materials testing technician, a *certified* concrete field testing technician, I'll have you know, and I'd go out and I worked *really* long hours. The twelve hour day was nothing—that was kind of standard. I'd go out to different jobs, and test the concrete and the soils as they were working on them, and carry heavy objects around all day. And the lab work was really rigorous—pouring portions of sand into a special mold, and you had to pound it like twenty-five times on each of five layers with this heavy steel thing, and then check the maximum density and all that stuff. It was hard work. I wore a hardhat.

"I had a certain technique for introducing myself to a new job. I had my little Beetle then, so I could get into the middle of things. So I would drive it in really fast, and skid to bring up a good cloud of dust, and then I'd jump out of the car and slam my hardhat on my head with one hand (which is a technique you really have to practice at home) and grab my book and pencil with the other, and stride purposively over and start yelling at people. I wouldn't speak to anyone except the job super, and I might deign to speak to the foreman if I really had to direct him where I wanted the laborers to bring my concrete sample, and I would demand to see plans. They just weren't used to it. They were used to people who would schlep in there and be a pain in the butt. Then I would say, 'I'm doing my test *here*; I need a laborer with a wheelbarrow, *thank you*, and they loved it. They knew that the job was going to get done, and get done fairly, and that I kept really accurate notes, and I only had a couple of problems in the three years that I did that job.

"Well, I'd get invited to stay sometimes for beer at the end of the day, and of course I don't drink domestic beer because I can't stomach any of it; so they'd start ragging me about that. And if I was there at lunchtime or suppertime, everyone would pull out their stuff, and someone might offer me a marinated deer heart, or some specialty that they'd gone out hunting for, and I'd politely say, 'No thanks; but I don't eat meat.' Oh, God, they thought it was hysterical. I'd probably have peanut butter or a bean spread or cheese and lettuce. But they respected me because I wouldn't let anyone walk on me. So some of them would kind of think about it; but none of them was really interested in giving up meat."

When LINDA was invited to dinner, she softened her style, but did not back down. She said: "It was sometimes hard to eat out; people would make such a darned big fuss. They'd invite you for dinner, and sometimes you'd say, 'Well, I'm a vegetarian, so, you know, whatever.' And they'd go—well, first they'd want to cook fish, and fish makes me want to throw up. So then they'd go into these long, elaborate things, and I'd have to keep saying, 'Don't, please. Serve whatever you're going to serve, and I'll eat around it. I just don't want you to be offended when I don't eat the main course.'"

It is easier for a vegetarian to be a perfect host or hostess than to be a perfect guest. One way to be both sociable and comfortable is to invite friends to one's own house. MARCIA said: "I was always eager to feed people good and healthful vegetarian meals so they would see that you didn't have to go away feeling hungry, and all the things they feared. Things would be tasty, and I would explain to them that it's a much more interesting way to eat. I would deliberately work up Mexican recipes and Italian recipes and Greek recipes, and I wanted to be able to cook good vegetarian food. I would feed it to people every chance I got; I would have liked it if they did eat vegetarian." DAVID agreed: "I prepared vegetarian foods for people that they enjoyed, and a lot of them were oriented toward eating meat. They were surprised they could have food that they felt was nourishing and nutritious. They would feel full after eating a meal."

For vegetarians, eating with omnivores is not easy; but we need not eat omnivorously to eat with them. Nor do we need to insult them if we refuse. Somehow, we can be ourselves—with panache, with humor, with the simple truth. If compassion led to our vegetarianism, we can find a way to be kind to our hosts. We can act lovingly, even if not consistently with the principle that it is never right to risk offense; otherwise we will be constricted in everything we do. If we compromise who we are by setting aside our principles for fear of making others uncomfortable, then who are we? Over food, we do sacrifice the greater for the lesser good? A strained social situation is, after all, more easily mended than broken ideals.

13

Travelogues

*"Wherever I go, whatever people I visit, I bow to their kings,
respect their gods, and eat their viands no matter what.
There is nothing I will not eat or drink at least once."*
— Richard Sterling

*I*s it right to do as the Romans when in Rome? Does it matter what the Romans are doing? Just as we may be vegans at home, but omnivores elsewhere, we may protest the rodeo in our own backyards, but not the running of the bulls when we visit Spain or Mexico. If the Romans re-created the Circus Maximus, would we attend? Would we cheer the animal combatants from the stands, or deplore at the "door"?

Customs differ, but do right and wrong? Cultural relativity is a fact; ethical relativism is a theory. Anthropologists confirm the one; philosophers quarrel over the other. Pygmies, for example, believe it is "unmanly" to trap animals; but Innuit men do it apparently without loss of sexual identity. Pygmies also believe it is wrong to eat eggs, because they are the "seeds of life"; but we eat omelets for breakfast.

Does this mean that right and wrong are merely matters of belief? This is what ethical relativists believe. Because value judgments differ, individual to individual, and culture to culture, there are no universal standards; thus "right" means only "what is considered to be right" in a culture or by an individual. (Hence "cultural relativism" and "individual relativism.") If head-hunting is considered right in Borneo, then it *is* right—in Borneo. If clitoridectomies are considered right in Somalia, then they *are* right—in Somalia. If *suttee* is considered right in a remote village in India, then it *is* right—there. If food animals are beaten to death with sticks (as they are in Africa, according to JONATHAN, in the belief that it makes the meat more tender) then it is right to do this—there.

Because people can come to believe (almost) anything, ethical relativism is an unsettling theory. It could sanction—among other things—the mass extermination of vegetarians if everyone else believed we were wrong and that it was right to kill us. We might think we were right, but not have the might to resist them. If relativism were true, then words like "right" and "wrong" could be dropped from every language, for questions like "It is believed to be wrong, but is it?" would be meaningless. Indeed, if relativism were right by its own standard, it would be believed to be right only; so if we like, we can believe it to be wrong. If we do, there is an alternative. We could be objectivists in ethics, denying both that there are absolute standards and that right and wrong are opinions only. As objectivists, we would insist on a good argument for any normative statement. We can ask the Romans if they have good reasons for what they do. If their only reason is "it is customary," it is not reason enough.

If we are vegetarians concerned with our character, we need not shoulder the ponderous policy question of whether to interfere in a culture with whose practices we differ. The question for vegetarians is how to be true to ourselves and our principles when faced with food in a foreign culture. My favorite anthropology professor at Ohio State told a class of squirming students that he had eaten live maggots to avoid grave offense. As a married man doing field work, he was offered not only food, but also women. He admitted eating the bugs, but declined to talk further.

How far do we go? Are we not allowed to keep our commitments? Should we be accommodating abroad if it would hurt the feelings of the host if we refused a hospitable offer of sex ("as is customary") with his spouse? What if we were in a village where AIDS or ebola were endemic? What if refusing this "meat" were a greater insult than refusing the other? If it is a greater insult to refuse this "flesh," then the principle on which vegetarians sometimes act ("Do not hurt the feelings of the host") will be found to be wanting. The more committed we are to our vegetarianism, the more analogous unsought steak is to unsought sex. We could set an example by standing up for our beliefs, even if we are sitting down at the table. We need not preach, but only teach—about ourselves. If a Hindu refuses our beef, we tend to respect his beliefs: why should others not respect ours?

To Russia With Love

Rynn told a story about committed vegans, Helen and Scott Nearing: "The Nearings were card-carrying Communists and socialists most of their lives, and when everyone else was *persona non grata* in Russia, they were allowed to travel wherever it took their fancy, and they found they were traveling through Soviet Georgia, I believe, and their hosts were unaware of their vegetarianism, and they prepared these enormous carnivorous feasts for them which they had the strength of character to decline. In spite of the fact that it was most certainly an inconvenience to their hosts, they forbore to eat any of the flesh, even though it caused considerable consternation among their hosts. I think their hosts ultimately respected them for adhering to their beliefs, and they weren't terribly offended by it. I think it's a way of educating people to their own food prejudices, and if you don't assert your own principles, you'll lose an opportunity to educate them about the moral benefits of a vegetarian diet."

MARCIA also traveled to Russia, but told a different tale: "There was a time when I did eat meat once when I was a vegetarian. It was when we were in Moscow, just a few years ago. It was Russian Christmas, January seventh. Meat was very hard for people to get. This Russian family had invited us over for Christmas dinner, and I knew that she had stood in line for a long time to get the meat to put into a meat and potato stew, and I wasn't going to embarrass her by saying, 'I don't eat meat.' I thought she knew, because this is someone who had been here already, and had been at our house. Either she didn't realize that I never did, or she had forgotten. And so I took more of the potatoes, but I took some of the meat, too, and I ate it. It wasn't traumatic, because I knew why I was doing it. After someone's gone through extra effort, and it's their Christmas dinner, it just didn't seem like the time to—"

Other vegetarian voyagers see how the "mere idea of turning down meat when other people don't have enough is very much a decision of affluence and privilege."[1] JONATHAN said: "A lot of people I met were very poor people. They went out of their way to offer food to you. Poor people—they don't have much; but they're offering what they have, and if you refuse, they're bewildered. It will make them feel uncomfortable; it will *clearly* make them uncomfortable if you refuse their food. They'll think, 'Oh, he's a rich Westerner; he's used to the finest food; and of course they equate good food and rich people with eating meat. So that's an unfortunate problem there. They may purposely give you meat rather than the rice and beans they have because they think, 'Well, this is what you're going to like the most.' So it's hard to refuse."

Rynn would say that we ought to educate them; but it may be Christmas Day. If we want them to turn over a new leaf, perhaps we ought to wait until the New Year. JONATHAN would say we ought to educate ourselves by immersing ourselves in another culture to widen our views: it is we who have lessons to learn. MARCIA's lesson was that compassion for hosts in far-away lands may weigh more than compassion for animals killed in far-off places.

Le Voyageur

Nepal; Tibet; Viet Nam; Cambodia; Thailand; Hong Kong; Japan; Mexico; Belize; Ecuador; Guatemala; Nicaragua; Mali; Senegal; Ghana; Burkina Faso—all these places JONATHAN has visited or lived in during the last several years. He calls himself "Le

Voyageur."

"In a foreign culture, you are the only representative to the people you visit. I was very interested in these other cultures. I didn't want to be just an alien foreigner. I wanted to try to fit in a little bit, so it was 'thinking like a native.' In travel situations, it makes it easier to find something to eat, and to share food with people, and so not to be such an outcast. Living in these foreign countries, it was more natural; when I come back, it's not the same. It has to do with choice.

"Actually, I went to fairly extensive lengths not to eat meat in Africa, which was pretty tricky because you'd be served these stews, and sometimes I'd have to pass on it because there'd be chunks of meat in it. This would have disgusted me, even just fairly recently. Sometimes they'd put these sauces on my rice and beans, and obviously it was partly a meat gravy, and sometimes there'd be chunks of meat. I'd pull the meat out of it, but I'd still eat the gravy. I could see the grease in it, and it was obviously fat from animals. I would have thrown up if I had eaten that in my initial years as a vegetarian; even in the last five years, I wouldn't have eaten that. I've become adaptable to the circumstances I'm in. I have a traveling persona of some sort, a traveling identity that's a little more flexible when it comes to diet."

JONATHAN tries to compromise by eating fish, but not other flesh, when traveling. "I still refused the meat. Other travelers who were formerly vegetarians at home would go the whole hog and literally eat that swine." One forswore the pork, but ate all other flesh. "A girlfriend who was ovo-lacto lived in Mexico. Prior to that, she had been vegetarian completely; but living in Mexico, she also ate meat because of the cultural situation: she had a very intense cultural situation living with families. She came there as a vegetarian and ended up eating everything except pork because she had an aversion to it. She told them she was allergic to it; but she ate all other meat, not really enjoying it, but because it made her fit in better."

JONATHAN is also accommodating in his own country (sometimes accidentally) when visiting other "nations." "There was a time

I went to a Native American Sun Dance and they served some buffalo food. It was at night. We were sitting around the campfire, and they passed a plate, and without thinking, or seeing what was on the plate, I started munching into something that had a very strange mouthfeel. After a while, I realized, 'These definitely are not beans!' It turned out it was buffalo."

JONATHAN is now planning an around the world tour during which he knows he will not be able to be "purist"; but he sees his lapses abroad as accommodations rather than as breaks in his vegetarianism. "I still try to keep to the fundamentals," he says. For some, travel is the ultimate escape, for we can leave behind not only our countries, but also our identities when we leave home; but JONA-THAN does not so much leave his vegetarianism behind as he occasionally travels lighter without it.

The Dog Show Hamburger

Sometimes eating meat abroad is not a matter of consideration but of survival. When our choice is fasting or feasting and fasting is impractical or impossible, then we may have to eat meat. LINDA said: "A couple of years ago, I was on a very arduous bike trip around the Bahamas, and there was no place to eat anywhere on this whole trip. Finally, we ended up at a Kennel Club Dog Show, and the choice of food was: potato chips, hamburgers, and soda. That was it; they didn't even have cheese. We didn't pack a lunch, and it was twenty miles to food. I tried a pack of potato chips first: I knew I wouldn't make it. I hit the wall once before on a bicycle, and I never want to do that again. 'Hit the wall'—I ran out of steam. I passed out.

"Part of it was: 'This is ruining my record' and part of it was: 'I'm so hungry, I don't care what I eat!' The last time I had eaten meat was fifteen years before. I ate a hamburger, and two packs of potato chips; I had them put everything on the hamburger so I wouldn't taste it. It got me back to where there was some *real* food to eat. I think we landed on some fruit from one of the vendors that line the wharves: they had a lot of vegetables." (Produce: "*Real* food for real people"!)

LINDA survived an arduous trip by accepting meat; others make their trips arduous by refusing it. ROCKY said: "Several years ago, I was going out with a woman who was vegetarian. I thought sometimes she was very unrealistic about it because she was, you know—no dairy products, no butter; and whenever we ate out, she had to make sure how everything was cooked, and what it was cooked in. There was a time we traveled to Mexico together. There were some things you couldn't help. She would just be very black and white about it, and I'd say, 'We're not going to be eating for the rest of the day: eat the darned thing!' Like on the airline. There'd be some food, and cheese might have touched it. Even if a fork was in the cheese, she wouldn't touch the fork. 'Come on, you're not going to get sick from this—eat the damned thing!' I could have used words a little stronger."

China Doll

When availability is an issue, what is a traveler to do? There are two poles to which we could gravitate: "Local Flavor" ("I'll try anything once!") or "Pack Your Own"—treating the trip like a picnic. On an extended trip to China with her father, INGRID decided to do the latter. Her travel diary illustrates not only the importance of food in her life, but also her resourcefulness.

"Today we will take a boat to Macau. I think the boat ride and the thirty-six hour train ride to Shanghai will be the highlights of the trip for me. I'm really glad I brought extra food. I supplemented the too-small plane meals with Familia, almonds, dried pear, shredded wheat. I could have used more than the quart of filtered water that I had—seventeen hours on the plane is dehydrating.

"This morning at breakfast, Daddy ordered a fried egg, easy over. After several minutes, the waitress came back. "Just a few minutes, Sir. The cook is . . . in the bathroom.' Honest, right? Tonight I used my food cards (index cards with English on one side and Mandarin characters on the other) for the first time. Mandarin is completely different from Cantonese, the main language here; but many understand Mandarin. 'PLEASE PREPARE MY FOOD WITH NO SUGAR AND VERY LITTLE SALT.' 'STEAMED BOK CHOY.' 'GREEN VEGETABLES.' 'NOODLES AND VEGETABLES.' They seemed amused by these cards. They took a long time studying the cards I showed them. I was curious to see what would emerge. I got a plate of garlicky, salty broccoli, very yummy, and a plate of about fifteen little bok choy plants. Then came a bowl of noodles and broth with bits of meat. When I pointed to the meat and shook my head, did they take the bowl away and bring the right thing? No—the waitress stood there and carefully removed most of the meat chunks with chopsticks. Interesting, huh? I laughed. It was fine.

"My friend here is considering opening a macrobiotic-vegetarian restaurant in Macau. For me, she was like an angel had come. When she picked me up at the hotel, she had a bag of food for me in the back seat—millet and squash, rice balls, arame, and carrot and lotus root. I was especially missing brown rice (I've only seen white so far) and soft sweet vegetables, so this was a god-send. Later she dropped off at the hotel two bags of food—two pounds of rice, some millet, muesli, puffed rice, rice cakes, amaske. She really encouraged me to ask for what I need. When we were at the Bella Vista for breakfast, I asked for carrot juice, and they said they couldn't do it. 'All you need is carrots and a blender to make carrot juice.' And sure enough, they brought it out, and it was so sweet I thought it might have sugar in it—but no, they are carrots from Australia. The carrots from here are much more watery, less tasty.

"I walked all around Macau with my friend. She pointed out all the different vegetables and foods. I held onto her arm as we walked by ducks getting their heads chopped off on a stump. We had fresh tofu—so good.

"We're leaving today for Shanghai. I'm all stocked up with my brown rice and carrots (the hotel cooked them for me last night with no problem), muesli, nuts, ume plum, miso, fruit, water. Last night Daddy had two little quails baked to a crisp and several little octupi—he said like a mouthful of rubberbands. I had rice balls (sweet aduki paste inside), Indonesian deep-fried rice cakes, and Moslem-style rice (no meat/pork, just rice and peas). I'm so relieved that they could cook my brown rice and carrots for the trip. This is the land of *white* rice, noodles (very white), bread, cakes, and pasta.

"I'm not sure how careful I need to be in China with food. Like is carrot or orange juice relatively safe? The vegetables and fruits are sprayed heavily with pesticides. There are no regulations like in America. Food poisoning happens. About twenty people recently got cholera and died from bad fish in Hong Kong. I was told I shouldn't eat street food, but I got lax about it toward the end of our trip, buying raw greens on the street and rice balls in bamboo leaves. Daddy wants to eat local yokel—he wants to eat cat and dog and snake and that kind of thing in places with 'atmosphere.'[2]

"I'm glad I brought all my own food. Daddy and I had lunch right here at the hotel in Shanghai. We sat at a table overlooking the Huangpu River. I ate a duck's tongue from Daddy's plate. I didn't like it too much. I ordered crab dumplings. The two men at the next table said they mix the crab with pork because the crab is so expensive. The interpreter eats and prefers a Western-style breakfast—toast, eggs, milk, fruit. Chinese is more like congee—white rice soup—I like it, very smooth and soothing—and dumplings, noodles; but he likes noodles for dinner. He doesn't eat brown rice. He said people in the rural areas eat their rice unwhitened. I asked the Korean if he eats brown rice, and he said 'yes.'

"On Monday, Daddy and I walked down some neat streets —real atmosphere. All sorts of vegetables, food and people. We watched a man stretch dough into noodles and toss it into boiling water. We ate huge bowls of noodles at this place for about five yen for both of us (about sixty cents). We saw vats and vats of eels and fishes, and lots of stuff I had no idea what it was.

"We're going home! I can't wait to cook for myself! I ordered fruit plates for all my meals on the way and brought rice and instant oats and sweet pea sprouts with me. It worked out great."

INGRID is intensely interested in food, and believes we are identified by what we eat. She said: "Yesterday, eating my corn chips dipped in refried beans, a friend said, 'So, you are a vegetarian!' I said, 'No, I'm not.' I felt like screaming, 'DON'T JUDGE ME BY THE FOOD I EAT!' I don't want food to be such a big part of my identity, but as I write, I feel, yes . . . food is a big part of our identity. It's so intimately connected with who we are, our very essence. I am different from the bacon and eggs for breakfast, bologna for lunch, meat and potatoes for dinner kind of person. I wouldn't want to relate closely with a person eating that food."

Who am I? And how much does what I am have to do with the food I eat? "We are what we eat" means something different to IN-GRID than it does to a nutritionist or to a physician. Who we are has to do with our choices; so when we have a choice about what we eat, how we dine, in part, defines us. Richard Sterling, who has been called "The Indiana Jones of Gastronomy," says, "I find it curious that we define ourselves, to a greater or lesser degree, by the foods we eat. When we say that 'we are what we eat,' we mean it literally, figuratively, spiritually and even politically. And by the same token, we define ourselves by what we do not eat."[3]

Most of us would not eat what Sterling eats, and indeed goes out of his way to find. In the Philippine town of Pampangua, he asked for "their best," and was served "Dinuguan," which looked like "river silt" and tasted like "a rich beef stew cooked with a lot of red Bordeaux wine." It was blood soup—coagulated, cooked blood, and nothing more.[4] He says duck's blood is best, and is happy to offer the recipe—as well as one for another Philippines special—simmered dog. Served a puppy, "in a broth seasoned with garlic and vinegar," he joked, "A spot of Spot, ha ha." Even after hearing another dog "yip" as it "met the knife" somewhere "in the back of the restaurant," he savored his supper.[5] "I'll try anything once" has no better representative than Sterling, who is obviously a man of interesting definition, and perhaps sterling qualities, but not one INGRID would be likely to meet for dinner—even though he probably does not eat bologna for lunch. Conspicuous by its absence was a recipe for human flesh: nowhere in his tales of high culinary adventure does Sterling say he sampled it. We don't eat humans (or admit to it) even though young ones might be tasty—chilled wren, perhaps, but not children.

We are defined by our values, and if we value vegetarianism, we will be defined by it, at least in part; but sometimes when we travel, our vegetarianism also goes on vacation, not because we couldn't fit it in, but because we can fit in better without it. If we wish to learn what it feels like to be a Thai or an African, we may choose to eat like one, not out of gluttony or curiosity, but out of empathy. If JONATHAN, an importer of drums, eats meat in order not to lose an order, that is one thing; but if he eats meat to immerse himself in a culture, that is another. Deep learning is not a spectator sport: eating like the natives may be one way to really understand them. (Sterling says it is easier to understand others through their food than through their art.)

If vegetarians find native customs abhorrent and refuse to participate in them, they may miss one thing in order to gain another: the choice is not a simple one when the gain is courage of conviction and the loss is insight. I could not imagine eating meat, and would likely starve before eating a cat; but I have not, as a vegetarian, lived in foreign lands. I would be tortured by empathy seeing live crickets or locusts tossed into boiling oil, and then seasoned like chips, or seeing tribal peoples catching bugs, pulling off their wings and legs, and carrying them for when they need a snack. But I am aware that my vegetarianism is a luxury—not only because I can afford to make choices, but also because I could afford the education which showed me what the choices were. Others are not in a position to either eat or think as I do, and I do not begrudge them their diet of circumstances. Perhaps we should not cling too tightly to our diet of privilege in their presence. It is a matter of the subtlest social finesse to explain our ways without causing shame; but if our vegetarianism means more to us than absorbing another culture by sampling its

viands, we will find a way to live, and let others live on what they need
to eat if they are to live at all.

Bangkok Banquet

Sometimes we are foreigners in our own countries. The country mouse who moves to the city finds a world as alien as the world of
the East is to that of the West. Such a country mouse is PATCHRI, a
twenty-five year old Thai woman who moved from a remote village to
Bangkok to enter the ninth grade. Uneducated and formerly isolated,
she was thrust upon customs very different from her own. Through
an interpreter, she said: "I started being a vegetarian at age ten,
because my grandparents are Chinese, and vegetarian, and it's a tradition. It's good because you don't have to kill animals or hurt them,
and it makes your heart feel glad. I felt pity for the animals." Yet
immediately after she moved to the city, PATCHRI broke her vegetarianism of a dozen years with pork and chicken.

"In Bangkok," she said, "it's very hard to find all-vegetarian
places to eat." My research assistant there confirmed this. After living
in Thailand for six months, Gary found no vegetarian restaurants, but
only an advertisement for one in the *Bangkok Post* (an English-lan-
guage newspaper), "obviously for tourists." "If you eat like the lo-
cals," he said, "you eat everything." Gary ate fried locusts, chicken
feet, "stomachs and guts," "fermented" (rotted) flesh, horseshoe
crabs, and jellyfish. Everyone he met was Buddhist, and all, including the monks, ate meat.[6]

"You have to survive. Your body loses protein; meat is good for
you," said PATCHRI. "Now I eat everything that I can eat, every day.
I feel like a normal person, like everyone else. Now I'm hungry! I
don't think I'll go back to vegetarianism because in the future I will
have a family, and being vegetarian will make family eating difficult.
You can't force anybody to do anything; it depends on each person's
heart. Everyone has different beliefs, and everyone has different
minds. I don't want to change anything."

PATCHRI's vegetarianism was rooted in tradition rather than

in conviction, so she was able to give it up without a struggle. Now in an environment where no one is vegetarian, PATCHRI's pity for animals has been swallowed whole by her culture, so she is able to swallow the animals she once pitied.

Sometimes we do what others are doing and sometimes we may have to do what most others would never think of doing. PATCHRI encountered a new set of rules and decided to abide by them; but sometimes we find ourselves in situations where there are no rules at all. Philosophers call the most extreme "desert island cases." Rynn mentioned the infamous one of the "the Brazilian team in the Andes where life was in peril: they committed cannibalism." He added, "I think it is preferable to eat dead human flesh than to kill an animal for its flesh, certainly." Most people would not be so certain, but we can be sure that vegetarianism is, as ELLY says, "a choice of circumstances like any other." It is arrogant to think otherwise just because we have been blessed with circumstances which others are denied. We may find the thought of eating a corpse disgusting; but it might be the only thing which could keep us alive. If we ate only "manna from heaven" and it rained only cats and dogs, we would have to eat them. Perhaps we should all go on a walk-about with the Australian Aborigines, and eat only what we find along the way. Then we will "know in our bones" that we may have to break animal bones in order to survive.

But issues remain. When we travel, to what extent do we dissent and to what extent remain silent? At what point does our education turn into condescension? Must we be actors abroad, acquiring, like JONATHAN, a "traveling persona," and only be ourselves at home? Is personal identity also a luxury? JONATHAN said: "We tend to over-romanticize native cultures. I was amazed to see the ways that animals were treated, and what was clearly animal abuse. People just don't think that animals have feelings. We have a long way to go to educate people about animal suffering. The whole world has to learn about how we relate to living things."

JONATHAN saw laughing children trampling an eel in Africa while adults looked on, smiling, perhaps an analogue to our children playing "Mortal Kombat" or "Primal Rage" while adults look away. But JONATHAN said nothing and did nothing, not wanting to interfere with the lives of others or impose his ideals. But inspiration is not imposition. We have no moral duty to help others persist in their illusions or to bite our tongues for fear that speaking out will let trouble in. I have lived in a number of urban ghettos, and in one, saw children dousing insects with lighter fluid and igniting them for fun. When I offered my view that these little lives were worth something to the creatures living them, the children listened to me, wide-eyed. I never saw them amuse themselves this way again. One can stop short of a "heated" debate and simply share one's view. If the whole world has lessons to learn, we can begin to teach them.

This is not to say that we should forcibly uproot the traditions of others. DAVID said: "I met a woman in Israel and I was explaining to her the values of vegetarianism, and she said yes, she thought vegetarianism was really the right way to live, but she said, 'On the Sabbath, I really like to celebrate, and I really like to have meat.' I look at this woman in Israel who said, 'To glorify God, I like to have a meal of meat,' and I felt there was a rightness to the relationship: I don't think it has a simple answer."

Whether or not we would express our religious convictions with omnivorism, we neither have to be silent nor agree. JONATHAN "only sent peaceful vibes" to the children playing with the eel; but at a meal, if offered meat, he would say that God had told him not to eat flesh, and his hosts would be satisfied with that. (*Inshallah*: "As God wills.") We can say simply that our own spiritual practice includes harmlessness, and so we abstain from meat. What harm could that do?

During my (nearly) twenty years as a stage actress, the characters I played were often women who wore furs or who ate meat, things I did not do. As a character actress, I entered passionately into their worlds, each one a foreign country. Dozens of women from "far away places with strange-sounding names" used my body to be born in on stage. I became them. If they wore furs, they were not skins on my back, but on theirs; but if they ate meat, a substitution was always made. (Fake furs would not have "read" in our two hundred seat house, but fake flesh was fine.) During rehearsal, an animal skin on my back was insult enough; eating flesh would be too much to bear. The coat—which belonged to "her"—could be left in the costume room; but the meat would have gone home in me.

When we travel, we may have to don a mantle to cloak our disapproval; but we might not have to eat meat. In those "intense cultural situations" where we have decided to live with a family or to "think like natives," it makes sense to eat as the natives do; but then our choice is not so much to abandon our vegetarianism as it is to let it lie dormant while we grow. Then perhaps there will be more room for it to flourish when we return to our homelands and to ourselves.

To travel is to find out who we are; in Western societies, where individuality is so highly prized, we may find out that both our vegetarianism and our personal identities are luxuries. For the plateful of sprouts, for the choice of teff, amaranth, or spelt, or barley or corn or rice or rye or wheat or oats or millet, we must be grateful. How fortunate we are to have the variety which so many others are denied, either because of poverty or because they are mired in tradition. Our vegetarianism is our privilege and our right; this does not make it right, or everyone's duty, but a blessing for which we ought to be grateful.

14

The Way they Were

*H*ow did the youth at the ashram become the man eating ham? How did the disciple praying over brown rice and fasting until her ribs showed at yoga become the one basting ribs on the backyard grill? For too many, philosophies are childish things too quickly put away. Is the source of vegetarianism the innocence of youth? If we trace it to its root, what do we find? Hippies—now eating sushi—or flower children, now tasting nasturtiums in trendy cafes?

Was their vegetarianism part of a life "style" which went out of fashion like their bellbottoms and love-ins and psychedelic art? Was it a costume they tried on, only to find they were in the wrong play and that the lines stuck in their throats like bones when they tried to say, "Please, no meat"? Was it a flirtation, or a foolish fad they followed and failed to pursue, or did they fail themselves somehow?

Who are we when our tastes and values change, our habits— and our diets? Neither people nor rivers stay the same, but inside every former vegetarian may remain a vegetarian, trying to get out. That they tried at all sets them apart. Having been vegetarian leaves its mark: Is that a lapso we see buying organic meat at the natural grocery? Is that a vegan who reneged selecting "free-range" chicken and eggs? Were they ever vegetarians at all, or just pretenders? As soon as there were contenders, did they go another way?

Once passionate, we become prosaic. We say we "get real." What happens to our ideals? Where is that dreamy child who loved animals too much to eat them? Is that really she with paté on her plate? Finding only omnivores among us, do we stop making such a fuss? When our dates and mates eat steak, do we partake? Do we see our vegetarianism as a mistake? Contrasting "before" and "after" pictures is revealing. Who were they in their vegetarian days?

GAIL said: "I began when I got out of college, as many people of my time did. I went to California. I went to the West Coast to explore the whole counter culture life style that was happening. That idea appealed to me. By becoming a vegetarian back then, you turned your back on a segment of society that was politically and ideologically more mainstream. It was part of plugging into an alternative society. You got away from a lot of junk food, and also it was a more conscious thing to do, a more thoughtful way of living—living thoughtfully, questioning the mentality of what was linked to what we called (one of the buzzwords) 'the military-industrial complex.' To be a vegetarian was associated with eating better food, learning how to get away from fast food and prepared food and grocery store food—ESTABLISHMENT food.

"Even though I don't remember hearing a lot about humaneness toward animals in any of the vegetarian ideology that was going around, I knew there were good reasons not to eat meat. It was a spiritual thing and it was part of the search for a more evolved lifestyle. And it felt *great*. It felt great to be exploring all the wonderful things you could make with the whole grains and the legumes and the tofu and the tempeh and the wonderful vegetable stews and all the salads. I learned about the wonderful world of ethnic foods—seasonings, tastes, ancient nutritional discoveries of other cultures: it was a culinary wonderworld being a vegetarian. I stayed with it all through my twenties.

"I've always been a bookish, dreamy, romantic kid. For some reason, I had very little contact with kids like that growing up. I was alone with it, and I found it hard to get close to most kids. Most kids wanted to do very different things than what I did. They were very sporty and they watched really low-brow things on T.V. most of the time, and they didn't like books that much.

"So I created my own world. I spent a lot of my time as a kid alone doing a lot of artwork and a lot of crafts, a lot of reading, a lot of collecting, a lot of studying. I always had my schoolbooks all read the first month of school. I read every one of them. I had very, very few friends growing up, so I created a fantasy world. I read everything, fiction and non-fiction, and I surrounded myself with beautiful things that I made or collected. And the whole counter culture thing came out in the sixties, and all of a sudden that was *me* and I felt kindred spirits. *I had found my people.*

"It tied in with the peace movement. The peace movement was big when I was in college. But there was one thing that kept me isolated a great deal, and that was that I never did any drugs at all—ever. Just a few marijuana highs. That was absolutely it. So even with the hippie generation, I was a real outsider, a real loner in many ways. You really couldn't get close to hardly anybody. People didn't trust you and thought you were mainstream. So I still lived a lot in my own world; but the whole hippie thing was the closest I ever got to soulmates.

"It was a good test of whether or not this person was going to be a real friend, whether or not you could discuss vegetarianism with them. The boomer generation: there were so many of us. There were many counter culture people. In college, it was easy; in California, it was easy; in college towns, it was easy. Trying to work in my family's business, outside of the customers, it was harder. A lot of people were on their way to becoming what we now call 'yuppies'—the white collar kind—and that was a little hard. It was hard meeting people of my mindset."

As GAIL was on the West Coast, NANCY was on the East. She

said: "It was part of the whole hippie and counter culture thing. I started off because it just made so much sense to me at the time. It just seemed right; everyone was talking about it at the time because it was a big consciousness, part of the whole awakening of consciousness. I did psychedelic drugs, and that opened a lot of doors." Opening doors to people who came into the health food store she opened with her husband helped to maintain her vegetarianism. "That helps a lot; you're involved with a lot of vegetarians and you're involved with the whole consciousness movement." GAIL and NANCY discovered their vegetarianism in similar ways, and each carried it into careers in the natural foods industry; but in the end, each developed candida and gave up what began in idealism for realism about their health.

At about the same time, in the late sixties and early seventies, ROCKY became interested in Eastern religions. He "practiced a little TM," and was influenced by Sri Chimnoy, who ran health food restaurants including one called "Love and Serve." He said: "Later on—and I was ridiculed by my friends—but there was a young boy from India whose name was Guru Maharaji. I followed him for several years. I lived in an ashram—The Divine Light Mission. When we were living at the ashram, I was strictly vegetarian—no eggs, no fish—nothing like that." After living in the ashram for six months, ROCKY was vegetarian for another four years. "I shared houses with friends who were also vegetarians; we would have eggs and dairy products though."

ROCKY chose vegetarianism because he "was involved with Eastern religions at the time. I was on a search, I guess for myself, for inner happiness, and it tied in with the Eastern philosophy. When I was vegetarian, I thought I was doing good for myself, something mentally healthy, because I was involved with smoking a lot of pot— harmless stuff like that—but which is kind of brain dead, really.

"I think I was waking up and becoming more aware of the world around me, that things weren't quite as they were taken for granted for being. There were a lot of things to know, and I wanted to know them. The spiritual path was a big part of it. Back in the seventies, animal rights wasn't such a big issue.

"I read *Diet For a Small Planet* several times. I felt great. I wasn't sleepy all the time and I had a lot of energy. I felt like I was doing proper acts: I was more sincere in my actions at work and with my friends. I felt like I was in touch with myself all around. When I worked in the factory, I stayed vegetarian during that time. I would get up in the morning and meditate before work."

To this day, ROCKY retains some of what led him to vegetarianism. He said: "I treat everything with respect. If there's a bug in my house, I'll take it outside instead of squashing it. I've always been like that." Nevertheless, for the last fifteen years, ROCKY has been eating meat often, "every couple of days, probably. Every other day, I'll have some form of it whether it's in a sandwich or whether I have a meat sauce from the great Italian deli across the street. I use various oriental noodle dishes, so it's a little different from the Standard American Diet. At least in the mornings, I eat grains—cereals. I shop at Food for Thought. I'm not just going out and having eggs and sausage for breakfast.

"In the summertime, I like to use the backyard grill. I like grilled chicken. I like spare ribs, stuff like that, but I don't go out and buy steaks of filet mignon or prime rib. At the Christmas party, everybody eats prime rib. It's a chunk of rare stuff for me. It doesn't appeal to me at all—big hunks of red meat—flesh. It is of no real interest. Frankly, I'd prefer some great sushi, which I enjoy immensely." Without support, ROCKY left his vegetarianism behind; his world today bears little resemblance to the world of the ashram or to the Eastern religion which, like his former diet, once nourished him.

Neither ROCKY nor TONY went to college, but each found, on his own, ideas which circulated among students and intellectuals at the time. TONY said: "I was trying to get a handle on Eastern thinking, in terms of benigness coming from what we put into our bodies, so along that basis, I decided to give it a try and see what it was like. As I got into it, slowly it just took over. I was very happy to do it. It was fine. It was what I was looking for as a person in terms of the philosophy to follow, going down the road on this planet. Vegetarianism seemed a good course because the people were all pretty benign.

"It raised new questions about looking at things in a different light from what I had been raised into which was all very nice. It's not until we get to a point of leisure in our society that we can become introspective about it. My family was locked into centuries of history where they had come from and because of always being workers: you don't have the time for introspection to see where all that comes from. I saw myself as evolving and I felt culturally removed from where my parents came from."

TONY was influenced by Alan Watts and *The Way of Zen*. "The simplifying of it all—in other words, eating like we eat in our society is a very complex, costly affair and it's not necessarily healthy. Vegetarianism simplifies it to a great degree: you're not as encumbered by a food culture. Vegetarianism becomes very ritualistic in some ways, but I like it because it simplifies your thinking even though it takes an enormous amount of thinking about your food. It was nice; you saw food differently."

When TONY became a vegetarian, he was living in New York City, singing in the opera and doing road shows. "It was a good time in my life. I was doing a lot of shows, feeling that life never ended: you were immortal. It was a very good time of life. Of course I did my share of Häagen-Dazs, I've got to admit that." Although life as a vegetarian was good, like ROCKY, TONY has been a lapso for fifteen years. He moved to the country, where he stayed, living in a cabin with few amenities for the last twenty years. He said: "I don't eat meat that frequently. I still wander back to wanting to simplify even at this point and I think that I will probably go back to a type of vegetarianism for myself. I can no longer see that deeply into the future, but if I was going to stay here, I would have a milk goat and I would grow most of my sustenance. With the cheeses and milk, all I would need is some vegetables, and existence is pretty total."

Three physicians—two medical doctors and one chiropractor—share similar roots in spiritual practice. DAVID said: "I became a vegetarian at the age of twenty-two mainly for moral reasons. It was a really, really rich time in my life. It was very dynamic—a sort of changing time in my life. It was a time when I came to the point where I realized that I was the master of my destiny and whether my life was meaningful or not ended up in my hands. It was a good time of my life because when I was in college I was not very happy. I got out of college and started studying Zen. When I was in medical school, I used to get up at four-thirty in the morning, do yoga, then would bicycle down to the Zen center to do Zen. It was a fairly rich time in my life. It was when I started understanding concepts of karma and that's still becoming richer every day.

"People saw me as somewhat of an eccentric and in some cases, as an oddball. It was a very formative time in my life when I started understanding some of the karmic relationships of things. One of the things that drew me towards vegetarianism was realizing how complex these relationships are. From a standpoint of how it affects world view, it was a truly righteous thing to do."

Although DAVID has now been eating meat for six years, like TONY, he believes he will return to vegetarianism. He said: "I mostly eat fish when I eat meat, and I occasionally eat beef. I very rarely eat pork. I eat sushi occasionally: I like sushi. I'm maturing in my relationship with food. I think as I do that, I can return to a diet that is much more meaningful. That I realize is a very personal choice and it can make the whole process of being a vegetarian more nourishing than it was before."

ROBBAN, another physician, said: "It was actually part of a spiritual organization that I belonged to at the time. It's basically a study of the teachings of the Ascended Masters. It was highly recommended to go on a macrobiotic diet to balance yourself spiritually. That was the best way you could get in touch with a higher spiritual level. There was a spiritual leader who was advocating a vegetarian diet. I did it because it was advocated in order to raise your vibration:

my goal was to be enlightened." Enlightened or not, ROBBAN could not stay with the diet for reasons of health; but if she could have, she would have.

PETER, a chiropractor, also traces the roots of his vegetarianism to Eastern traditions and like ROCKY and INGRID, lived in an ashram. He said: "I don't remember where I got the idea that being a vegetarian was a healthy thing to do other than it was generally in the air those days. Also in the air was the kind of lifestyle I was interested in pursuing. People I was interested in tended to say, 'Oh, you're supposed to eat a lot of brown rice and you don't need to eat much meat.' And I experimented with that. I found out that it worked for me and it was a very short time before I realized that I didn't want to eat meat again. I felt better without it."

In California, PETER lived at the ashram for five years, studying "fairly high-level metaphysics" with Yoge Shwar. He said: "My spiritual life revolves around my relationship with people and my internal experience of the divine: eating a fleshy diet doesn't stimulate a healthy, meditative lifestyle. In the ashram, I ran the kitchen for awhile; I made the yoghurt. We ate in a certain way and that was a common understanding. Our guru talked occasionally about the importance of a healthy diet. I was in a teaching position, actually teaching a course on holistic lifestyle at the ashram; so people who were interested in what my guru had to say would enter the course and study tapes and do lessons. Anyone who came along and said, 'Gee, I'm interested in yoga,' I'd try to convince them that's what they ought to be doing with their lives. The diet was a major part of the yogic life. I would encourage them to do their yoga every day and meditate and how to eat better. Many of them changed over."

With an M.A. in philosophy and the ashram behind him, PETER entered chiropractic school in the midwest. "I've always been a pariah—no, I don't think I was a pariah," he joked, "but when I was going through chiropractic school, I was known as 'Doctor Spirulina' because I was in the habit of carrying my blue thermos around all the time filled with apple juice and powdered spirulina which no one else in Davenport, Iowa could have ingested."

Today PETER eats fish regularly (because he believes it is good for him) and poultry on very rare occasions, mostly to please his family. He explained: "For the most part, eating meat is so distant from my consciousness that I don't even entertain it. It's like, 'Would you like to smoke a cigarette?' It's not a question of like or dislike: there's nothing there. It's just not there. But there are other times when having a bit of turkey doesn't sound so bad to me. Red meat I never have a desire for." PETER may return to vegetarianism later in his life if he begins to live in a simple, meditative way, far from the energy-draining flux of the world.

When INGRID lived at an ashram, she had already abandoned the vegetarianism she had begun as a child of ten, influenced by her older sister. After battling bulimia as a college student, she began eating fish and chicken. "In college," she said, "I was suddenly immersed in a much more liberal, thoughtful environment. My friends were toward the left. I did protests, felt like I had to save the world, and felt totally exhausted and hopeless and desperate over it. My health declined, for many reasons . . ." Shortly after graduation , she took up residence at a Yoga center in rural New England.

She said: "I had just graduated from college in December of 1990, and moved into an ashram. They don't serve any flesh food there. Gurudev felt that for the spiritual path it's very important not to eat flesh foods. I had already started to eat fish and chicken, so when there, I had an appointment with Resident Health and they told me where I could get organic chicken and where the fish store was. It felt really good for me to have some chicken and fish. So I would go. I remember buying this already cooked piece of chicken and sitting in my car in early spring, eating it. Oh! It was so good! I felt like it would be really weird if I brought it to the dining chapel. I might have brought a piece of fish.

"There were a lot of older residents who were starting to eat meat; they were getting tested and finding that their B12 levels were low, and they would have cans of tuna in the kitchen. Once I went out to have some fish and there was another male resident there eating fish. I felt so funny. He said, 'This is the second time I've been here today.' When we were having dinner, he mentioned two older female residents and said they gave him the idea, because when they started eating meat it felt so good. 'When they came here for lunch, they came here the same day for dinner.' So they just liked it. It was funny, because we were eating our fish there.

"I remember residents boiling eggs in the kitchen and taking them to the Dining Chapel every now and then. One resident was having fish in the kitchen, and another resident said it was like the smell of death; she had gotten really sensitized to that. Gurudev ate a lot of dairy—yoghurt and all of that. His lineage is Indian; traditionally, they don't eat meat. The religion for most Indian people is Hindu, and they don't eat meat. But for a lot of us, we're European, and our ancestry and our digestive systems are used to some meat. So it didn't work for us.

"I was getting really exhausted and was trying to get as much rest as I needed and take naps. When we were there, we had a Meditation Training with Rish Prabhakar. He came to visit to do this Resident Retreat—meditation retreat—to lead it. He was talking about raw foods and this whole raw food thing got started—making 'energy soup' with sprouts and apples and avocados all blended up. But it wasn't enough. I would go out; I loved getting tuna sandwiches. I never felt you had to eat vegetarian there. I feel really connected to God, and I eat meat. Being connected to God feels like a certainty that I'm in the right place: everything is right where it should be. It's not a complacency, but a calmness."

Like INGRID, VICKY was exposed to new ideas as a college student, but found her vegetarianism at school instead of abandoning it there. She said: "The wonderful thing about this stage of my life was the introduction of so many new thoughts and people. I felt I was opening a big box of toys and I could choose anything I wanted. Vegetarianism was one thing I chose to take for myself. Toy is an appropriate metaphor, though, because of the way I tried it, and put it down.

"College was the first time in my life when I had the freedom to choose what I ate, even when I was in the cafeteria program. I was intrigued by new life choices. I had a close friend who had been vegetarian for years before college, because she loved animals and didn't want to eat them. I figured, I loved animals, too; why DO I eat them? I had no good reason for eating them. I had to acquire tastes for some things I never had before: tofu, kidney beans, soy nuts, couscous, and the aforementioned Brussels sprouts. In terms of philosophy, my reasoning was: If you have a choice of what to eat, why eat something that caused fear, pain, and death for a sentient being?

"I felt that the unexamined life was not worth living, as Thoreau said. At least I was starting to examine mine, my reasons for doing things. I felt there was less on my conscience if I was not living off the deaths of others. Books that influenced me were *Be Here Now* by Ram Dass and *On Walden Pond* by Thoreau. I also read a book by Alan Watts; I don't remember the name. Buddhist philosophy was a big influence on me; the idea of not killing a single mosquito, not stepping on a single ant, never mind not eating a cow. There was a sense of joy from deciding to let another creature live, no matter how indirectly.

"There was a time when my roommate baked a chicken and I looked in the oven to see what was in there and the sight of it made me nauseous—all the bones and the juice. I still vividly remember how horrified I was! I didn't ask her not to eat meat, but we did have an agreement that she wouldn't cook it when I was home. I think that was awfully considerate of her. But baking chickens do not make me sick anymore. I don't get grossed out washing raw chicken parts. I don't eat meat when I'm with vegetarians, though—unless they say, 'Go ahead; it doesn't bother me.'

"I didn't eat meat often ever again. I eat meat maybe once a week now. I eat all kinds of pork, beef, chicken, and fish. I still don't eat veal or lamb. I don't buy raw meat to cook unless it's for special occasions; mostly I eat meat that's in prepared food, like sandwich meat, tuna fish in cans, pepperoni on pizza, and most of all, restaurant food. I just about ALWAYS eat meat when I eat in a restaurant. Part of the reason I eat meat is when people give it to me as a gift or when I am visiting them. *If this animal died so I could eat it, I'm not going to just throw it away.*

"I reconsider my views on this subject every time I encounter someone I consider wiser than I. For instance, Mother Teresa would not eat meat except that her priest told her she must, to take care of her health. (She obeyed the priest because she considered HIM wiser than SHE.) Peace Pilgrim decided not to eat meat; she was a great person. I have met people who have showed disdain when I told them my behavior was just following some wiser person's behavior; but I think we have to do that sometimes. I hadn't decided what was right; but I was trusting that this wiser person was likely to be right.

"Spiritually, I continue to keep an open mind about this and all issues, which I think is a virtue a lot of people lose with age. My view of people who eat meat has not changed except that I don't put them all in the same basket. Now I know that some people who eat meat HAVE made a conscious decision to do so. I still think it's better to be a vegetarian, if you can do it. It's just a lack of will power that makes me eat meat; I'm just not crazy about vegetables. I've never regretted being a vegetarian; but for all the good I thought I was doing then, I'm sure I do a lot more good in the world now, in different ways, because now I have the resources of money, time, and skills I didn't have ten years ago."

MARCIA also traces her vegetarianism to her college days, as a graduate student in Chicago. She said: "I began being a vegetarian when I was twenty-one. I usually told people it was a combination of economy, ecology, concern for animals, and health. I was your typical poverty-stricken graduate student. Meat was expensive, and that annoyed me. The final thing that made me thoroughly vegetarian was that I decided to share an apartment with a woman who had recently come back from teaching English in Bombay for three years. She was (at the time) vegetarian, ovo-lacto, and I decided: Well, why not? I didn't have a taste for meat; but I used to have protein deficiencies as a teenager. I was big meat eater as a child; I liked meat and it was a favorite food in terms of taste and what I craved. The other kids would go get a nickel and go downtown for a candy bar. I'd go buy beef jerky or cheese because I always craved the proteins.

"So I had to learn something about vegetable protein to overcome that, and I guess my body didn't need it as much as I grew older. I was fine. I've never been anemic since I've been vegetarian. I also met some people who were involved for a while with a guru in Chicago, and I was sort of a hanger-on with that for a year and a half, maybe. It was nice to meet people connected with vegetarianism. We lived on carrot and potato and cabbage curry. Very cheap graduate food. I hope I never see carrot, potato, and cabbage curry again!"

BARBARA also found her vegetarianism in the stimulating milieu of graduate school, but in a more academic way. She said: "It was primarily a course that I had taken in political science—Eco-politics. I did a paper for that course, and in the course of my research, I began to be aware of the issues around food consumption—how much ENERGY it took to raise beef and issues around world hunger. So that paper really got me interested in the whole idea of giving up meat. In that paper I wrote, I can still remember some of the images that I had. The image that I held in mind was the image of living on a spaceship. We were eating algae. That really got me aware of how interdependent I was with my natural surroundings, and that in turn got me into being much more open and really hearing the issues around using land as a resource to raise cattle, and how inefficient that was.

"So it was really a kind of poetic image that first sparked me, and made me more receptive, and gave me the energy perhaps to make that jump, because it was a big transition for me. I was an avid meat eater. I was raised on meat and potatoes, so it was a real challenge for me to reconsider the way I was eating and the effect I was having on the environment. I've been married the whole time, so I lived with someone who was not vegetarian for close to a decade. I went through some real struggles of not imposing my values on him. He was not going to change his diet to please me; that was a real issue between us, and I had to respect that. At the same time, I was always sharing information, or suggesting that we go someplace like an Earth Day celebration, and go to a workshop. I think it was constant exposure and suggesting we do things and education. He was open to that. The more he learned for himself, he made decisions for himself. He's now been a vegetarian for six or seven years.

"Prior to becoming a vegetarian, there was a real sense of being disconnected somehow, of not being connected to something larger than myself. Since being vegetarian, it's been a spiritual journey for me; it's really the image of being connected that I spoke of originally, the strong image of: I've eaten this and in turn I am providing waste products to support life. This was a spiritual breakthrough for me; it's a wonderful sense that I belong in this universe."

BARBARA gave up her vegetarianism reluctantly, and only temporarily, for reasons of health; but others , like VICKY found that the world weighed too heavily upon the fragility of ideals. Of the first, new, almost-green of spring, Robert Frost said: "Nothing gold can stay."[1] For some, the delicate optimism of youth is quickly dulled; for others, convictions are only imitations, a too-easy way of appropriating identity. INGRID "followed" her sister's example, perhaps admiring her sister more than the example she adopted. Although she practiced a strict vegetarianism in high school and in college, like spring's new gold, it did not stay.

She said: "I remember three years ago, I was at a restaurant in New Jersey with my family—ten of us. I ordered venison. This was the first time I had red meat in seven years—and everybody CLAPPED! 'Yeah! Ingrid's going to be O.K.! Ingrid's coming to her senses!' The venison was *really* good. It was five cookie-sized pieces of meat, round pieces of meat. I don't know what part of the deer it was from, but it was really savory, and well-seasoned and rich, and a little reddish on the inside. I remember chewing it and thinking, 'Wow! This is good! I can't believe I'm eating this, but, oh, it feels really good!'"

I asked her to imagine what the ghost of INGRID past would have said if she witnessed this. The ghost replied, "I can't believe you're doing this. Deer are so beautiful and such innocent creatures, and I'm really surprised that you're doing it. I never thought you would do this. You're really beautiful now, and you've come really far. You've grown into a really thoughtful person, and you look healthy. It seems like it feels good to you—like a really positive change. I really look up to you. You're doing great."

INGRID (present) said: "I believe that towards the end of my life, I might not eat meat anymore, or after I stop being reproductively fertile." But for now, she eats all sorts of meat. She said, "I actually went to Tops last week, to the butcher, and got a pork chop. I hadn't had a pork chop in sixteen years; but I felt like I really wanted one. A week before, a friend had gotten pork chops for dinner, and it put the idea in my mind. Oh . . . pork chops . . . It wasn't as good as I thought it was going to be. It was really tough and I didn't know how to cook it. I just put it in water and boiled it and added onions and carrots.

"In growing up, I didn't think about it too much. I was looking through old cookbooks to see how to cook pork, and a lot of the meat recipes were circled, so I guess we used to eat that stuff a lot. My mother served ham and pork chops and *Hackepeter*—ground beef with egg mushed up with onions.[2] I remember having that regularly and thinking nothing about it. My mother is surprised that I will eat lamb. I eat it because I feel like it is good for my physical health: I'm trying to heal my body."

To the pig who provided the pork chop, she would have said: "I hope I can appreciate you enough and take you into my body and use what you give me to the fullest. I feel a little sorry that you were killed for me, in part, and I'm sure that the way you lived your life wasn't wonderful. I don't know how you were killed, but I felt I was really wanting to have a pork chop."

We change, sometimes beyond recognition, but metaphysically, some core or kernel of ourselves remains the same. All lives are in flux; the extent to which we "go with the flow" or try to direct it is, if we believe in free will, up to us. Appetites do alter. A woman may love in her youth what she cannot endure in her age—just as she may eat when older the meat she could not abide when young.[3] INGRID may someday change: perhaps in years the spirits of the animals will tell her that the way they were is not the way we allow them to be any longer, and she will lose her taste for their chops and loins. Perhaps someday they will tell her what a beautiful and thoughtful person she is as she again makes a conscious decision—to be vegetarian.

15

Reasons and Rationalizations

*"Even in the most logical realm, it is
insight that first arrives at what is new.*
—Bertrand Russell

"Idealism is not the result of logical thinking."
—Clemenceau

ven the wise are taken for fools if they are alone. Vegetarians are often alone among many meat eaters. They may or may not be wise; but they have their reasons. Meat eaters have their reasons, too, good reasons or bad, and they have their rationalizations, which are not reasons at all, even bad ones, but excuses.

What is a reason? Philosophers are apt to favor the premises of sound arguments; but a reason can be what makes something understandable (or "rational") and so can be a cause or motivation or an explanation. It is easier to explain vegetarianism than to prove it right. This is not because there is something wrong with vegetarianism, but because we cannot prove that anything is morally wrong or right. Questions of ethics, like all philosophical questions, can be argued in many ways, but none can be conclusively answered.

An argument is an invitation to argue, not necessarily an invitation to seek truth. Some philosophers believe that if arguments for vegetarianism fail, then we have no "reasons" to forgo meat. ("The argument is the basis of their eating practice, so that, if it is compromised or rendered doubtful, they *per se* have no reasons to abstain from meat.")[1] If our reasons fail to compel meat eaters, we are told to "re-think" our "positions," as though an infallible argument were the same as a sensible choice. Presumably, if we have no argument, we have no reasons, and if we do not, then they have no reason to forgo meat, and so can continue to enjoy eating it.

Such invitations to argue both misconstrue vegetarianism and overestimate ethics. My own vegetarianism flows like a river from my heart; it does not arrive like a caboose at the end of a train of syllogisms. Arguments are peripheral, not the heart of the matter: as far as living goes, the heart of the matter is not logic, but heart. This is not to say that a philosophy of life like vegetarianism is a matter of emotion rather than reason; it is to say that philosophies of life are not matters of reason, but of living. Why should we expect what we live to be logical when living itself is not?

Reason is the mind's yoga: intellectual stretching is good for us. We enjoy following arguments just to see where they lead, and to see whether they succeed. Logic is a good arbiter and a fair judge when we argue; but logic is limited. Even the assent we make to the conclusion of a good argument is not done with the rational mind. Logic is for testing arguments. If they fail its tests, they are flawed: "the center cannot hold." But for people, the center is something else. We cannot touch this center, our being, with logic: it doesn't reach.

We may have reasons for loving someone (or something) but we do not *deduce* them.[2] Nor do we stop loving if we evaluate arguments in its favor and find them wanting. Reasons for loving, and indeed for living, are different sorts of things than evidence. In the 1930's, Darrow and Foster debated optimism and pessimism: "Is Life Worth Living?" Dostoevsky's Kirilov blew his brains out for want of an answer.[3] But such questions are not to be decided by deductions. One reason for living may be to enjoy the utter "unreasonableness" of so doing. Another may be to enjoy the paradoxes we can generate with our reason.

We can argue for or against vegetarianism; but we are vegetarian in the way we are in love: we do not have to justify it if we do not wish to. Yet we are also *not* vegetarian in the way we are in love, for while most of us do not wish others to have our lovers, we do wish others to have our diets. But why? If vegetarianism cannot be proved "right," how are we justified in wanting to share it? The reason (apt to disappoint philosophers) goes beyond good reasons for vegetarianism: it is because we want company. We would feel less alone and more at home in the world if others shared our view of it.

A vegetarian typically undergoes what I call an "inner paradigm shift." Startling new facts change the vision, and we never see the world in the same way again. We cannot *argue* anyone into seeing a Gestalt transfer in another way. Vegetarians should not wish others to follow their arguments as much as follow their example. We are much more like escapees from Plato's cave than devotees of Aristotle's logic. A friend once called Aristotle's syllogisms "silly-gisms"; he was being silly, having fun with the word, but as the years pass, I see the wisdom in his lo-"cute"-ion. Deductive arguments do not *take* us anywhere: if we want to see the light, we must move out of the cave. Facts (and sometimes slim figures), not formal arguments, guide us.

It would be irrational for me *not* to be a vegetarian, given the way I see the world. My vegetarianism grows out of me as organically as the plants I eat grow out of the earth. It is not a "personal" choice in the sense of a taste about which there is no disputing, but is personal in the sense of "who I am." To explain my vegetarianism to others is to explain *myself*. Explaining our vegetarianism does not mean that we can show why anyone else must lead a vegetarian life: it only justifies our choice to others. It is an accident of our culture that vegetarians stand out and are questioned. In a plant-eating culture, it would be carnivores who would be "grilled." If we say simply that vegetarianism is our way of life, that we like what it makes us into, we may be met with hostility: "How *dare* you be so different? Are you implying there is something wrong with *me?*"

Who is right? The omnivore saying, "Prove to me that meat eating is wrong"? or the vegetarian saying, "Prove to me that meat eating is right"? Perhaps neither. But if we insist on ethical arguments, we will debate the "burden of proof": on whose shoulders should it fall? Vegetarians are asked to shoulder it because they are "different"; but philosophers know that popularity or numbers prove nothing right. If unnecessary killing and suffering are wrong, then the moral burden falls on meat eaters. They and those who turn the shoulders of others into chuck should shoulder it, uncomfortable though it may be.

When we feel uncomfortable or threatened, we rationalize. While a reason explains, a rationalization excuses. With rationalizations we try to explain our actions by defending ourselves for doing them—a sort of reverse *ad hominem*. Rationalizations are stories we tell ourselves to justify what we do. Freud saw them as "defense mechanisms": they create illusions so we can live more comfortably with ourselves. We all edit the stories of our lives as we live them; but if we rationalize, we lie to ourselves and to others. Reasons bring things to light; rationalizations hide them. We may not see the difference, but this is the difference between them.

Meat eaters often resist and rationalize. Some years ago, a colleague, noting my "glowing complexion," graciously told me I looked "half my age." When I replied (after thanking her) that twenty years of vegetarianism might have had something to do with it, she quickly changed the subject. Had I told her that I had discovered a new face cream—tested on animals, no doubt—she would have listened; but she would not discuss vegetarianism.

Some people are what Socrates called "misologists"—haters of reason—for reasons can uproot rationalizations. In our culture, we believe it is wrong to eat persons, but we do wish to eat animals; so we do not call them "persons" in spite of their similarities to us. Can we justify this—or are we just rationalizing?

MICHAEL said: "The line that one talks about in which monkeys would be nearer the pinnacle—although eaten in some places—and fish are at the bottom—we really have no way of knowing, if it's a matter of consciousness we're worrying about. We don't have the faintest idea—nobody does—of how consciousness works, how it's constituted, and what's got it. There is no basis whatsoever, not the tiniest shred of evidence, to assume that a cow is conscious and a fish isn't, rather than the other way around. We simply don't know; so as a legitimizing device, it's merely rhetorical. It's not based on anything that can be called 'evidence.' I use it for peace of mind; but the 'empirical evidence,' so-called, simply isn't.

"We not only have no idea of what consciousness is, but we also—and this is very disconcerting—know that we never will have any idea, because the whole point about consciousness is that it is something that defines the self only—which is available to self only. If you can ask a fish, 'Are you conscious?' and the fish says, "Yes!' we still don't know if the fish is telling the truth: it could be a machine for telling lies. And there can never be a way beyond that. The empirical process—the scientific method if you like—by its very nature must stop at determining whether an entity is conscious. So to state, 'X entity is conscious,' is a political and rhetorical device.

"I had a chat with my doctor in London four years ago. He went further in this agreed-upon, although ill-founded, scale. He eats fish, but doesn't eat birds at all. 'To me, the chicken is worse. The more it looks like an animal, the worse it is for me. With a chicken, I can see the whole thing delineated there. At least with a cow, it's just a slice removed from the animal, so that's easier.'"

JOHN said: "I'm petting a dog right now, and I have no intention of eating you, Elmo; I want you to know that." PETER agreed: "There is a part of me that feels the more conscious a creature is, the worse it would be to kill it. I couldn't imagine killing a dog to eat it. I couldn't imagine doing that. And if you put me in front of a cow, and asked me to kill it, I couldn't do it, certainly. Fishes and chickens are even more distant; I don't know what goes on in their consciousness; I just don't know . . . From a gut feeling, there's no way I'm going to kill a dog. And from a gut feeling, I'd have a really hard time with a cow. So there is a hierarchy for me; but it is not a finely-tuned, metaphysical one."

ROLF hesitated when I asked, "Is there a hierarchy at the top of which would be an animal whose flesh you would not eat?" But I persisted, and our dialogue consisted of this:

K: If you went to a house, and they were serving a Downs baby for dinner—

R: I wouldn't eat human flesh, certainly.

K: Why not? If it were legal, and available—why not? And if one of your friends served it to you, and they did it without suffering, and if it were an extra human? There are too many on this earth anyway, so there's no ecological problem, and it would really help, given that this is the flesh of a human killed in an industrialized society. So why *not* eat human flesh if it were good?

R: My reasons are not principally rational, but just kind of immediately emotional. It's utterly revolting to me.

K: I knew you'd say that.

R: But in terms of a hierarchy amongst animals, I think I would be very queasy eating primates or something like that. It would bother me.

K: Why is that? Why?

R: Because I identify with them more strongly than I identify with chickens or something.

K: Why is that? The emotional life is closer?

R: The emotional life. The mental life. I think a large part of our ethics comes from what we identify with and it's a kind of empathetic bond that's very valuable.

K: So, not a human, not a primate—how else would you construct the hierarchy? Mammal flesh you *do* eat—

R: I can, yes. I would not refuse to eat it.

K: So there's less of an understanding between the mental life of a cow for you than a chimpanzee or a rhesus monkey. So the less you understand a being, the more likely that you would eat its flesh. (My goodness, on that principle, I should eat the flesh of some of my former lovers! The less I understand someone—watch out!) How do you feel about hierarchy in general?

R: It's a tricky—it's a very tricky question. I think there is a sense of hierarchy in nature, and it's represented in the trees that represent the animal kingdom. I'm not sure whether trophic relationships—food chains—really constitute a hierarchy; they certainly resemble one. The value of an individual animal life is ethically significant to me; but it loses its significance as one moves down the evolutionary scale."

ROLF seems to invoke Darwin, but Darwin chided himself for speaking of "higher" and "lower" animals "up" or "down" on the evolutionary scale.[4] We could say instead "earlier" or "later" or "more" or "less" complex; but "sub-human animal" has persisted in our language, just as The Great Chain of Being has persisted in our consciousness. As apes, because we are not pure carnivores, we are not at the apex, as much as we would like to think so. If we are on a ladder of life, and will eat only what is "below" us, then it is convenient to place ourselves at the top, or just below God or angels, who, presumably, do not need to eat.

Flesh-eating for some is practically a religious obligation, to show our superiority in the hierarchy. GAIL said it was considered "sacrilegious" to care too much for animals, and ROBBAN believed that God put animals on earth for our use. BARBARA had to unlearn the dogma that animals are beneath us. She said: "Vegetarianism went hand in hand with some changes in my religious upbringing, getting away from that sense of dominance: they were on earth for us, for our consumption, and coming to realize they have a right to life as much as we do."

MARCIA believes we can learn such lessons from our pets. She said: "I think most people like animals. Not everybody does, but most people do, and if you can get them to extend from their pet animals and realize that anything that looks at you the way an animal does is like your dog or your cat that looks at you — there's a soul in there. You can see it in their eyes; they're looking back at you." Would that it were so simple: we don't eat our pets, but we eat other animals. In Korea, pet dogs are escorted to a yearly picnic, hung by the neck until dead in trees (by the children!) and roasted on spits; everyone but the roasted dogs, presumably, has a good time. In our culture, farm children like ROBBAN make friends with future dinners, and even MARCIA, who wept, ate the farm's chickens, and relished the venison from the dead deer she caressed. Even when they are among us, animals are outsiders; that is why they end up inside us.

In our culture, we eat the sheep, but not the sheep dog; Angora goats or rabbits, perhaps, but not Angora cats. Do we have good reasons, or only rationalizations? In Thailand, people eat cats and lizards, and in China, snakes and dogs. INGRID, a long-time vegetarian before she traveled to China, wrote: "The menu is amazing if you're counting kinds of animals and parts . . . sliced pigs' ears, tripe, pigeon, fish, duck, dog, pork . . . Daddy and I shared a five-snake soup. I had two or three bites."

We eat what is available; but how do we justify what we make available? It cannot be anonymity, or family farms would be out of business. It cannot be the scale of being, for a horse is too much like a cow, and a pig like a dog. Anthropologists suggest that the first great conceptual divide was not night and day, or male and female, but edible and inedible. How do we decide? Are certain animals, like horses and dogs, totems, whose qualities we admire? Do we eat a turkey (and break its "wish-bone") because we wish not to be called one? If we eat strong and beautiful animals like deer, is it sympathetic magic, and not the magic of sympathy that moves us?

If we play the game of "consistency" about what we eat, there will probably be only losers. LEONARD said: "I sometimes wonder whether vegetarians who are using Brewer's yeast don't realize that they're little animals, that they're microscopic little animals. Baking yeast are feeding on the sugar, on sweetness, when they're rising your bread. They're feeding on it, and the gas bubbles are produced through their alimentary tracts. If you don't mind, that's O.K. with me. Risen bread has baked little animals in it. They're dead. They *were* alive."

Whether or not yeasts are "little animals" (and what if they were?) the reason we eat what we eat is probably because we do not think about it much; if we did, we might eat something (rather than someone) else. Rationalizations feed on denial as we feed on what we deny. LINDA had to make sure her beef was, "thoroughly disguised," and BARBARA said, "I always had to buy it in ways that I didn't see it was beef; that was my only way of dealing with it." FRANK could only accept meat in forms which did not resemble flesh, and JOHN said, "I go through this whole charade at times, which is why I prefer hamburger to steak—if I'm going to have my meat, I want it ground into a form where I just don't recognize it." It's a rare person who can grill a hotdog, and laugh, "Snouts without the kraut!"[5]

BARBARA ate meat "in delicate situations" (ironically, at family funerals and wakes); GAIL did not want to "offend" or "make waves"; LEONARD ate it out of "nostalgia"; VICKY ate it "rather than throw it away"; JONATHAN, MARCIA, and TONY did not want to offend the pride of the poor who offered it; DAVID wanted to stop hurting his mother. Their reasons may be good or bad; but they are not rationalizations.

Excuses, excuses. Omnivores make more of them than vegetarians; but if anyone has a good reason for eating meat, it is a former vegetarian. Vegetarians think they see more clearly than omnivores; but what about those who see what they see and do otherwise? Have they turned their philosophies inside out now that they've "come out" and again eat the insides of animals?

Rarely defensive, and with refreshing candor, lapsos do not hide from the facts of death or beg to be shielded from unsettling sights which unsettle stomachs, crying, "Idon'wannaknowaboutit!" They say: "I didn't want to be elitist." "I didn't want to be 'pure.'" "I wanted to accommodate others." "I wanted to understand other cultures." "I wanted to achieve a harmony." "I didn't want to set myself apart from others." "I didn't want to make my behavior an accusation." "I didn't want to get into an 'ism.'" "I don't want to draw the lines of 'right' and 'wrong.'" "I needed it to be well." "I wanted to heal my body."

Omnivores, on their side, offer: "It tastes good." "It's an ingrained habit." "It makes me strong." "It's convenient." "I need the protein." "I like the mouthfeel." "I was brought up to like meat." "It's part of my cultural heritage." "It's what everyone eats." "It's natural." "It's an antidote to dietary boredom." "What else would I eat?" "Everything in moderation: I don't eat *that* much meat." "The Bible says it's all right." "It's already there: I didn't kill it." "They're just dumb animals: their purpose is to be meat."

ELLY saw that "people eat meat because they like it and don't want to think about where it came from." In general, when omnivores justify meat, they justify their *liking* it, while former vegetarians justify their *eating* it. Although some lapsos lapse for reasons of convenience, and some omnivores eat meat for "health," the contrast is striking: excuses show themselves as such.

Philosophers cannot argue anyone into love or out of hypocrisy, although value clarification exercises or a field trip to the killing floor might help. It is we who are rationalizing if we think otherwise. There is no better knock-down proof of the unwholesomeness of a meat-centered diet than the knock down of a heart attack, or an environmental one as powerful as the knock down of a rain forest for pasture. There is no philosophical argument which mandates (or womandates) vegetarianism. We cannot argue anyone into it; we can only argue *about* it.

Arguments have their purpose, but one does not argue in the face of true love or true wisdom, inspiration or revelation. One does not argue a philosophy of life. One takes it in or rejects it; one inspects it; but one does not subject it to the canons of proof. If we had reduced SIANNA's story to syllogisms and critiqued them, would we have been the wiser? If we shared the critique with SIANNA, would she? SIANNA had good reasons to eat meat: she didn't need arguments.

Insight is swift; argument is slow, and most of us are impatient. But patience is not the issue: seeing clearly is. The captives of Plato's cave could have argued endlessly, or gone outside and looked. Philosophers overvalue philosophizing about value. Some believe a sound argument that meat eating is wrong would cut through the rationalizations and lead to vegetarianism. But people do not refrain from wrongs because arguments are right; most people do not follow arguments at all. They are "good" because they "see" something wrong with being "bad." And if they do not, they will cheat, lie, steal, and murder no matter how strong the arguments forbidding them might be. Trying to convince people that "meat is murder" is as likely to lead to guilt over eating it as it is to vegetarianism. People change only when they "see" for themselves.

Philosophy is not spiritual surgery: logic cannot perform change-of-heart by-pass operations or personality transplants. Vegetarianism is a way of living according to the ideals of compassion, reverence for life, nonviolence, peacefulness, and respect. Logic cannot inject or graft these, nor can it prove that omnivores lack them. It is unreasonable for philosophers to expect a "proof" of vegetarianism although it is not unreasonable for them to try. Just because reason cannot prove that God exists does not mean we cannot play with our minds and work up arguments. If the arguments fail to convert, that does not make faith foolish; if arguments for vegetarianism fail to convert, that does not make the commitment faddish.

To some extent, we have to take vegetarianism on faith, not because it presupposes the supernatural, but because we cannot be certain that it is "right." We cannot be certain that it would bring a balance of good into the world, or that universal vegetarianism would be best for all concerned. Maybe it would be a disaster. Maybe it would be the dawn of a New Age. Nor can we be sure that near-vegetarianism (or an evolved form of omnivorism) would not be as good or better. I prefer to live in a world of peaceful people, but philosophers have argued that universal peace would not be good for us.[6] But then, who are we? And what about the rest of the world?

Those trained in philosophy can be the first to see its limitations. ROLF said: "What got me interested in philosophy in the first place was a desire to be more intelligent and reflective and deliberative on how I live; but the philosophy I was trained in was mostly an academic exercise in which any sort of utility was looked down upon. Ethics had nothing to do with how one lives; it's just how one analyzes the concept. So the gap between life and philosophy is absolute.

"My philosophical interests have tended to drift toward those kinds of problems that were really relevant for my personal life: the more theoretical problems I just let go of unless I was involved with them for teaching. In an environment where I'm studying philosophy with other philosophers, I can get interested in academic problems; but I find myself completely unable to sustain those kinds of interests on my own. I don't believe that ethical choices are or ought to be purely cognitive. They arise from compassion and things of that sort."

ROLF *said* he was convinced by the "arguments" in John Robbins' book, *Diet for a New America*, but meant otherwise: "For example — and I used to have a whole bunch of these facts in my head . . ." demonstrating that the drama of data, not the finale of form convinced him. I, too, read the book, and remember only examples: neither of us recalled a single "proof." ROLF gave as his reason for being a near vegetarian that he wants "to live in a way that gives as much room as possible for other things to live, including other people." Like ELLY, who didn't "separate the idea of logic from the idea of emotion," ROLF bases his decision on "a combination of thought and feeling" and says he "does not like to divide the two very much."

PETER said: "I grew up as an atheistic Jew with socialistic parents and discovered philosophy first as a possible answer to the question, 'Who am I?' which my parents were answering only in a material sense and not in a spiritual sense. Socrates was my first guru; but finding that philosophy in the modern tradition had become analytical and essentially linguistic masturbation, I searched for something more and found that in the Eastern traditions."

If we look at the human and animal "conditions," we might have revelations. For centuries, sages in Eastern traditions have struggled to reach a state of enlightened bliss, emptying their minds of logic and language. But this is just the state of the animal mind all the time! To what we aspire, they are already! If we do not want a saint or a sage on our plates, why are we eating them? Perhaps instead of eating them we should be emulating them. This insight was not the conclusion of an argument, but simply something "seen"; but this is not to say that Western philosophy with its emphasis on what can be (not so simply) shown is without merit: a mental workout can be just as joyous as a physical one. As long as we do not tyrannize others into thinking they have no "reasons" if they have no "logic," then it has its place.

Given that vegetarianism is not a philosophical position but a way of living, it should not matter to vegetarians whether arguments for or against it fail; and because omnivorism has not yet been articulated as a philosophy of life, calling for high ideals, it is not yet a contender. But understanding vegetarianism as a philosophy of life shows the true connection between vegetarianism and philosophy: an unexamined philosophy of life is not worth living.

16

Consistency and the Coherent Life

An inconsistent life is a lie; but a coherent one is not the same as being truthful: it is living one's truth. If we are not truthful, we deceive, and are not true to our word; if we betray our ideals, we falter, and are not true to ourselves. If we say one thing, but do another, we are inconsistent, and may be called "hypocrites" or "liars"; when our actions belie our beliefs, especially what we believe in, we are not living coherent lives, and may be called "ingenuine" or "insincere." A consistent life has more to do with honesty than with truth; a coherent one more to do with integrity than with proof. Our lives are not formal systems which forbid contradiction. Logical consistency may be difficult to fulfill, but the concept is simple: the coherent life is complex.

Truth-value is one thing; what, in truth, we value is another. If we are unaware of our values, we may not know if we lead coherent lives; but living a coherent life and being who we are come to the same thing. If there is no pattern, there is no person: to the extent that we lead coherent lives, we *are*. That a coherent life brings potentially conflicting values together in us does not mean we have betrayed ourselves or that we do not know who we are; it means that to maintain or to create identity, we must juggle our ideals.

We may love animals, but eat them. We may or may not be inconsistent; we need to know what else is "at steak." If we value compassion, but show no mercy; if we value harmony, but cause dissension; if we value peace, but make war, then we do not act according to these values; but we may balance them against others. We may value justice more than peace, and go to war; we may value truth more than harmony, and make waves; we may value our lives over compassion, and show no mercy to what threatens them. We may love animals and eat them (or love some animals and eat others) because we value our lives more than theirs. Thus what appears to be inconsistent may be part of a coherent life.

To import the rules for inference into biographies treats them unreasonably as still-lifes. Inconstant people betray ideals, beliefs, themselves—and sometimes us. We call them "inconsistent"; but this is not the inconsistency of logic ("non-contradiction"). Logical consistency does not admit of degrees; but people can be more or less consistent, or consistent more or less of the time. Our lives are not closed structures; as they flow, we grow.

Although there is a "logic" to life, it is more like the "logic" of art or of nature than the logic of formal proof. If we study a coherent life, we find its meaning; yet that pattern or order was not set down according to rules, but evolved over a series of decisions. We respond to the world by ordering and re-ordering (and by inventing and re-inventing) our values. The world is too rich relative to any final, fixed arrangement. Its complexity "rules out" such simplicity. We are not inconsistent with our former selves: we grow out of them. But while no one is expected to remain forever the same, for one to be someone, there must be some order in one's life.

We do "contain multitudes"; but we cannot use Whitman's poetry as an excuse for contrariety. If the multitudes we contain change with bewildering rapidity, then who are we? Human relationships thrive on some degree of predictability. When others profess what they do not live, we become angry. If we charge them with inconsistency, it is a much more serious business than finding flaws in their arguments, for we are doubting the people themselves. We need to know what to expect from others — and from ourselves, if we are to have self-identity.

Yet we should not strive constantly to be constant. Indeed, it may even be inconsistent to do so. Compassion may be our ideal, but if we worry too much about living consistently with it, we may not have time to be compassionate. Living consistently with values is valuable, but over-valuing consistency is not. It is not unreasonable to decide not to let reason decide everything, and threaten the spontaneity of our lives.

Thus living according to ideals has little to do with deduction and everything to do with construction— of lives. Inconsistent positions self-destruct; inconsistent people can self-perfect. Inconsistent positions are dead; but inconsistent people are alive, and may be interesting. Inconsistency in formal proof is illogical; inconsistency in lives, at its worst, incomprehensible.

If we think we value something, but do otherwise, we can only fool ourselves (and others) for so long; when things are important to us, our actions tend to show it. We may be blissfully ignorant of our contradictions, but eventually a counselor or a friend (but probably not a logician!) is likely to catch us.

PETER said: "Consistency in logic is valuable in doing philosophy, in thinking philosophically. It's important; it has its place. I do not have respect for people who insist on speaking in paradoxes, and throw out contradictions as if they didn't matter. But the truth itself is an experience to be had when one lets go of logical thinking;

it's not in virtue of our logical prowess that we reach the truth. So the only consistency that matters is the consistency of our own lives. For me, a strict vegetarianism is not part of that harmony. The inconsistency of eating food prepared in anger is more a block to my kind of personal growth than logical consistency. It is the activity of harmony and love in our diets that's more important than what we eat."

ELLY said: "You can talk philosophy, and you can talk philosophically if you want, but your basic beliefs are first principles which can't be subject to proofs anyway. All our most basic, fundamental beliefs are not philosophical. They're based on faith that one can find the 'right' in that particular decision or in that particular principle — and it can't be parsed down any further.

"My decisions have been made on the basis of reasoning, feeling, and intuition; but I don't distinguish among these. I apply this kind of subjectivism to my principles: I believe what feels true to me. While I use terms like 'right' and 'wrong,' I think that any person's ethics is contingent on their circumstances as well. I don't see ethics as necessarily being absolute at all; I think they can be contingent. Even when I was a vegetarian, there was relativistic veneer on my vegetarianism: I wasn't absolutist in my vegetarian beliefs. I think vegetarianism is a choice of circumstance like any other.

"I noticed that non-vegetarians were disconnected, but I could appreciate them for other values they had; it wasn't all-encompassing. I wasn't a one-issue person like your average abortion-rightist. My vegetarianism was a source of comfort and well-being because I was acting in conformity with some of my deepest beliefs. If I felt close enough to someone, I would talk to them about the contradictions in values I might sense. I found that if they were truly consistent with their values, they would be vegetarian."

Whatever our tolerance for inconsistency, we will sometimes struggle with it. LINDA said: "It's a definite inconsistency for me because I think all life is sacred, and here I am using these animals. Working in a dairy farm made me realize that we are *using* these animals. You breed them, and you take their babies away, and you make veal out of some of them, and you take the calf's milk away from it, and you milk the mother cow. You're just blatantly using these animals, and they don't have any say in it. And yet I participate in that.

"It's a pretty major conflict, and I have to say, from the organic farming side, we are using these animals, too, because you're using their manure—and you use it by the *truckload*! We're not just talking about having a cow, and convincing it to walk across your land. You *need* these animals to produce that much manure to compost to put on your fields. I guess I see that things are a lot more complicated than I would like to imagine that they are, and that I'm willing to compromise my values a lot farther than I ever thought I would. Maybe I'm just getting close to forty."

MICHAEL offered: "If we are talking about moral probity, being vegan is the only way to do it. I suppose I could get all my protein from milk. But, but, but. Were does the milk come from? It comes from cows, and if all of us drink the milk, what happens to the cows? Are we really going to waste all that good protein walking around? So the person who says, 'I'm vegetarian because I don't hold to the idea of killing animals, but I do drink milk and eat cheese and butter and so forth, that person is being a hypocrite, because they are doing something which leads, as night follows day, to animals which are going to be killed. That person is an accomplice, let me say.

"As to moral issues with regard to animals, I embody the reason why they used to say, in the 1960's, 'Don't trust anyone over thirty.' Because I think as one gets older, one ceases to believe in the perfectibility of the world. One makes one's premise; one abides by it, and toddles on through life. There is nothing else one can really do.

"I personally accept that animals might well be sentient, and they might not enjoy the process of being reared for food and killed in the end. This is where I make my moral compromise. And I see it as a pettier, or tawdrier or less supportable moral compromise when the animal walks around on the land, and looks at me with appealing brown eyes than when it looks like a machine for pecking things on the ground. I use the term 'red meat' as a legitimizing device. I use it as an abbreviation for anything that doesn't fly and doesn't swim, so it includes not eating rabbits, hare, and all sorts of things of that kind. It is limited to avians and pisceans—that is right. Once I make a tatty compromise, I want to support it; but I'm aware that the logic can be unraveled."

Inconsistency may take the form of betraying our values; but it may also take the form of denial. Sometimes we deny with the language we use, learning from our culture how to refuse to face the truth. MICHAEL said: "In German, you have the noun '*Schwein*' which means 'pig' and you have the noun '*Fleisch.*' And the word for pork is '*Schweinfleisch*' and the word for veal is '*Kalbfleish*' and so on, and there is no barrier at all between the two. And I must admit that for an English-speaking person learning German for the first time, there is something slightly eerie about these terms—'pigmeat' and 'calfmeat.' It's more honest and direct than what one is used to. They're slightly eerie words."

FRANK said that in Japanese and in Chinese, the terms for meat are also literal. "The word for pork is '*butaniku.*' The character they wrote the flesh-word with—and most people don't know this—was, etymologically, a picture of a carcass hanging from a frame. I'm interested in that, but the native speaker just learns it the way we learn the alphabet. We don't think that the letter 'D' was a picture of an archway door turned around."

FRANK explained that after the Norman Invasion, Anglo-Saxon words were replaced by the euphemisms of the higher-class conquerors. "The Normans became the courtly group. They used their word for flesh at the table, and the people who had been conquered identified with the enemy, the conqueror: they began to use the more elegant word. The fact that it caught on does say that we are more comfortable with it—or some people were."

"Beef," "pork," "veal," "poultry," and so forth are euphemisms but are not euphonious, for as words, they are short and harsh; but like evening gowns they dress up the actual in an aura of the fanciful:

they create illusions. To our ears, "roast beef" sounds better than "roast cow" and "veal" better than "calfmeat." (Would we eat dog if it were called "chien"?) To the extent that our language shields us, we hide from what we do; if we feel ill at ease upon hearing the literal rendition, especially when eating, we are ingenuine. VICKY said: "I felt fine about eating meat again. I only felt bad when eating with vegetarians who called my dinner 'flesh' or 'that dead bird.'" But if we do not or cannot admit that we are eating a dead bird, are we honest with ourselves?

Sometimes our inconsistencies are more subtle. We can, like FRANK, eat fish caught with worms, and value butterflies, who are worms with wings. FRANK said: "I gathered up three caterpillars at the end of fall, because they were going to weed the schoolyard. They were Eastern Black Swallowtails—a phenomenally beautiful caterpillar—and they went into chrysalis almost within a few days. One of them came out over Christmas break, and I felt so guilty because it got a little too warm where it was and thought it was spring. It came out: they're supposed to overwinter. I put the other two in the garage where it's cold, and I felt responsible for this *being*. I consulted a lepidopterist from Yale and a couple of other people, and I was comforted to find out that they usually only live from ten days to two weeks as adults anyway.

"Normally these things would just fly around, mate and croak, and that's its life-cycle; but now I saved the caterpillar from the weed whacker, and now I'm responsible for it. It's alive. It's been three weeks, and it's still alive. I fed it sugar water to simulate the nectar, and it's sort of battered: the scales are coming off the wings, and the swallowtails are kind of torn off. I mean, these things are food for birds by the millions, and I know that intellectually; but now that I've raised it, I'm its parent. I thought: Should I bring it to a greenhouse? At least it could have a few hours flying around in the flowers."

FRANK would probably "parent" a salmon fry in the same way even though he is willing to fry salmon. Although he values consistency in doing science, he does not turn his life into a testable hypothesis: his compassion expresses itself both in his near-vegetari-anism and in his nurturing of insects. He never said he was "perfect." As if to illustrate this, he added: "And milk. The whole idea of nursing from a cow! It's the wrong species; it has the wrong immune factors. And now it's doubly worse because we feed hormones and pesticides to the animals. It's ludicrous. Completely. Of course I'm not willing to give up cheese. Although tofu cheese is pretty good."

MICHAEL said similarly, although less humorously: "The reasons I do not eat meat are two-fold. One, there's the problem of what the animals have been fed on, and how they're reared and so forth. The second issue is that I find blood and guts extremely distasteful. The messy, fatty, sinewy, bloody, gristly business of getting the meat off the chicken is one that I find aesthetically displeasing. I eat chicken, yes." Here MICHAEL is more honest than he is inconsistent, for he admits his "moral compromise" even as he acknowledges the "lack of logic" in it.

Both ROLF and JOHN see the interplay between conflicting values. ROLF said: "You can't have a coherent theory unless it's logically consistent; the concept of a coherent life has more to do with living in harmony with nature, but also with society, and I don't know if it's possible to do both at once." One might accuse ROLF of inconsistency because he refuses to buy meat to cook at home, but eats it elsewhere; but he is really balancing two kinds of values. At home, he eats no flesh, thus achieving a "natural" harmony by not contributing to meat's damaging effect on the environment; but away from home, he eats it to achieve a "social" harmony. Rather than accuse him of inconsistency, we should see how he serves two moral masters.

JOHN said: "I wish the whole world were vegetarian, because in the purest sense, I really do think that philosophically, it would be preferable—for the animals, for the ecology, for the health of the people involved; but simultaneously, it is really a desire on my part not to separate myself from the mainstream of the world at large." Thus JOHN, too, is not so much inconsistent as he is torn between the demands of two ideals.

When JONATHAN saw some of his inconsistencies, he exclaimed: "You can't put a logic to it!"; but when our lives include arguing about how we ought to live them, then logic has its place. Logic stands in relation to debate in the role of a fair arbiter, allowing us to disagree without accusation. ROLF and I illustrated this during part of his interview.

The Sound Of Two Philosophers Talking

R: I don't think I'd eat veal—

K: Why not?

R: Just because of the horror stories I've read about how the veal are raised. That seems to me—

K: But if other animals were raised in ways that you considered horrific, would you then draw your line, and exclude those animals, too? If you learned that the sow or steer was also—

R: Probably not in a social setting like that.

K: What would be the difference between cruelly raised veal and cruelly raised chicken?

R: I wouldn't buy such meat; but if somebody served it, I feel that in eating a portion of that, I'm not really contributing to the destruction—

K: But you wouldn't eat *veal* at the other person's house. That's what I'm trying to get at. How do you make the distinction? If each were raised—

R: No one has served me veal. No one has actually served me chicken, I don't think.

K: We're getting off-track though. Go back to what would be the reason. If I served you veal, you'd refuse it. Why?

R: I was sort of surmising that I might. The situation has not arisen. Certainly, I would not feel good about that; but Thanksgiving, I was at someone's house, and they served me a turkey which they had bought at a natural foods store. It was a free-ranging turkey—that sort of thing.

K: I'm still trying to wedge back into: If the pork or the beef or the chicken were raised in ways you felt were as bad as the veal, would you accept that at someone else's house, using as your reason, "I didn't buy it; I didn't contribute"?

R: Probably on a single occasion I would.

K: Right. And probably on a single occasion you'd eat Veal Marsala or Parmesan.

R: I would have trouble with that.

K: So I'm still trying to find out why—as a philosopher. I'm not asking to make you defensive, but just, philosophically, what the argument would be—the distinction.

R: In what reading I've done—and I haven't read a great deal—about the way in which meat has been raised—most of what I know is from John Robbins' book—and it was the veal story that seemed to me the most horrific.

K: But that's why I gave you the conditional. *If* you knew that the other animals suffered as much, *if* they did, would that make a difference in your being hospitable?

R: Yes; it would.

K: That's all I wanted. I'm a philosophy teacher, too. Sorry! Two of us together!

It is one thing to argue; it is quite another to accuse. TONY said: "Somebody one day woke me up, hit me over the head, as I stated I was a vegetarian, and they noticed I had leather shoes on, and they conked me over the head with that. I felt that even if I didn't eat this creature, the parts which were made into my shoes would have been there anyway, so it didn't matter at the point. Wearing leather didn't matter because it had already come from someone who had eaten the steak. So that didn't bother me."

Such accusations sometimes illustrate what logicians call "The Fallacy of False Charge of Inconsistency"—taking an apparent contradiction to be a real one. Sometimes such accusations illustrate the fallacy called "Ad Hominem Circumstantial"—arguing that one's position is wrong because of one's personal circumstances; yet one could wear leather, eat steak, or even work in a slaughterhouse, and still put forward a credible argument in favor of vegetarianism. Logicians are interested in arguments, not in how the arguers live their lives. The advantage in logical thinking is that one can evaluate reasons on their own, no matter who offers them, or what the circumstances. Philosophers "attack" not people, but positions. Seekers of truth attack nothing at all, but listen to how people live their lives, in order to understand them.

A zealot, eyes flaming anger, approached me at a vegetarian conference in a red passion to convict me of contradiction because I feed my cats fish. Because I care about cats, and also about fish, he thought he could impale me on the sharp, pointed stick of inconsistency and watch me squirm (something he would not do to a worm). Instead he could have asked, "Why do you do that?" Then we could have had a conversation instead of the confrontation he intended, but which I ended by walking away from it. Although there was something "at stake" (something to teach and something to learn) I dislike the burning of witches on gibbets: enough people have died in bonfires already. I sometimes sense that militant vegans would roast nonconformists in a way they would not roast beef.

Had I been given the opportunity of conversation without accusation, I might have told the zealot that I did not invent "tiger, tiger burning bright," and that carnivores have a right to be who they are. I might have told him that I hate waste, and so do not find the refuse left over from the fishing industry any *more* objectionable than meat by-products going into the asphalt over which I (and he) drive and into the cars which I (and he) own. I might have reminded him that if the heads and guts of fish did not end up in the cans, they might have been turned into fertilizer for his vegetables or for his houseplants. We might have discussed whether turning cats into vegans was a form of animal experimentation (a practice he would not defend) or whether boycotting (or girlcotting) by-products would negatively affect the industry as much as it would the cats.

Feeding fish to cats may be "wrong" or "bad" in some senses; but it is not necessarily inconsistent or part of an incoherent life. When a vegan feeds her dog a bone, she may be urged to bring her life more in line with her principles; but already the rules are closing in. Perhaps she loves her dog more than she values a strict adherence to principles. Perhaps a glimpse into the flat, sad eyes of an ailing vegan canine convinced her to provide a carnivorous option—or perhaps she realized that imposing on others what we choose for ourselves gives others no choice.[1]

I would love to meet a vegan who said, "You must really love your cats to feed them what you deny yourself: how do you justify that?" Asking people how they live is more important than asking what they do. If we stopped looking for frozen, timeless truths and accepted flowing, contextual views, what seemed like flaws would appear as clues.

A world where there is no room for interpretation is a small world indeed. We need to venture outside the bounds that "define" us if they are not to confine us. All too often, vegetarians narrow their focus; but a philosophy of life is not so much right or wrong as it is big or small: a large vision is better than a grand mission. Living in the confines of a closed system stifles us and can make us mean-spirited. If we have compassion for cows, but are cruel to the people who eat them, are we "consistent" then? If we love sheep, but shame those who wear wool? Perhaps life ought to imitate art; but if it imitates logic, it will lose its magic. It is better that life imitates nature, for nature flows, allowing profuse change and wild growth without disorder. Codifying a philosophy of life condemns it to death. We would not put animals into tight little boxes, but that is what we do to our beliefs when we try to conform. Our beliefs need to breathe if our philosophies of life are to go on living.

When our compromises compromise others' lives, we may have to rethink our values; but a change in vision must come from within. Why should we force the square corners and sharp points of individuality into the round holes of conformity? If our only answer is that fitting in is comfortable, we are all in trouble. *Sapere aude!* (Have the courage to think on your own!)[2]

Consistency makes for healthy arguments, but can poison people. People are not arguments, or even like them, even though we like to get into them. No vegan who lives in the world can ever be consistent. The most innocent-seeming items contain animal by-products. Consumer "goods" contaminated with animal "bads" are everywhere.[3] So few, if any, vegans who charge others with inconsistency are consistent themselves. One may be a warbler-watcher and a duck-defender, but also a photographer whose film is coated with gelatin from factory-farmed hooves and horns. Vegans may think they have hidey-holes for cover, but they remind me of nothing so much as cats in bags, heads in first, tails protruding, feeling invisible. The most consistent vegans have no bones to pick with others.

Without obsessions, what need for confessions? The ardor of the vegan zealot is a kind of blood-lust for victory, an irony given what they wish to be consistent about. Moral crusaders are too often filled with hatred even when they crusade for universal love. Would vegans fight to the death for a world with only vegans in it? The vegan zealot's life can be meat-a-phor for violence, and hence incoherent at its deepest level.

Demanding consistency from others is a march to war: we become scouts for contradictions in armies of accusation. If we find rules beautiful, then we may become ugly when we discover the inevitable exceptions. We should not so much conform to our values as to devalue conformity. This is not to say that we should idolize inconsistency, for we need to avoid anarchy as well as tyranny. We all know people whose words mean nothing a day, hour or even minute after they utter them. Predictably unpredictable, they use their "freedom to feel" and to change as a form of power, or as an excuse for their vagaries. Usually they do not know who they are.

It is a challenge to rationally justify a life; but it amounts to a "vain" pursuit in more ways than one, for as long as we are alive, we are not finished, and only what is complete can be completely understood. Contradictions can craze logicians, but people live them (and live with them) comfortably enough. If others challenge our integrity, we can show them how we live and what we live for: if the story makes some sense, we are living coherent lives. When we stop pretending we are pieces of logic, we can avoid the madhouse—as well as the steakhouse—and proceed with our lives.

The world is full of inconsistency: the true nature of things is probably that in some sense everything both is, and is not, and that whatever is true of something in one sense is false in another. Inconsistent arguments are "full of holes" yet holes in arguments do not let the light shine through, but rather obfuscate them. It is the opposite with both people and the world. People shine when striving, and become dull when they think themselves complete. In the cosmos, "worm holes" may lead to worlds without end. (Amen.)

17

Morals and Moralizing

"Those who still eat flesh when they could do
otherwise have no claim to be serious moralists."
—Stephen R. L. Clark, *The Moral Status of Animals*

"Does one know the moral effects of food?
Is there a philosophy of nourishment?
—Nietzsche, *The Gay Science*

The meek who shall inherit the earth will not eat meat. The omnivore will lie down with the lamb and not think of mutton. Here's our Bible: The Vegetarian Gospel. Good news for animals—good news for you! Read our parables and enter the kitchen of heaven. There is life without death. Eat peas for peace of body; eat right and see the light!

You are kept in the dark by an evil industry. There is an enemy! The Forces of Darkness to subdue! Join us in our righteous fight. There are no dues. All you have to lose is your shame. Repent! We will absolve you of your sins of flesh. It's not too late. Put some vegetables on your plate. It won't hurt you. It may convert you!

Bad food does you no good! Give it up! Quit it! It's an addiction! You'll never miss it! We will initiate you into the mysteries of meatless cuisine. See what we eat! You'll be healthy, just wait and see! Just look at me!

Hear ye! Hear why cows and sows are not allowed to walk. Let us talk: learn why chickens must lose their beaks. Let us speak: see what's real and you won't eat veal. Heed our fire and brimstone of heart attack and stroke. This is no joke! Believe and you shall have eternal health for as long as you shall live.

Omnivores often express an interest in vegetarianism, but say they do not wish to be identified with fanatics. In effect, they do not stay away from vegetarianism, but from vegetarians. They recoil from holier-than-thou missionizing and zeal and feel unclean around it. Indeed, if vegetarians had preached to me, I would have silenced the sermon and resisted remonstration: I'm much too willful. It was just because it was not demanded of me that I was able to make my own decision. Omnivores often like our "product" but hate our sales pitch. Too often vegetarians are pests instead of paradigms.

ELLY said: "I refused to proselytize. It's the same way with my daughter in terms of her burgeoning vegetarianism. I taught her to love animals; I gave her what she wanted [to eat] and I always hoped that she'd find her way toward it—which she did. PETER (whose sons eat meat) agreed: "I wasn't going to starve them just out of my ideals," and added, "I don't have an ethics on it; I don't have a general judgment for people." JONATHAN said he would never "harangue" people; but others, like TONY, admitted being "obnoxious" or like BARBARA, trying to "convert." VICKY adopted her short-lived vegetarianism trying to live with an "obnoxious converter."

MARCIA said: "I do think it's counterproductive to be too moralistic about it around other people. You don't need to make people feel horrible if they eat meat. I like to tell people why I don't and encourage them not to. I just think it alienates people if you treat them as though they're some kind of horrible creatures if they continue to eat meat. It would be counterproductive to come on too strong about it. I'd rather show by example."

JOHN encountered too many of the "counterproductive" types, including one he said needed a "smugness meter." He said: "Any former vegetarian who really loves to pursue this down a philosophical path is going to have to admit that ultimately he or she has been unfaithful to the intellectual premises they set out on. I suppose it's like being a lapsed Catholic. Happily, I don't have that problem at least: I'm an atheist. There are those born-again types who make the argument that there is no morality without religion, and one of the reasons, over the years, that I've decided to stop calling myself an agnostic and come out of the closet, as it were, is precisely because that infuriates me, that argument. SAYS YOU! I can be as moral or more moral as you—probably more moral if you're saying I'm *not* moral, because I think people ought to treat other people kindly. There. The end.

"And so it goes with vegetarianism. As the religion is to the morality argument, there's this sense of philosophical purity that goes with vegetarianism; but I want to say that it's possible to be philosophically pure and a meat eater. It is important to remember that just as it is possible for atheists to be moral people who treat other people decently, so it is necessary for vegetarians to remember that they don't have the lock on the nobler aspects of human nature."

We may be sympathetic to vegetarianism, but not living as sympathetic vegetarians. We are not sympathetic if we impose our views and refuse to let others come to their own conclusions. To moralize is to treat others like some treat those whose flesh they eat—with little sympathy or compassion, herding them over to one side of the gate. It is our claiming to be right that divides us from others. To be "right" builds barriers; only when people feel they are not being judged "wrong" will they relax long enough to listen. Forcing good ideas on them is just as bad as forcing good food on those who are not hungry.

Vegetarianism may have its roots in religion; but it does not have to become one. Rynn said: "I think you have to return to the original teachings of the Buddha and Mahavira in which they lay down the first precepts: to cherish all life and to do no harm. There's nothing abstract about that. That was to be taken literally, to be acted upon. To return to the original teachings of the Jains and the Buddhists where the moral imperatives were very clear, they tell you, the Buddha and Mahavira, that the first precept of their religion and belief system is not to harm others, to do no harm."

ELLY admitted the religious roots of her principles, but adopted them as her own. She said: "I don't think you find the source of your belief in a revelation or in a text: that would be religious. But perhaps that is where I get mine, second-hand, by default, because a lot of my principles have a religious source, even though I might not believe in them for religious reasons. I'm not saying, 'Believe that because it's in the Bible.' I believe that because it feels true to me—the same principles that other people might accept by referring to a reve-latory source."

Even if we believe what others once preached, we should prac-tice without preaching, instead of "practicing what we preach." Even if we are invited into the pulpit, it is better to teach than preach, for what we are allowed to find on our own we are likely to keep. We may think our way of living is heaven, but make it hell for those who have to listen. If we preach, we in effect give others the answers before they have time to think of the questions. To the extent that vegetarianism is perceived as a religion, others may resist not only the practice, but also the principles which inspire it, asserting themselves like JOHN, and vowing to oppose it. In the end, moralizing comes to nothing compared to a gentle example.

MARCIA saw that vegetarianism is something "people have to come to in their own time," and TONY said about vegetarians as exemplars: "I think vegetarianism is wonderful, and I'm glad you're there, because you remind us that there are other ways and that you're surviving. The fact that you're surviving means other people can survive that way; you're in good spirits and your intellect isn't harmed because you don't eat meat. You have all this wonderful energy and you're in a good place. Whatever vegetarianism is doing for you, it keeps you happy and humorous. I think it's wonderful. Those are the things we like to see—differences, healthy ones."

More than a religion, vegetarianism is a vision; but it is also treated like an ethical position. Ethics and the world have long been involved in a pitched battle. Ethics says: "Don't do what is done—do what you ought!" The world says: "Go mind your own business. I've gotten along without you for billions of years." If idealism challenges realism, realism fights back. JOHN said: "If the devil wins out, it's winning out on the basis of, 'Don't take that otherworldly tone with me! You're in the world! Why don't you admit it to yourself? Relax and have a good time!"

It might be wrong to have a good time over a feast of meat, but a deeper issue is the extent to which vegetarianism is a matter of ethics at all. If it is, it becomes the secular equivalent of religion—or the philosophical equivalent of law. Right and wrong replace good and evil as legal and illegal replace the sacred and profane. To do the right thing, must we be vegetarian? ELLY said: "It is easy and possible for me to express my love and reverence for animals through choosing vegetarianism; it is neither easy nor possible for other people to make that choice."[1] If it is "easy and possible" for us to choose vegetarianism, do we have a moral obligation to do so?

There are compelling moral arguments against factory farming and arguments forbidding the fruits of such systems. But is it fruitful to argue others into meatlessness on moral grounds? Killing animals for food, no matter how "humanely," may be wrong when other food is available; but is it unethical to eat flesh? Is it wrong, for example, to eat the flesh of animals who die naturally? Sometimes birds suffer heart attacks and fall out of the sky. For those who need protein, they might be mallards from heaven. Would it be wrong to eat blubber from a beached whale or venison from a highway collision? What is immoral about eating roadkill?

If no rights have been violated; if no pain and suffering has been inflicted; if no oppression or exploitation is involved; if no environmental damage has been done; if such flesh were inspected and safe to eat, what principle would we violate if we ate it? We might be revolted at the prospect or find it aesthetically unappealing; but these are visceral or perceptual compunctions, and not ethical injunctions.

This is not to say we could argue, "I didn't kill the fish. I just took it out of the water; it died on its own," or "I didn't kill the calf; I just tethered him away from his mother so he could not nurse." But what would be the harm in eating an animal who died on its own? If eating such flesh is not wrong, then eating flesh is not always wrong, even when other food is available. Thus vegetarianism, if it involves the complete abstinence from animal flesh, would not be morally required. Birds from heaven or beached whales could become meals without violating moral principles.

Philosophers want moral arguments for vegetarianism because moral arguments have force: If vegetarianism is a moral demand, then we can argue people into it. But to what extent is vegetarianism a moral issue? And do we really want to "force" it? PETER said: "It's not a moral issue at all"; but what he meant was that it is not a moral obligation, and he is right, for if we think that vegetarianism is morally required, we mistake the kind of thing it is.

Vegetarianism is a philosophy of life. As such, it is not so much the right thing to do as it is the living of ideals. It is neither a religion nor an ethic, but a species of idealism. If vegetarianism is the right thing to do, it becomes a demand rather than an inspiration. (Imagine a world where love were the law.) Most of us resist demands, but are hungry for inspiration. Sufficiently inspired, we may even hunger for vegetarianism.

A philosophy of life cannot be forced. We can force action, but not compassion. We can force people to do the right thing, but not to be good. Living according to ideals cannot be required, but only acquired in the course of living. Vegetarianism grows from within, out of perceptions and emotions, out of sentiments and moral feelings, out of sympathy, empathy, and respect, and ultimately, out of personal conviction—the desire to live consistently with our principles. We could argue people into meatlessness, perhaps, but not into vegetarianism. SIANNA once said that we "cannot pry open the bud to get at the flower." To say that vegetarianism is morally required is like saying that optimism is required, or good cheer, or love.

We are not "wrong" if we do not live in a certain way; we are "wrong" only if we do (or do not do) certain things. A philosophy of life is the bridge between moral philosophy and biography, and hence is not itself a matter of right and wrong. Vegetarianism does have to do with value and virtue; but in itself, it is morally neutral, because it can be practiced either well or ill. If it is practiced out of love, then the reason to be a vegetarian is because love is a good thing, not necessarily because vegetarianism is a good thing. Even idealism is bad if practiced in the wrong way.

When the ideal is lived in the best possible way, it transcends both the religious and the moral and becomes spiritual—something not only good but also beautiful. The health conscious vegetarian asks, "What would be injurious to me?" The ethical vegetarian asks, "What would injure others?" The religious vegetarian asks, "What would violate the rules?" The spiritual vegetarian asks, "How can I live my ideals?" If, as the Danish philosopher Kierkegaard said, the moral transcends the aesthetic and the religious transcends the moral, then the spiritual transcends the religious. Ironically, because people who live their ideals are like artists creating works of art, if what they create is beautiful, the spiritual resolves into the aesthetic, the "highest" into the "lowest," leaving the normative (both religion and ethics) behind.

Like the law, ethics and religion are each external to us, even if their sanctions are internal (bad conscience) instead of external (going to jail or to hell). Philosophies of life are different from the carefully contrived arguments of moral philosophers and from the teachings, dogma, and tenets of religions. When "ethical" vegetarians cry, "Meat is murder!" they suppose that people can be convinced by moral arguments, backed by good reasons, like soldiers marching to the front. But if vegetarianism is ethically "defensible," we are readying for battle, and if it is a defensible "position" we are in a position to wage war. What ideally springs from peacefulness, ironically is cast in military metaphor.

It is no accident that "ethical" vegetarians (like members of the so-called "moral" so-called "majority") can be militant; but if we try to argue others into peacefulness, we contribute to a violent world.

Taking sides, something philosophers do naturally and well as a means, is actually inimical to the ends we may wish to achieve by arguing. It is just because "ethical" vegetarians think in terms of right and wrong that we sometimes find among them high ideals juxtaposed with cruel zeal; but if we stop seeing vegetarianism as an obligation, we will also stop moralizing. Just as some food is not good for us, some ideas are not good for us either: that vegetarianism is morally required is one of them.

We can be concerned with doing the right thing, or instead, with living in the right way. And we can live in the right way without ever doing the right thing, and even without thinking in terms of right and wrong at all. Indeed, to the extent that we stop thinking in terms of right and wrong, we might be living in the best possible way, for only when we believe we are "right" do we think we have the right to force our views on others.

The reason I find something wrong with eating meat is not because vegetarianism is right, but because eating meat goes against my principles. (In principle, I could eat a roadkill, but I have developed an aversion to meat.) I cannot prove that the way I live is the best way of living, any more than we can prove to the pessimist that optimism is better, or move the curmudgeon with a sermon about love. At best they would listen, but would not give in. If vegetarianism were an ethical position, we could try to prove it; but we cannot prove a way of being.

It may be wrong, in the context of vegetarianism, to speak of right and wrong; but there is a better way. We could speak instead in terms of better and worse. Vegetarianism may not be a matter of right and wrong, but it is a matter of better and worse like any other choice. ROLF said: "The choice not to eat meat is a morally better choice," and MARCIA agreed that "it was better, mainly because of the animals." Vegetarianism may not be required as an action, but may be a good choice as a reaction against killing animals for food. Although not morally obligated, we may feel obliged to be vegetarian, as a symbol of solidarity, or to express outrage, to engage in boycott, or even to establish credibility so that our arguments against modern meat will be taken seriously. Our eating beached whale blubber or roadside raccoon is not morally inconsistent, but others might be resistant to our arguments if we ate it. So even if vegetarianism is not a moral duty, it might be politic to adopt it.

The real moral issue is not the rightness of vegetarianism: it is the wrongness of meat production. Because we eat animals killed for our consumption, even philosophers (who ought to know better!) argue that vegetarianism is required of us when what may be required is non-consumption. If everyone were vegetarian, but purchased factory farmed meat solely for the purpose of burying it in backyard gardens to fertilize vegetables, the problems would remain.

It is not the eating of meat but the meat that we eat that is the problem. Modern meat involves exploitation, so even if vegetarianism is not a moral obligation, eating meat has moral implications. We cannot say, "What I eat is a personal choice; do not engage me in dialogue; it is of concern to me only; it is out of the ken of ethics." Although PETER said vegetarianism was "not a moral issue," he immediately added, "On the other hand, I do tend to be sympathetic to the view that to raise animals for our eating pleasure is both un-natural and immoral."

Indeed, while some "ethical" vegetarians (like Rynn) refuse meat because they disapprove of killing animals per se, others protest the industry. ROLF said: "I don't want to support the meat industry because I don't like the way in which the business is run." ROCKY said: "I think vegetarianism is a great alternative to the meat industry, to the dairy industry. I'm not really there—big business, period." PETER spoke of "the unnaturalness of man's raising creatures for his own needs in such unnatural surroundings," and GAIL said, "A cor-ollary is wanting to support righteous business as much as possible."

BARBARA agreed: "I didn't want to be part of promoting that kind of care for another life form. That really upset me terribly. I learned how animals are raised and I didn't want any part of that. I just would see a lot of abuse of another living creature, and to give my life energy by consuming that kind of energy really upset me." VICKY said: "I do feel I am responsible for the death of an animal even if someone else killed it for me," and ELLY said, "In our society products are produced on a supply and demand basis, so there has to be some level of responsibility." ROCKY agreed: "You could say if there's no market for this, it wouldn't be there, like many other things in the world, like cigarettes. I could go along with that. In theory, yeah, in theory."

Do we have a moral obligation to protest what we detest? And is the best way to protest to boycott? It is often argued that modern meat production is like slavery,[2] so just as we would not support one, we should not support the other. But buying meat is not wrong in the way that slavery is wrong; it is wrong in the way that purchasing a product produced by slaves is wrong. Thus buying meat is related to but is not itself an absolute evil like slavery or owning a slave.

But even if consuming meat is not an absolute evil, is it not morally wrong to support industries which violate rights or do great harms? Are we obligated to disassociate ourselves from this? The problem (unfortunately) is the enormity of the world's evils relative to our ability to resist them. On the principle, "What counts against all, counts against none," if we are obligated to boycott modern meat, we are obligated to engage in all sorts of other negative actions as well, such as refusing to drive cars, pay taxes, put money into banks, take out loans and mortgages, pay utility bills, and purchase almost any consumer item, especially those from overseas markets where they are made with the equivalent of slave labor and without environmental controls. R.G. Frey, a philosopher critical of animal rights and of vegetarianism, says that such a "severe view" of moral consistency demands too much of us: "it's extent destroys its force."[3]

ROLF struggled with the implications of a severe moral consistency. He said: "To me, the agonizing dilemma in a technologically advanced country in the late twentieth century is that we need to deviate most radically from the way in which people live in our society because we are not living in a way which is (a) universalizable and (b) sustainable. And that particularly applies to things like driving an automobile. I spent some months agonizing over the possibility of living without a car—which is as important an issue to me as is vegetarianism—and I finally decided that I wasn't going to do it, that I wasn't going to go it alone. It would isolate me so much and I would be so resentful and self-righteous that I just wasn't going to do it."

If we all stopped driving, the air would be sweet (and there would be no dead animals on the street); but are we immoral to drive? We cannot have an obligation to resist anything associated with evil, because almost everything is, and "ought implies can." With our purchases, we tacitly approve of much that we hate. ("What we will pay for as consumers is not always commensurate with what we would vote for as citizens.")[4] Which evils, if any, are we obligated to protest? Some say we have an obligation to boycott meat because individual life is of value and there is an immediate and obvious connection between animal death and an omnivorous diet. Driving animals to their deaths with our cars is as immediate and obvious, but far less frequent than driving to purchase them for our dinners, and it is not intentional: it is no accident that an animal dies so that we can eat it. Although there is a small anti-paving movement in response to current environmental concerns,[5] there are reasons for meatlessness rooted in ancient philosophies and religions whose precepts were laid down long before paved roads.

Sartre said that we are responsible for any evils we do not resist; but to be collectively responsible is not to be immoral, especially when we are far from the source, or have little choice. But if it is "easy and possible" for us to choose and we do not approve of agribusiness, should we not boycott it? Refusing to consume what is produced with abuse would not land us in jail as would forgetting to pay our taxes or isolate us as would going carless. Are we not wrong to buy factory farmed meat?

We should perhaps boycott it, but not because we have a moral obligation, for moral obligations are for one and all, and not just for a few of us. Ethics cannot require what most of us are incapable of doing. If we think on a global scale, and not just about the up-scale affluent and educated, with their means and their choices, there are too many exceptions to make boycotting a moral rule. Looking globally instead of locally, we find ignorance and poverty; if we think provincially of only ourselves, we see that we are the exceptions; so we cannot formulate a rule.

Boycotting meat is not a moral mandate; but some say that it is "supererogatory"—above and beyond the call of duty.[6] We are commended if we do it, but not condemned if we do not. For others, it is neither a duty nor supererogatory, but a matter of moral consistency: some actions do not violate duty but rob us of integrity. The more loudly we denounce a practice, the less justified we are to buy into it. Those who condemn factory farming violate their own principles if they knowingly support it.

Former vegetarians sometimes do boycott factory farmed meat, acting on principles (especially environmental) which led them to vegetarianism in the first place. KIVA buys only "free range chicken, Happy Hen Eggs, and dolphin-safe tuna fish." BARBARA said: "I do get organic chicken and drive out of my way to get organic beef—about an hour south of here." Putting aside the issue of driving long distances for organic meat, theirs appear to be the better choices; but other lapsos know as much about factory farms, yet revert to buying their meat. Having heard their stories, it is hard to call them "unethical"; but even they admit their inconsistencies. ELLY found "contradictions in values" and "emotional disconnect"; LINDA noticed a "definite inconsistency"; MICHAEL found "a lack of moral probity"; and FRANK saw the lack of "a defensible position." ROCKY laughed when he said: "Put the handcuffs on me; I'll sleep tonight"—perhaps at the contradiction in his images. ROLF said: "I wouldn't say I cannot live consistently with my principles. I say I've chosen not to and I'm morally culpable for those choices. I don't know that many of my peers would hold me responsible, but I expect future generations to hold us profoundly responsible for the damage we've done."

Our buying into cruel systems is not the same as approving of their cruelty or ourselves being cruel; but even if we are not morally wrong to buy meat, there may still be something wrong, for inconsistency is a mistake, and hypocrisy is a vice. People who care nothing about the world's evils are not inconsistent if they do nothing to stop them; but those who care cannot consistently do nothing. Those who hate the system and who want to "stop the slaughter" feel obliged (but are not obligated) to resist in some way—passively, by boycotting or actively, by protesting. Neither is morally required; but we require it of ourselves in order to become who we wish to be. In effect, we write the law we ourselves must obey.

Even if boycotting meat is not morally required, some believe it is a great moral triumph. Rynn said: "I think the act of not eating meat is a great moral achievement. The person who doesn't eat meat is doing a great deal more than one gives him credit for. I think one should give a vegetarian more credit because he's having an impact on the preservation of animals' lives—not one, but thousands and thousands of animals are spared—and he also sets an example for the community. So I think one shouldn't minimize the moral force of a vegetarian or a vegan who is content to abstain from taking animal products. I think it's easy to belittle that and magnify the achievements of the non-vegetarian philanthropist."

I agree that vegetarianism can be a "great moral achievement"; but I think vegetarians take more credit than they deserve in some ways, and not enough in others. Our diets do not stop live "stock" from dying; our boycotts do not liberate animals, much as we like to think they do. There are no happy hens or heifers enjoying their lives now because I refused to buy their flesh. At best, they were not born into the system to suffer; but even that is moot, for transnational businesses advertise to create demand and open up new markets worldwide as fast as vegetarians can say, "No more meat!" If all current vegetarians had renounced meat in concert, the industry might have noticed; but the gradual ebb and flow of our numbers hardly affects it. So we do not really, but only symbolically, "save thousands of animals" we do not eat. They are not alive and well to thank us.

If refusing animal foods does not save animal lives directly, then what good is it? It is easy to think we have done positive good with our negative actions; but if we do not save lives or change the system, then what good have we done? We do not contribute to or abet evil, so perhaps we are not responsible; but in what way are we moral?

When we have a choice, what we eat is a matter of morality in one of two senses: what we do or who it makes us into. Even more important than disassociating ourselves from violence is becoming nonviolent ourselves. There may be little or no justice in the world, but that is all the more reason to become just or fair people. We cannot act compassionately unless we are compassionate persons: to do compassionate acts is to act out of our compassion. The more often we act this way, the wider the sphere in which we practice this virtue becomes. Only a fool would think that if suddenly everyone became virtuous the world would be no different.[7] Practicing vegetarianism out of compassion may not release animals, but it creates people who ultimately will; although we may free no animal from its stall or crate, we free them from being thought about as objects. The more widely that thought circulated, the more likely that animals would be liberated.

Ethics is about ideals, not about the here and now; it is not about what is, but about some improvement upon it; it is not about what we have, but about what lies beyond us.[8] By its very nature, vegetarianism is not required by an "act ethic" telling us what we should do, but suggested by a "virtue ethic" telling us how we could be. No ethic can force us to feel what we do not feel, or to live an ideal, but it can inspire us.

If we are inspired to become compassionate, we can no longer resort to moral cocooning, thinking that as long as evil befalls others, but not us, or befalls other animals, but not us, that all is well with us, even if not right with the world.[9] We will see that what befalls one, befalls all, and that we cannot escape the pain of the world, even if we do not feel it, because the world is full of pain, and we are in the world.[10] A world which contains confinement units and cages is the world we live in whether or not we are confined or caged. Ultimately it is not meatlessness, or even boycotting, which will change the world, but it is changing ourselves, for cruelty and callousness do not exist in the world, but in us. When we are compassionate, we do not forget those out of sight and far away, for we know that in a world where there are cages, no one is truly free.

18

The Correctly Politic Vegetarian

Vegetarianism can be too easy, and can be a symbol, a beautiful symbol, like placing a flower on a grave; but perhaps more vegetarians ought to put down their flowers and take up their spades, first to uncover the brutal truth about brutal industries—and then to bury them. If we make our cause simple by thinking in symbols, we may think we don't have to struggle. The world does not need proof of our sincerity as much as it needs reproof of the meat industry.

Making others aware of what made us into vegetarians is more important than making others into vegetarians. One does not have to lead a vegetarian life to fight the meat industry. Most people buy meat, but many dislike big business and government subsidies, and almost everyone cares about the environment and health. Politically, broadcasting what goes on in the world is more important than what goes into our bodies. If we pursue anything, it should not be potential vegetarians to convert, but industries to subvert. On the buddy system, it is true, there would be twice the number of vegetarians; but vegetarians are not the only ones who hate animal exploitation and will oppose it. Lapsos show that vegetarians come and go, but this does not mean a political movement could not grow. If we join in, we should worry less about losing converts than about losing momentum.

When MICHAEL, an English citizen who has been living in Portugal, came to the United States to teach International Law in Washington, D.C. he was incredulous to find widespread ignorance about how our food animals are raised. He said: "There is a huge market in England of people who are absolutely disgusted by battery farming and would not *dream* of buying or eating a battery bird. Now then I come to the United States and I find a complete unawareness of the issue. In England, if you say, 'I prefer not to eat battery bred animals,' they will either say, 'I feel the same,' or 'Yes; I understand you. I just find sometimes it makes life awkward and difficult.' Where if you say that in the United States, most people will look at you with blank incomprehension and say, 'What's a battery reared animal?'"

In fairness to the U.S., citizenry, my own experience is that we have heard the expression "factory farming" more often than the word "battery"; but to what MICHAEL said about the general level of ignorance in this country I can attest, having taught these issues for nearly twenty years. It is fine to resist; but we also need to persist in exposing abuses.

The problem is culturally sanctioned, institutionalized cruelty, and the solution is to end it; but how do we decide what to do based on what we know and what we value? Some think the issue is diet; but the real issue is standing up to giants. Taking on the meat industry does not mean reforming it, but dismantling it. Women talk of "taking back the night"; vegetarians and other concerned citizens ought to think in terms of "taking back the food supply," decentralizing it. No more factory farms! That would not mean meatlessness, but it would be an improvement.

To be radical, Marx said, is to grasp things by the root, and rightly, for the word "radical" is rooted in the word for root. The root in this case is not the individual or even the collective actions of meat eaters but the conglomerates which produce meat. If I were the owner of a giant agribusiness corporation, I would be relieved to see that vegetarians were putting all their energy into vegetarianism and ignoring me. What if they put all that plant-based energy into embarrassing and discrediting me? What if everyone knew how the system worked, and who profited from it, who the winners were and who the losers, humans and nonhumans alike? If they advertised that, they might endanger me. Telling people about rainforest ranches and calves in crates and billions of fluffy yellow male chicks suffocated each year hurts me more than their converting a few more vegetarians.

The irony about modern meat systems is that the animals are enslaved by (and for) people who are also slaves of the system. Focusing on the farmer is like blaming the soldier for the war. Huge issues of economic and social injustice and corporate and political power underlie the meat (and egg and dairy) industries. The "other" is not the slaughterer or the omnivore; it is those who run these businesses, not those who work for or buy into them. Neither meat packers nor meat eaters are the "enemy"; the enemies are animal industries and the ideologies behind them.

ROLF said: "Vegetarianism can be isolated from other kinds of activities that are equally important, and that for me would involve things like concern with social and economic injustice among human beings and future generations of human beings." Vegetarians need to see that working for human rights—getting people out of spiritless and toxic jobs like meat packing—is necessary, for when we liberate them, we liberate animals, too. "ANIMAL LIBERATION IS HUMAN LIBERATION" has long been a slogan of the animal rights movement; but it is also true that "HUMAN LIBERATION IS ANIMAL

LIBERATION."

In capitalistic countries like ours, where citizens are consumers, subjected to the propaganda of advertising, our tastes and preferences molded to fit markets, giving the lie to the supposed relation between demand and supply is difficult; but unless we tell, people will think all is well with the farmer in the dell. People hear a buzzword like "humane slaughter" and think they do not have to bother. Not everyone wants to be an activist, but we can all be educators. Instead of telling others to be vegetarians, we should tell them what is wrong with the system: its abuses are so odious that the disabused may change on their own. As a result of showing a single film ("Down on the Factory Farm") in an Organizational Ethics class where I treated the issue as one of business ethics rather than one of animal rights, a young woman became both a vegetarian and an activist, something I would not have known had I not met up with her years later at a protest.

If we want to live in a peaceful world, we may have to fight for the right—not with bombs but with facts. The truth will set the animals free, as MICHAEL's story shows.

A Political Parable

"England is a net exporter of calves and the reason for this is that England has a big market for milk and milk products and a relatively smaller market for beef and veal. And the veal market is somewhat reduced because for a good number of years, the crate method of rearing calves has been illegal. It's been illegal for years and years and years. Veal—the so-called 'milk fed veal' reared in crates—can be imported into England in small quantities, but the demand is not great.

"So what's been happening is that calves have been exported from England to the European continent where the crate method is not illegal, and where they are raised in crates after often being transported for many, many hours without food or water. They die on the way and so forth. Now *officially* this export cannot be limited in any way because England is a member of the European Community and there is free movement of goods just like there is in the United States from one state to another.

"For the last several months, there have been riots in England directed against one ferry company across the channel. (The companies transport people and goods across the channel to France, Belgium, or Holland, and also to Germany.) And the sit-ins, demonstrations, riots, political action has been aimed at getting the ferrying companies to stop carrying calves. And they have succeeded. It is now virtually impossible to transport calves across the channel. England is being very active in the European Community in trying to get a solution for what is seen as a problem—and the solution they are pushing for is banning the crate method in Europe and also including strict laws on the number of hours that animals can be transported without food or water.

"Interestingly, it's a north/south divide in Europe. The northern European countries are perfectly happy with regard to food and water and having I think about eight hours between stops—eight hours for food, water, and so forth. And the southern European countries where the tradition is that you treat animals simply as a commodity and the idea of worrying about cruelty to animals is preposterous, all are fighting against this attempt by the northerners, particularly by the English, who are seen as being preposterously soft and sloppy about animals. So there you have the story."

Just being vegetarian, while not as dramatically effective as political action, does change us, and we do change the world, slowly, just by being in it; but if we want results at a faster pace, boycott works better than diet. We could at least let the truth be known: if the English had never heard of veal crates, crates would not now be illegal in England. I did not become an activist because of any moral argument or because I knew any vegetarians, but because I read about factory farms. Initially, my vegetarianism was not spiritual, but political; I boycotted meat as I had, a few years earlier, boycotted table grapes.

Becoming a vegetarian is a step, but if small steps to a worthy goal are good, are not large ones even better? The radical does not want a world where there are larger cages or even empty cages, but a world where there are no cages at all. Should we reform or abolish? Reformers who want to ameliorate rather than eradicate might do more harm than good, not for individual animals whose conditions might improve, but by helping the system to engulf more animals. If people thought veal calves were more comfortable, they might buy more veal.

For the abolitionist, it is a straw issue and a question-begging one to argue (as does Frey) that if we want animals to have straw bedding, we ought to get them straw bedding, and that simply refusing to eat them does not make them more comfortable.[1] Only if our end is reform does this make sense. It is a version of what I call "The Doggie in the Window Dilemma." If we buy one poor puppy, saving him from the cage, he benefits; but the puppy mill churns out another puppy. Atomistically, we did right by one doggie, but wrong holistically by encouraging the store to order more. If we love animals, we move in one direction, and if we hate the system, we move in another. Thus it is difficult for an activist to decide whether to be a welfarist or an abolitionist—especially when welfare is more likely to produce results. But even if we move in different directions, we could converge on the system.

Vegetarianism alone is not the best way to protest because if we practice it badly, we can lose more than we gain, and it is not the only way to protest, because omnivores can fight, too. Nor is vegetarianism enough, for many practice it in quietude, not adding to the problems, but not working for solutions either. While not "politically correct" in all their gestures, omnivores, like MICHAEL, who is a lawyer, can be useful, and activists, no matter what their diet, could do more for animals than those concerned only with meatless meals, for their riots could topple giants. Thus vegetarians should not divide the world into "us" and "others."

Being vegetarian can be a metaphor for our lives and can inspire us; we can borrow Shaw's image of being followed to grave by all the animals we did not eat;[2] but we need to remember that most of those animals ended up in the graves of other people's stomachs and so were not saved at all. If we want to "STOP THE SLAUGHTER" or to "LIBERATE ANIMALS," there is more we can do than just refuse to eat them.

By being a vegetarian and doing no more, we can waste energy which could be put into useful activity. Think of all the time spent making sure our soy cheese contains no traces of casein, or our veggie patties no iota of albumen. It is one thing to refuse to bring home the bacon, but another to labor over labels lest we take a minuscule amount of some bad thing home. We could match the time we spend reading labels with work to prevent animals from becoming the products behind the labels.

We can put much energy into studying nutrition, keeping our hands clean, and trying to conform; but perhaps we should worry less about what we put into our bodies and more about what is happening in the world. (There are activists so busy doing good works that they do not even notice what they eat.) Vegetarianism can be an exercise in vanity and a kind of narcissism: we may regard our slim shapes and clear complexions with no regard for fattened animals dying with clearly pained expressions.

About factory farming, LEONARD said: "There's nothing much I can do about it; I don't condone it." But he is wrong. As an organic farmer; as the owner of a health food store which stocks "stock" which is "free-range" and organic (not best, but better); as a competitor against big business, always supporting the small and ethical; as a reader of magazines like *Acres,*[3] sharing everything he knows, he is doing much to stand up against the industry. And so can we.

We do not wish to contribute to harms with our money and so we boycott meat. Thus we avoid harm-money, but we can also achieve a harmony by joining with omnivores. If we stop ambushing them at table, and treating them as outsiders elsewhere, they might at least boycott factory farmed meat. If we leave them alone in one way, we might work together in another. Our educating others must stop short of telling them what they must eat, for this is too much like telling them whom they should love. Instead of embarrassing omnivores for eating meat, we should meet on common ground to embarrass the meat industry.

GAIL said: "In a perfect world, if I had time to do everything I wanted, I'd study and work for legislation for kind treatment of animals. I get angry thinking about inhumane treatment of animals: it's not necessary. We don't have to do that. I think of that as one of the bad facets of humanity—that we can just get callous like that. That's a side of humanity that I *don't* like: 'Let's not feed them any [of] this, and if they peck their neighbors because they don't have enough iron, let's cut off their beaks. It's just to make a little better bottom line. That's why I stayed in this business. I like the idea of supporting a little more of an altruistic way of being on the planet. I like having my life contribute to that movement, in that direction."

The vegetarian movement, unfortunately, closes out the conscientious omnivore, and perhaps for the same reasons, loses its vegetarians. Because people are leaving, it is more important to know why there are former vegetarians than to know why some people never become vegetarians at all. It is easy to believe that non-vegetarians know not what they do; but lapsos have seen the glare (of the battery house) and the darkness (of the veal barn). It is easy to think that so-called "pre-vegetarians" have not had previews of coming detractions; but former vegetarians have seen the whole horror show and have gone back to eating the horrors.

What they knew could not keep them because it is not knowledge alone that makes vegetarians: there is a gap between seeing (and even believing) and assent. Because a philosophy of life like vegetarianism is personal, we must have our own reasons to live it. Likewise, there are personal reasons for leaving it: some no longer wish to be associated with vegetarianism or feel uncomfortable with the label. Understanding lapsos can help political vegetarians and social activists plan their strategies. Former vegetarians are in a unique position to teach, for they know what we know but do not do what we do. We need not expend energy educating them: it is they who should educate us. If we shield ourselves from their reasons for leaving, we will not be telling the whole truth about vegetarianism.

Unfortunately, vegetarians are somewhat less than welcoming and see differences where there are similarities. Readers' responses to Drew DeSilver's courageous *Vegetarian Times* article on former vegetarians drew complaints. Although one reader, a near vegetarian, called it "outstanding"; "accepting"; "non-judgmental"; "open-minded"; and "accurate"[4] another said, "I was outraged by your January article . . . What a slap in the face to pick up this issue and find such an article . . ."[5] Another wrote, "upon opening your latest issue, I couldn't believe my eyes. My *vegetarian* magazine had printed an article called 'Putting Meat Back on Their Menu.' To say I'm appalled would be an understatement. Publishing that article in *Vegetarian Times* is like the National Rifle Association publishing an article with the headline 'Why All Guns Should Be Destroyed . . .' This article has no place in a magazine dedicated to those of us who choose a meatless diet."[6]

But according to Amy Clark, promotions manager for *Vegetarian Times,* 56% of the magazine's 325,000 readers are not vegetarian.[7] JOHN, a former vegetarian who says he is still convinced by the philosophical arguments for vegetarianism, but who lapses for reasons of convenience said: "We still subscribe to *Vegetarian Times,* strangely enough, or maybe not so strangely." It is unfortunate that vegetarians want vegetarianism all to themselves. The vegetarian movement would have more of a following if we shared it. Just as one does not have to be a vegetarian to enjoy vegetarian food (as three recent cookbooks, *The Occasional Vegetarian, The Almost Vegetarian,* and *The Gradual Vegetarian* suggest)[8] one does not have to be a vegetarian to want many of the things that vegetarians want.

Business people have a practical sense of things which philosophers are often lacking. According to Carole Sugarman, *Vegetarian*

Times "is going after the quasi vegetarian crowd"[9]—to sell them magazines. This large "crowd" is part of the vegetarian family and should not be excluded from it on technicalities. If the magazine wants them, so should we, not because we want their money, but because together we could do more to save the world.

The vegetarian movement needs diversity, but ironically, some degree of conformity as well—and therein lies the danger. Coalitions and organizations facilitate social change; we probably won't get what we want unless there is a movement and there won't be a movement unless people conform. Yet the kind of person an organization needs is not the best kind of person we can be: it is best to be open, and conforming can close us. Even when their ends are noble, political movements are not always healthy for people, and themselves lose vitality without variety. What starts as inspiration can become catechism: vegetarianism is in trouble if vegetarians are not flexible.

The vegetarian movement needs discourse most of all; without diversity, it loses integrity. Vegetarianism needs to be regenerated constantly out of dialogue if it is to remain resilient and strong; otherwise, it will be uprooted by a new fad, new medical knowledge, or a new political movement. We should not all be of one mind. At a vegetarian conference in 1994, four hundred vegetarians burst spontaneously into applause when it was announced that a giant food corporation was now marketing a new vegetarian burger. (The big businesses think: If we can't sell them beef, we'll sell them beef analogues.) As far as I could see (or hear) I was the only one to remain silent. Meat analogues are fine and should be widely available, but should they not come from businesses which are ethical, the small competitors, not trucking literally or figuratively with meat? We need to debate this.

JOHN said: "When I see people so passionately one-sided about something, it always makes me want to stand back somewhat." Many vegetarians would shudder at examples of political or religious fervor, closed minds and persecution; but many in fact practice how they wish others would not preach. Whenever a platform provides

---

simple answers or becomes a single issue, we should beware. Vegetarianism needs dialogue, not indoctrination, dialectic, not heretics. Vegetarians need to see that people working for Amnesty International (while eating some meat) are moving in the same direction as we. Working for peace is a broader issue than peaceful diet—and it is hard to feel peaceful if we fear violating dietary taboo.

Too often vegans set themselves apart from vegetarians and vegetarians from omnivores; but if we could erase lines of demarcation, identifying ourselves, perhaps, as "against modern meat," our numbers would swell. The contributors to this book, at least, should erase the stereotypes of what flesh eaters are like. Think of what a revitalized movement including such people could do!

Vegetarian societies should welcome the views of those critical of vegetarianism, and vegetarian journals should publish them. A philosopher at a vegetarian conference is bound to suffer, not at the healthful lunches and suppers, but from the absence of healthy debate. Critics are not invited and the messages are the same: it is a bit like being in church. But as philosophers should listen to "unreasonable" people, vegetarians should listen to omnivores, not because they are unreasonable, but because we cannot understand ourselves or our positions until we understand them and theirs. Fires of disagreement may ignite, but in their light we will be able to see better. One hunt saboteur I know subscribes to *Outdoor Life* (which he calls "Outdoor Death")[10] for just this reason. We should read *Meat Magazine* as well as *Vegetarian Voice*.

It is easy to think that anyone with our knowledge would be like us, or that only vegetarianism is rational. JONATHAN said: "I felt it was pretty disgusting to be eating meat, and all I could do was hope that this was going to be a movement and eventually create mass converts to vegetarianism. To me, it just seemed the most logical thing to do: anyone who would think about a situation would see that we can't be killing animals for food."

Poets in literary guilds do not ask everyone to write verses; flower fanciers in garden clubs do not tell everyone to grow roses; but vegetarians often want a world with only vegetarians in it. But should the vegetarian mission be a world without omnivores—or a world without oppression? Even JONATHAN, who thought the assent to vegetarianism was a matter of logic, also saw that even near vegetarians would change the world. He said: "If everybody was eating the small amounts of fish that I do, the impact would be so much less. It's still helpful. If eventually everyone became a vegetarian and ate fish a few times a month, it would be a better world than not making any changes." Whether "pesco-vegetarians" are vegetarians is not the issue: changing the world is. The issue is not converting people to vegetarianism: it is achieving the ends of the vegetarian movement.

Adopting vegetarianism as a way of life is the symbolic side of meatlessness: it is like wearing an armband to show solidarity. But symbolic gestures can turn into an energy sink of being "politically correct." At conferences, for example, all are in cotton, and none in silk, although most cotton is sprayed heavily with insecticide which kills individual animals. Silk also kills individual animals, presumably as they sleep unaware in their cocoons (in a kind of worm abortion) so arguably in a way which causes less suffering and certainly far less environmental damage, especially in closed-loop systems based on fish, ponds, mulberry trees, and worms. But vegetarians are often more interested in solidarity than subtlety, in the symbol rather than the actual. Subsistence beekeepers are decried, but agriculturists who grow our grains, fruits, and vegetables are spared, even though they may spray to protect their yields.

We can fool ourselves with food, feeling good about what we avoid. We may drink coffee without cream and feel benign, for there is no ghostly flesh floating in the mug; but coffee plantations displace forests, and all their fauna is floating there invisibly with the caffeine. Coffee is not a symbol, like milk is, but it could be. There is even ambiguity in bread: when the threshers come for the yield, they also come for field mice and voles, and caterpillars who will never be butterflies. It is not a catcher who comes through the rye, but a grim reaper, harvesting that organic grain.

It is a nuisance when we talk about vegetarianism and people look at our shoes, ready to discredit us so they can discount our views. This is illogical; but it is how the world works, so there is pressure to conform. Vegetarians often herd together for social safety like the animals they collectively replace with rice and soy, thinking that with a dozen symbolic gestures (no silk, no wool, no leather . . .) they are all they can be or doing all they can do. But our symbols, which make us feel spiritual, can give us excuses not to change the world, excuses not to do more, excuses to polarize our thinking, and excuses to feel good about ourselves. Our symbols can stifle us and slow our progress.

Vegetarians may convene in plastic shoes instead of leather, unaware that they play two sets of criteria against each other. Respect for individual animal life is one parameter; the impact of non-renew-able "resources" on nature (and hence on animals in nature) is an-other. ROLF claimed: "I have never had intense moral convictions about eating animals," and added, "What I was thinking about is the whole ethical question [of] holistic vs. individual ethics. My inclina-tion is toward a holistic ethics." We might see ROLF in leather shoes and judge him unfairly, not knowing he teaches eco-philosophy and how close to vegetarianism he is. Likewise, we might catch KIVA, NANCY, or BARBARA eating chicken, or ELLY eating beef, but miss their vegetarian philosophies. We might fault FRANK, PETER, or MICHAEL for eating what swims or flies, but not realize why they refuse to eat four-legged "landflesh." We may begrudge DAVID his pork or TONY his lamb, but not know that each is on his way back to vegetarianism.

KIVA said: "If they're a meat eater, they think you're a fanatic, that you'd risk your life for the sake of a cow." It is the unthinking conformity among many vegetarians that creates this social stereo-type. But we can distinguish the myopic fanatic from the visionary radical. The fanatic wears blinders and has tunnel vision, seeing only the side that is her own. The radical may also overzealously pursue consistency, but does so to get to the roots of things: for the radical, consistency is a tool, like Descartes' methodological doubt, and not a goal. So when a radical digs in her heels and won't let go, or holds a position to its extreme limits, it is more like finding borders, seeing just where they are, than creating boundaries which obstruct the flow of discourse.

Vegetarians can have small minds and live in small worlds, but the more open-minded we are, the better (and bigger) the world will be. Vegetarianism is not for everyone; it is not a moral mandate, but something we must take on faith, and to keep any faith alive, we must doubt or question it if only a little bit, for otherwise it will turn into certainty, or zealotry, and then ossify, an ironic situation for vegetarians who eat nothing on bones. The beauty of vegetarianism is that it is not required: when it is practiced out of peacefulness, it is a gift we bestow upon the world. It is our way of bringing value into it, but others may have their own ways: if we are blind to their truths, how can we be students of the universe? If we want to liberate animals, we must first liberate ourselves: if we shackle ourselves to our beloved ideas, how can we be free?

19

Eating Animals Again

"The food was silent and rigid.
Bathed in its own broth.

And tinged slightly with regret, as spice.
I have now become meat,

it would have said."

—Richard Grossman

There is a difference between eating animals as we always have and eating them again, after we have been vegetarian. Those who were never vegetarian usually know little about the life and death history of whom they eat. They do not know what the beings were like, what they suffered, or of what they were deprived before they became supper. All is a blur—the faces, the eyes, the cries, the brutal feel of the system, the push and pull of the speed of production, the lack of commiseration (and sometimes the sadism), the commodification of animal life. As unaware as confined animals are of the world outside, they only want to eat in peace pieces of animals who neither lived nor died that way.

But lapsos know: they ate unforbidden fruit and forbade themselves flesh knowing too much about it. They found reasons for vegetarianism, and may agree with them still, yet they eat animals again. KIVA said: "When you're a vegan, you stop seeing animals as food; then you start seeing other animals as food." It may be difficult to fathom, for once we have come to see in two ways, we cannot pretend there is only one. First we see meat as just food, but then as from animals; thus we can never see meat as just food again. "Now you see it, now you don't" implies that sometimes we do see it.

Yet even lapsos try not to see it. INGRID said: "I ordered delicious white perch which came out whole with white pins where the eyes would be. They put the plate down with the fish staring at me. I chose to turn it around." When we return to meat, we turn around, or we turn the animal around: we cannot "face" each other. What Carol Adams calls "the absent referent"[1] must be out of sight as well as out of mind if it is going to go into our bodies.

When we eat animals again, we cannot deny as others do—although we may try to. KIVA said: "I still have a problem with it. I tried to prepare it once. My boyfriend bought a whole chicken and I tried to lift it up, and my whole body shook and I couldn't even eat it. So there's still denial because it was a carcass." As a vegetarian, VICKY excused flesh eaters on the grounds that "they didn't really think of what they were doing. They didn't think of meat as a former animal. They didn't think about the way it was treated or the quality of its life; they just didn't question the social norm." When lapsos return to meat, they return to the norm—but they do not unequivocally accept it.

When we eat animals again, we know it is animals we are eating, and that each was once a who, even if we do not know just who it is we are eating. Lapsos who eat animals in full knowledge often do so with deep regret. KIVA said: "Even now, when I eat animal protein, I have a really hard time and usually go through a period of depression right after I eat it because I feel like it's in my body; I don't like the idea of meat inside my body. It's a very large experience whenever I eat it; I have to really psyche myself up. I don't think I *can* eat [meat] casually. I don't think I'll ever be able to do that because I can't divorce meat from death."

We can suffer because we know—and because we don't know. DAVID said: "I think that for most of us the relationship to meat—if we really start to look at it—is a painful experience"; but DAVID feels less pain realizing he sustains himself in ways which cause suffering than he feels for people who are insensitive to animal suffering. He said: "Those people are really suffering; there is a sense of needing to reach out to them because they are suffering." Thus what we don't know can hurt us, although not as much as animals hurt in order to feed us.

What we know can also change us, and sometimes incline us again toward vegetarianism. DAVID said: "I think someday I will be a strict vegetarian. In a complex world that's so *troubled,* I have a lot of respect for people who have tried to direct their way to what has some kind of healing effect on the world, and I think, in principle, vegetarianism does that. Life is so complex. There's a lot of pain in life. One of the reasons I'm attracted to vegetarianism is an appreciation of [this]. I think I'll be drawn once again to vegetarian lifestyle. I'm moving in a direction where vegetarianism would be a really joyous thing for me, when it would be a really joyous thing for me to be vegetarian. It will bring a sense of lightness and joy to eat vegetarian food again."

If we eat animals again, we can be vegetarian again. Lapsos are less tied to meat than other omnivores are, and say if they go back to vegetarianism, it will be in a different way. TONY said: "I think I will return to a *type* of vegetarianism for myself." KIVA said: "I'm still battling with my ethical part and I think it's quite possible that I'll be vegan again, but it won't be like, 'I'm VEGAN now." For lapsos, the decision to eat animals again is not a firm one, but one open to revision—like their vegetarianism.

Because vegetarians are not just people who eat no meat, when they return to meat they may still embrace a vegetarian philosophy, and so differ greatly from those who were never vegetarian at all. Thus the titles "lapsed vegetarian"; "former vegetarian"; or "ex-vegetarian" are appropriate to distinguish them. ROLF said: "My *attitude* hasn't changed since I started on this path. My convictions haven't changed. I think it's best to eat a vegetarian diet." JONATHAN saw "nothing wrong with the fundamental tenets of vegetarianism or of veganism for that matter." JOHN said that although he is "no longer as far out on the philosophical limb," when he looks at vegetarianism "in a distant light and from an appreciable distance, when the option appears, it appears as a higher option." Thus lapsos may keep on one level a connection they have broken on another.

Significantly, lapsos do not become lovers of meat when they again become eaters of it: none ate meat in a passionate way, choosing it solely for its sensual pleasure. Although LEONARD mentioned the "exquisite flavor" of some fresh organic beef, he was appraising the meat, putting it to the test, rather than simply enjoying its zest. He said: "Everybody has their own feeling about life. To me, eating meat is not enjoying life." TONY did find his mother's lamb "delicious," but never spoke of lusting for flesh itself. Although ELLY never lost her taste for meat, other benefits decided her and the other former vegetarians. ROBBAN, KIVA, and LINDA said that meat "felt right" in their bodies, although not all felt right about eating meat: to like eating meat is not the same as liking the meat we eat.

Even those with the most positive attitudes toward meat (like ROCKY who sears it on his backyard grill or TONY who eats "charred flesh") were also repulsed by some forms of it, and all differed markedly from gourmets who can take pleasure in what they know was produced with pain. It strikes me as a kind of perversion to feel ecstasy eating *pâté de foie gras*, lobster or veal, or a crab eviscerated alive, but there are some who do. No lapso relished animal flesh: none craved the savor, the texture, or the mouthfeel of meat. No one chose meat for its *flavor*. Frey, a philosopher who says we "take great pleasure" in "meat dishes," laments that if vegetarians have their way: "Gone forever will be *petto di pollo all crema, scaloppine zingara, saltimbocca romana, coda vaccinara, carré d'agneau paloise, tournedos Rossini, filet de boef poivre à la façon du Moulin, lapin bonne femme, dinde à la creme, médallions de veau biscayenne, entrecôte bourguignonne, mutton tikka, chicken tandoori, regan gosht, sheftalia, moussaka,* and *Peking duck.*"[2]

All this sounds elegant, but it's a cover-up for rabbits and birds and baby cows. (Perhaps this is why the French are famous for their sauces.) Perhaps Frey ought to sample KEN's "cuisine mirage" to see if he could savor the illusion as much as the real thing. As we wear faux pearls, we could eat faux animals, with the same flourish and with the same fine wines. Gourmet dining is, after all, with its linen tablecloths and candlelight, just another illusion. While some do find (real) meat really delicious, and scoff at the idea of a tofu "steak," lapsos stand out in sharp relief from gourmets and gourmands: the contrast is as startling as the difference between boiling lobsters and boiling corn.

While the retronym "real meat" should inspire vegetarians, the opportunity to replace the real thing can appeal to both vegetarians and former vegetarians. LEONARD said: "It looked like a beef stew, but it was red potatoes and onions and rutabagas in a gravy—a vegetable gravy. It was at someone's house. There was no meat on the table—no meats or eggs. It wasn't even on the table, so I was very happy with that." Fake steaks and ersatz goulash may please LEONARD and other lapsos who differ from the omnivore forever who does not ever want to be fooled.

The contrast between the forever-omnivore and the former vegetarian also shows in the language lapsos use to describe eating meat. When people feel reverent toward the animals they consume, they often use the expression "taking into my body" (BARBARA spoke of "taking in the flesh"), language which suggests welcoming, a warm greeting, sheltering, a bird taking a nestling under her wing. When we incorporate animals in this way, we do not destroy them but (symbolically) give them a home in us: this is not a violent act. This is close to SIANNA's vision, "Eat me, but love me first!" To eat an animal could be to rob it of its life, or to give it the gift of being incorporated into the human, as SIANNA suggests.

Construing meat symbolically involves philosophy. Former vegetarians are in a unique position to articulate omnivorism as a philosophy of life, for as they once thought philosophically about vegetarianism, they could now think philosophically about omnivorism, making explicit the principles implicit in their practice.

Such a philosophy of life might also be derived from environmental or nature philosophy, from the philosophy of biology or ecology, from a theory of the wild, or from mystical religion. Any view of the world which sees reality as the interpenetration of being could be its core.

What if there were a philosophy of omnivorism? There is a practice, but no principles, no theory. Buddhists and others have philosophies compatible with omnivorism; but there is no omnivorean way of life as there is a vegetarian way of life. We may practice *ahimsa* and peacefulness by not eating animals; but omnivores may eat them to celebrate being in the world or even to practice an idealistic way of living based on how they see reality. ROLF said: "I very much think of myself as simply a part of a much vaster natural system that's been here a long time before I came and will be here a long time afterward, and I try not to think of myself as very separate from that. I like to emphasize the interconnectedness between myself and all other beings."

FRANK sees this in terms of the "re-cycling of molecules." Lawrence Shamblin, in a letter to *Tricycle*, agrees, and sees what the basis for an omnivorean philosophy could be: ". . . it may include animals in a vision of life in which eating and being eaten are all part of the same dance of 'interbeing.' It may express an attitude toward life full of reverence and respect, and which takes into account the necessary sacrifice of one life to another. It may be a view that celebrates animals as food for humans as well as humans as food for animals, including vultures and parasites and worms in the ground."[3]

FRANK saw how a philosophy of omnivorism could be compatible with certain ways of eating human flesh. He said: "In Heinlein's *Stranger in a Strange Land*, that character, the human who was brought up on an imaginary Mars by imaginary Martians—sort of a reverse feral child—to him, if somebody dies, you all ate the person so as to become part of him, so it was a very intense, moving, and beautiful ritual. It's possible to view meat eating as an aggressive act, or it could be a beautiful 'thank you' for absorbing this fellow creature of God."

TONY said: "You saw people who eat meat as voracious predators, but at other times you realized it's not that way at all." Although Rynn thinks meat eaters "satisfy their lower, baser needs" and that meat eating is a "capitulation," joking that "in ten years [the lapsos] will all either be raw foodists or cannibals," others are more reverent, like BARBARA who said that when she eats meat "a sacrifice has been made for my life."

Because meat eating involves not only meat eaters but also those eaten, a philosophy of omnivorism would have to go beyond our attitudes: simply saying a prayer of peace over obscenely produced meat would be a mockery. A philosophy of omnivorism, if as idealistic as vegetarianism, would require that meat be provided (not "produced") *lovingly*. If "humane slaughter" is an oxymoron, then no animals could be slaughtered. No matter how reverent we may feel about meat, because meat producers do not feel reverent about producing it, it is not enough that on the receiving end there is thankfulness and love, for on the disassembly line, where meat is made like machinery, there is only cold efficiency and a lack of commiseration. No philosophy of omnivorism could justify this meat.

In theory, omnivores could practice their philosophy as idealistically as vegetarians practice their vegetarianism. The vegetarian issue could be revitalized if omnivores articulated their ideals. The converse of vegetarianism is not, after all, meat eating, but a way of life which justifies it. At present, the debate is between those with principles and those who practice; but how can a mere practice stand up to principles? The practice of omnivorism needs principles of its own for balance. Omnivorean principles could put vegetarian ideals into perspective as ideals among other ideals, not as ideals in a wasteland of blind actions.

At present, however, omnivores have few options to live an idealistic philosophy. Although some buy organically "produced" meat from animals who are slaughtered, they would come closer by eating the flesh of animals who died on their own, or perhaps the flesh of animals hunted when they are past their prime. Leaving aside the ethics of engineering animals, and for the sake of argument only, we could imagine creating a very small number of food animals who lived out full spans of life in freedom with others of their kind, and then at a pre-appointed time, instantly dropped dead at just that moment when their own natural (arguably more painful) dying process was about to begin. Vegetarians would prefer that we engineer steaks rather than steers, but on theoretical omnivorean grounds, the issue is worth debating.

AVA said: "We all sacrifice for each other; it is the nature of life"; but whatever else it involved, a philosophy of omnivorism would rule out hurting the world for our food. Even though "life lives off life," we do not have to live off of obscenities. Killing and eating are not in themselves obscene:[4] restraining, mutilating, confining, fattening, and "finishing" are. If we believe that life lives off life, and that "in order to prosper" (as DAVID put it) we must eat some meat, we must determine what sort of meat would be natural and respectful to eat. Life does not, after all, live off of torturing and demeaning: nature does not work by de-naturing. If we want to feel at home in the world, or want to remain in our home, the world, by eating some flesh, we ought to see how flesh is eaten in that world we want to be part of.

An omnivorean philosophy would not sanction eating the flesh of animals "produced" for profit: others profiting has nothing to do with our prospering (and indeed threatens it). KIVA said: "I have no problem with people eating meat in an ethical way," implying that there is an unethical way to eat meat. All is not fair for daily fare. As philosophical omnivores, we could no more eat factory farmed meat in an ethical way than we could keep a slave and treat him kindly. We could buy a slave and treat him kindly by freeing him; but we cannot own a slave and treat him kindly, because treating others kindly excludes owning them as slaves. If the omnivorean philosophy were, like vegetarianism, based on respect for individual animal life, animals could be neither owned nor slaughtered.

An omnivorean philosophy could be based on compassion, as

is vegetarianism: in that case, conscientious omnivores would be reduced to eating either carrion or mercy deaths (or perhaps flesh bequeathed by dead relatives). But it could also be based on holism, subordinating the value of the individual animal to the value of an eco-system. (Such thinking led ROLF to eating venison.) In that case, it would not be the animal we loved, but nature. An omnivorean philosophy based on holism would sanction respectfully hunting healthy animals for food; an omnivorean philosophy based on compassion would not. A holistically based omnivorism could be as idealistic as vegetarianism, but not as compassionate. Omnivorism could be based on holism or on compassion—but it cannot be based on both.

We can respect animals we hunt for food, but we cannot be compassionate toward them, even if we are concerned to ensure them a "clean" death. Although we say we "feel" compassion, compassion is very different from pity. We can feel sorry for animals, yet kill them for food; but we cannot be compassionate toward animals and kill them for reasons other than their own good. If we are compassionate, we can kill only out of mercy and ideally with consent, implied or expressed. We can slaughter food animals swiftly; we can reduce pain and fear; but if this is "humane," it says more about humanity than about loving-kindness.

We cannot kill animals for our ends out of compassion; but we can experience pity, sorrow, and a soft heart. Buddhists claim to take "painful responsibility" for the suffering of beings they eat with "broken heart" and "knowing mind";[5] but to suffer with the animals is to have sympathy for them, and not compassion toward them. In our culture where most people eat animals primarily for enjoyment and not out of necessity, we may feel bad for the animals or feel sorry that their deaths were the precondition for our pleasures; but we cannot be compassionate toward them because compassion, like love, involves an I-Thou relationship and an empathetic understanding which rules out using others for our ends.

Compassion is not a warm, mushy feeling, but a disposition; it is a way of being, not a soft emotion. It is not a sentiment, but a value we bring to life and into the world when we respect lives other than our own. We may feel sickened or upset watching something die, or be deprived, or otherwise made to suffer; but we are not compassionate until we are predisposed to act on its behalf. If we are compassionate, we help the animal; we do not just feel bad watching it suffer.[6]

NANCY said: "I can't even watch a program on TV that shows an animal suffering; it's very hard on me." NANCY wanted to live in a way which spared animals pain; but then her own suffering, and compassion for her own body, like the body of any other animal, led her back to eating meat. Is she compassionate or merely sentimental? Would she intervene, like ROCKY who gently carries insects out of his house or like FRANK who saved the caterpillar from the weed whacker? The thought of animal suffering is hard for her to bear, yet she sells organically raised meats in her store. What does she (or any of us) owe animals out of the softness of our hearts?

"LOVE ANIMALS DON'T EAT THEM" is an animal rights slogan; but it does not mandate vegetarianism. Although our love cannot turn animals into vegetables, or spare their bodies pain, if we practice omnivorism out of compassion or loving-kindness, there would be some (albeit little) meat we could eat. If we all acted lovingly, the world would be sweet, even if that meant that some would eat meat, for gone would be the veal barn and the farrowing stall, the battery cage and the battered raceway fish, the separation of mother and young, confining, degradation, and early death. Gone would be all forms of exploitation and oppression. The only animal flesh available would be from those who died naturally or were killed mercifully as they approached old age and death (something like ELLY's "Chicken Old Age Home" without the Home.) If small amounts of flesh were provided lovingly, then arguments against it, which vegetarians sometimes put forward hatefully, would lose their force, for we could not lovingly inflict pain, damage the environment, or violate rights.

Even if animals have a right not to be killed, we do not have to be vegetarian unless animals have a right not to be eaten; so omnivorism could be articulated on the basis of some of the same principles which seem to demand vegetarianism. I do not wish to expose fallacies in the vegetarian philosophy—only ambiguities. One can embrace a vegetarian philosophy without being a vegetarian, and one can eat meatless meals without being a vegetarian. It is good and good for us to remember that moral ambiguity is as healthy as healthful meals.

As a child, I ate my mother's organic vegetables fertilized with manure from a family friend's mink farm: I can think of no better image for ambiguity. Today many "ethical" vegetarians eat organic produce, like LINDA's , fertilized with manure from factory farms. The same person who buys into the system in one way feels superior to those who buy into it in another; but the line is thin. If we will have nothing to do with violence, we refuse factory farmed meat—but can we buy organic vegetables? One of the riddles of the vegetarian debate is: Why is the vegetarian debate riddled with ambiguities? The answer is that the difference between vegetarianism and a philosophically articulated omnivorism may be almost negligible.

There is also ambiguity in attitudes. Thirty years ago, I helped a young Israeli visitor break her life-long fast from pork. She begged me to cook bacon, just so she could "taste" it; I fried a whole package, and she ate the entire pound. At the time, I felt I was corrupting her; being young and extremely ignorant, I even took a little guilty pleasure in this. In robbing her of something sacred, I felt power, perhaps, in watching the smashing of an idol. In those days I was carnivorous, cerebral, and crisp, with no sense of the spiritual whatsoever. Looking back, I find much more wrong with what I did than with what she did, even though she was the one eating the meat, for in serving it to her, I acted in a self-serving manner, while she acted out of naive and innocent curiosity. If the pig blames anybody, it should be me, for my attitude. Everywhere there is ambiguity: not what we eat but how we live is the issue.

If we wish not to hurt the world (and/or to heal it) suddenly our lives are filled with many choices. We could articulate omnivorism on the basis of nonviolence; but some say that eating flesh *makes* us violent, no matter how the flesh is procured. If it does, should we choose to eat any meat? Even if flesh eating affects us if we eat it often, because a philosophical omnivore would eat flesh seldom there is not a problem—although there might be for some. On Earth Day, 1995, a student who had heard of my research approached me at the university before I gave my speech. He was, like KEN, a (former) former vegetarian—for just this reason. When he returned to meat, he "could not control his anger" and became "volatile and short-tempered." Frightened by this, he soon returned to a vegetarian diet which he said restored his peacefulness. Soldiers are fed meat rations supposedly to incite them to combat. If it is true, as ROBBAN says, that meat eating raises testosterone levels, and that increased testosterone levels can lead to aggression, then eating little or no meat could contribute to peace on earth. If "men in high places" forswore meat, then perhaps there would be a world with neither high nor low places in it. As Plato made stringent demands on the Guardians and on the Philosopher King in his *Republic*, perhaps we would be wise to make meatlessness a prerequisite for political office![7]

Whether or not meat eating makes us violent, eating some meat, even if it is tied to violence at its source, does not: saints, as VICKY saw, leave behind them a better world whether or not they eat meat. It can also be argued that vegetarianism is not the only way to act out of compassion for animals. If we believe we must return to meat, our initial compassion might be expressed in other ways: refusing to eat flesh is not the only way to love animals. If we wish to become more spiritual, we could find a more spiritual way to be a vegetarian—or even a spiritual way to be an omnivore.

What JONATHAN calls the "spiritual charge" of vegetarianism can diminish and need to be replenished in some way. He said: "There was an initial burst of power that I got from switching because it's such a transformation of thought and feeling; one just changes so dramatically in such a transforming way and that alone has such a charge to it. Now that my vegetarianism is old-hat habitual, I can't get the same spiritual charge out of it that I used to, and I have to look at other aspects of my life to get that, out of good works and actual spiritual practice."

Many lapsos channel their idealism into good works, for all their initial sensitivity may still be there, and have to go somewhere. Former vegetarians may do more for animals than some present ones, because, like VICKY, they want to *do* something, while vegetarians think they are already doing enough, overestimating, perhaps, the positive good they do with their negative actions. DAVID said: "If we live in a way that glorifies God, one of the consequences of that is changing the way we live, because we become sensitive to how deep our steps implant into the ground, how much we are consuming, how much we are hurting the world."

How we are vegetarian evolves with our insights. Vegetarianism is not perfect and may fail us by making promises it cannot possibly keep—to ensure perfect health, or to make us pure. It might seem to promise animal liberation or an end to animal exploitation in our lifetime, but these it cannot easily deliver. It may tempt us with a vision of peace on earth, or with special spiritual benefits; but it is not so easy. If we want a nonviolent world, we must make ourselves nonviolent and work for peace in whatever ways we can. We need to discover what about the world wounds us most deeply and set to work resolving that. If animal abuse, "the slaughter of the innocents," hurts us the most, then it makes sense to become vegetarian. If we are moved instead by the horrors of political oppression, we may find that our work takes us to a country where to be healthy we must eat some flesh; but we would be moving in the same direction as the vegetarian, even if not on the same road, for oppression of humans and other animals springs from the same flawed systems of belief.

When we live our ideals, we are guided by them in certain directions, and are not moved by our preferences willy-nilly. If we eat animals again we should be conscious, like KIVA, who said simply: "I didn't just think it was O.K. and I didn't have to think about it anymore." If compassion is one of our ideals, we may wish to express it toward animals by not eating them, or by refusing to eat any who were slaughtered or killed solely for our use. We may express our spirituality by choosing meatlessness, or a very restricted form of omnivorism as reverent as vegetarianism. Thus with how we eat, we could converge on the fundamental truths of compassion and loving-kindness, nonviolence and respect, bringing them into our lives, slowly making them real, changing ourselves, approaching the ideal —peacemeal.

20

An Appetite for Accommodation

"A mortified appetite is never a wise companion."
—Robert Louis Stevenson

The opposite of a polemic is what I intended in this book: enough diatribes have been written already. The vegan activist who offered: "Vegetarians will enjoy reading it so they can feel morally superior" will be disappointed. The vegan author who advised me not to write it, arguing: "Vegetarians will not be interested in non-vegetarians and non-vegetarians will not be interested in the subject," may change his mind—as may another vegan author who, while not unsympathetic, exclaimed, "How depressing!"

A vegan interviewing ex-vegetarians runs the risk of offending everyone. Some feared apostates would not talk freely; others that vegetarians would be tempted back to meat. Indeed, the thought that animals might die as a result of ideas in this book almost stopped me: Would I do more harm than good? If it is true that people with guns and not guns kill people, then it is also true that people with ideas and not ideas themselves do harm or good. Although I would prefer a world without guns, I would not prefer a world without ideas—even depressing ones. Ideas in the wrong minds, like guns in the wrong hands, can be dangerous; but more dangerous (and depressing) still is suppression.

Unlike Rynn, I did not find former vegetarians "a lamentable lot"; but I did find them a mysterious one. How could anyone abandon vegetarianism? To know vegetarians is to understand vegetarianism; but to know former vegetarians is to know it even better. Those who were never vegetarian at all do not offer the same richness of insight: we know more about marriage by understanding divorce than by understanding being single. Thus we should be interested in why vegetarians lapse for the same reasons we are interested in why relationships fail. Even a non-vegetarian may be interested in the same way that a loner is interested in the relationships of others.

From Plato we learned that "like knows like." Among vegetarians, it is a matter of those liking the same things liking each other; but if we put aside actual diet, we find that we like many of the same things that lapsos do, and so we ought to like each other. We have seen the same things, faced the same issues, come to the same decisions; we have been initiated into the same mysteries; we are family.

I did not, until recently, see vegetarianism as a philosophy of life. I simply, and mistakenly, identified it with meatlessness. Now I laugh when I read a statement like: "She had become a vegetarian except for bacon and hot dogs."[1] We should say instead: "She ate no meat except bacon and hot dogs" or "She embraced a vegetarian philosophy, but could not give up bacon and hot dogs."

Vegetarianism is a way of life; meatlessness is not; vegetarianism is a way of being of which avoiding meat is only part. More important than what we eat is how we eat. In a world which is dynamic, not static, we cannot know any "thing" until we know the "how" of it: the adverb is more important than the noun. All being is becoming; all is-ness, process; every "what" is a way. Vegetarianism is not a state or a thing, but an evolution; when it is not finished, it can flourish.

Philosophers should stop searching for what is true and what is false, and search instead for the ways in which things are true or false. If we wish to inquire into the spirituality of former vegetarians, we should not ask what they eat but how they live. How we return to meat may signal moral weakness—or be a sign of moral strength.

Of lapsed vegetarians who say they are "on a spiritual path," Rynn said: "They have learned to manipulate the jargon; unfortunately, they are using it for a self-serving end. They're misusing the terms to satisfy their lower, their baser needs. One has to satisfy the basic moral principles before one can transcend them; only then can you rise in the moral hierarchy." But if there is a moral as well as an evolutionary scale, then perhaps it is as true of the ethical as it is of the biological that (as MICHAEL observed) "the definition of 'pinnacle' and the definition of 'base' is itself politicized; it's not objective in any sense."

We do not condemn others for their tastes in art as we do for what they taste from their plates; we do not judge the "lowbrow" for not climbing the pinnacle of moral refinement we think we now occupy. The palette may be individual; but the palate is political. A philistine is not considered a bad person in the way that someone dining on veal is sometimes thought to be. If there are "slob hunters," there are probably "slob omnivores" ("chowing down two Big Macs in a row," as JOHN put it) although no one I interviewed was one of them. There is a difference between eating consciously and eating unconsciously, between eating rare steak and eating steak rarely. (For the low-impact, environmentally sensitive omnivore, or the "flexible" vegetarian who does not follow the diet to the letter, steak is too rare to matter.)

PETER said: "It's very clear to me that what we put into our mouths is a determinative factor in our spiritual consciousness. When I see people who devour great masses of flesh, that's gross to me; it's unconscious in every respect. I found people who ate meat on a regular basis to be just unconscious—not necessarily unethical; but they were missing something in life." But what we are "missing in life" (if we are not vegetarian) may be the pleasure of announcing to others that we do not eat meat—a pleasure just as "base" or "low" or "self-serving" as the ends Rynn attributes to former vegetarians. The "uncompromising vegan" may be less spiritual than the omnivore who, like INGRID, feels the pain of the world "as being disconnected from divinity" or less conscious than an atheist like MICHAEL who said: "I take responsibility for the way [an animal] is treated even though I may not be the one killing it."

If we understand vegetarianism as a political movement or as "the right thing to do," it loses its particularity; the wind gets knocked out of it; it becomes a stale subject for dry debate instead of a living option. ROBBAN said: "I was doing it because it was the right thing to do and I found myself really strung out over the diet, emotionally as far as trying to follow it, as well as physically getting sick from it. I had all these good, wonderful intentions; the problem was that it doesn't really take into account individual variation and health." DAVID agreed that "the whole concept comes down to a very individual process." When we understand vegetarianism as an individual *commitment*, we understand it for what it is.

I wrote this book as a peace offering, to soften the debate, to erase lines of demarcation, to trace ambiguity and nuance, and to suggest that being a vegetarian should not be so easy. Reality is much too slippery for either consistency or consensus. The distinction between vegetarian and former vegetarian is itself difficult to draw, especially when some who eat birds and fish call themselves "vegetarians" and some who call themselves "former vegetarians" return to eating the flesh of only birds and fish. It is hard to say whether MARCIA or JONATHAN, who eat fish on vacation, or PETER or ROLF, who eat it on occasion, are vegetarians. MARCIA and JONATHAN call themselves such; ROLF did before his interview, but not after, and PETER does not; but they all do the same things.

Because vegetarianism is not a doing, but a way of being, it can accommodate a few exceptions, like MARCIA's accommodating the Russians on their Christmas Day. MARCIA was not a former vegetarian for a day, but a gracious "queen" who ate meat as a loving gesture. JOHN laughed when he said: "There are some people who eat fish who claim to be vegetarians"; but we can claim to be vegetarians if we eat fish seldom. Someone living a vegetarian life could eat fish every ten years or even every ten months if there was a good reason for it; but if we eat fish every ten days, we should say, "I am a conscientious omnivore with a vegetarian philosophy."

Even Catholics who sin are still Catholics (up to a point); but because we have no sacrament comparable to confession, we cannot eat flesh as often as Catholics can sin and still call ourselves "vegetarian." We may still embrace the philosophy, but we should not, if we are honest, claim the label. Indeed, those who call themselves vegetarian while eating some flesh tend to have strong vegetarian philosophies, while those who refuse meat for reasons of health only are more likely to forfeit the badge when they lapse. The deeper the philosophy, the more room there seems to be for accommodation, even though it is true that many with the deepest philosophies never lapse at all.

Understanding vegetarianism as a way of being excludes some who call themselves "vegetarian" and includes some who do not. If those who eat vegetarian for health alone would say they have adopted "meatlessness" instead of "vegetarianism," it would both end confusion and restore to vegetarianism the dignity it deserves. It would also accommodate as family members those who adopt the principles but who do not practice.

Simply requiring meatlessness for vegetarianism is too weak, for some eat meat because there is none for them to eat; but requiring that vegetarians never eat meat is too strong, because a way of life can accommodate a few exceptions. Because there is more to vegetarianism than diet, a lapsed vegetarian may be closer to vegetarians than to omnivores. Indeed, there is more of a shift toward vegetarianism than away from it, for to become a vegetarian is to accept a philosophy we need not reject if we return to meat.[2] Lapsos differ in their actions from vegetarians; but action is only part of vegetarianism. Lapsos with vegetarian philosophies differ markedly from so-called vegetarians who avoid flesh out of narcissism or necessity.

After listening to lapsed vegetarians, I came to see vegetarianism as neither a moral duty nor as a spiritual *sine qua non*. I saw that just as not everyone chooses meatlessness for spiritual reasons, not everyone who has spiritual reasons for living chooses vegetarianism. I also came to see how the choice involves more than reason, and thus re-assessed the power of rational argument as a guide to life. Facts are fine; seeing is splendid; but no one can make anyone into a vegetarian. At best, we can argue others into meatlessness, or make ourselves into those who attract others with their questions. (When asked about vegetarianism, I'm in heaven.)

Understanding vegetarianism as a philosophy of life has changed the way I live it; it is now something I express, not something I espouse. Once I wanted my students to become vegetarians; now I want them to think clearly about meat. (The results have been the same in either case.) Never have I taken my vegetarianism in so deeply! I have also developed a great appetite for accommodation and a sense of family pride. I have come to see some meat eaters as relatively more benign and some who call themselves "vegetarian" as relatively less so.

Lapsed vegetarians are, by and large, people concerned with the fates and states of their souls; but sometimes the world with all its temptations is too strong for our commitments; something else becomes important, perhaps even the freedom to choose anew. Former vegetarians deserve our empathy, for saying goodbye to anything can be traumatic. There must be countless millions of lapsos world-wide, many in hiding, like VICKY, feeling guilty and ashamed to talk about it. Some may miss their vegetarianism for a time, but eventually it fades like a beloved face we once loved to look upon but see no longer. Some, like AVA, may feel bitter and betrayed by their vegetarianism, and leave it as we leave a partner who has hurt us much too deeply. Breaking up, breaking idols, breaking vows—so much damage, so many fragments. When I first heard a stranger (who turned out to be KIVA) express her break with veganism with such sadness, I knew I had to hear (and write) her story. After hearing it, I knew I had to hear many more.

Meat over-done; fruit over-ripe. Meat can be over and done with, but fruit not over and ripe with. No one struggles with the moral and spiritual implications of giving up fruit; but many struggle with the implications of eating or not eating meat. In the struggle itself, the spirit is strengthened; to the extent that lapsos struggle, their spirits are not weak. Anyone engaged in struggle is more alive than someone who thinks the problem of living has been solved once and for all. When we relax and settle into our convictions, we are not letting our spirits breathe. Thus those who have finished with meat may be less spiritual than those who have not finished with the issue.

There are comfort foods, and there is comfort in refusing some foods; but in doing so we may become too comfortable—and too complacent. The sea squirt floats about searching for a rock or reef to root on and then when planted "eats" its own brain.[3] Thus it blurs the line between plant and animal—something for vegetarians to think about. If we hold too fast to our philosophies, we are not living healthfully (or philosophically) no matter what our diet. Just because we love plants does not mean we should aspire to resemble them, at least not in this "incarnation." It may be nirvana, being a tree, but our complexity, our big consciousness, is our gift from nature—just as long, slow life is the tree's—and so we ought to use it. If we examine only our meals, and not also our souls, we are not all we can be. Indeed, if we digest our own brains, how can we be vegetarians?

Postface

*I*n *Beyond Violence*, Krishnamurti said: "Don't quote anybody. Living on other people's ideas is one of the most terrible things to do."[1] Yet here I quote Krishnamurti—but only to explain that I did not quote my interviewees to replace my own thought, nor to let them think for me, but rather to complement and in some cases crystallize my own insights. So I did not "live on" their ideas (in Krishnamurti's sense) although I was nourished by them: what they "fed me" inspired me to "cook up" ideas of my own.

Although I interviewed twenty-four people, this book was not a collaboration among the twenty-five of us: its design was implicit in the collection of transcripts as a whole (and my running commentary on them), its chapters emerging from common themes. I began with no plan, not even a definition, but ended with pattern; I did not set out with a thesis, but ended with one. I had no agenda, but only curiosity—and sympathy. Indeed, I was surprised to arrive at the view that vegetarianism is a philosophy of life, for I did not foresee anything as unified as what grew out of my survey.

Ultimately I knew I would use the interviews as an excuse to do philosophy, and that I would "use" people as my research for there is scant literature on ending vegetarianism.[2] The one published tale I found ("Much Taboo About Nothing") was as poignant as its title. (Twenty years of vegetarianism—begun with an oath on the Bible in 1920—literally wore the writer out: her optimism became "battered"; she too often "rose empty from the board"; people "burlesqued her arguments", chiding, "poor boiled cabbage . . ." until finally her "principles were completely gone.")[3] DeSilver's "Putting Meat Back on Their Menu" (published some months after I conceived of this book and the term "lapso" and after I had transcribed my first two interviews) contains sketches of several more.[4] If our contemporaneous efforts are an example of Rupert Sheldrake's "morphic resonance"[5] or a sign of "The One Hundredth Monkey Syndrome" in the making, perhaps we will hear more about lapsos in the near future.

Although some I interviewed were never vegetarian in the strictest sense, and so were not, in the strictest sense, former vegetarians either, listening to them I was enlightened. Without their variety, the text lost texture. Rather than select only the paradigmatic (and dramatic) cases of long-term vegans who return to meat (as was my original intention), I included other views so the reader could be enlightened, too.

I did not interview anyone whose material I did not use and used almost each line of every interview. Together, my respondents emerged "larger than life" with regional color and theatrical flair as though each were a character in a play; but each is real—and I intended the drama. The names were in every case but two their own: "GAIL" and "INGRID" are pseudonyms chosen by the interviewees themselves. Although I lightly edited sometimes ragged and wandering transcripts by rearranging sentences into coherent paragraphs, and wove paragraphs into the tapestry of the whole, my aim was always to preserve both meaning and the personality of the speaker. I did not always fix grammatical anomalies or unusual locutions, for I wanted the reader to enjoy the flavor of each speech.

My only research tool was my questionnaire—and my imagination. Statisticians might fault my sampling "technique" as "biased" because I knew most of my interviewees who were perhaps pre-selected on the basis of some similarity to me. I have known LEO-NARD and GAIL all my life; SIANNA and MICHAEL for more than twenty years; ELLY, LINDA, VICKY, MARCIA, and TONY for fif-teen; PETER, JONATHAN, ROLF, FRANK, ROBBAN, KEN (and Rynn Berry) for many, and JOHN for several "by sight". I have never met PATCHRI, AVA, BARBARA, ROCKY, or INGRID, but found them through contacts or through advertising. I met KIVA, NANCY, and DAVID when I began this project in 1994.

Such a sample is not random; but it is unbiased in the sense of not including or excluding on the basis of preconception: I listened to people as I found them, and stopped when I learned enough. Because those who contacted me after my research was complete offered stories similar to those I had collected, I concluded I had ample variety: given the differences in ages, backgrounds, and styles, I am not sure whether a stratified random sample would have served me much better. Statisticians might also fault my sample of two dozen out of many millions as "insufficient"; but it was just the right size for this book.

Marvin Harris claimed that "The lesson to be drawn from spo-radic episodes of veganism, as from the occasional appearance of those who deliberately starve themselves to death, is that such prac-tices are not only unpopular but they don't last long."[6] Other forms of vegetarianism, while more popular, end also; but the lessons we can learn go beyond mere numbers or duration.

In *Lila*, Pirsig observed: "Data without generalization is just gossip."[7] If I had published stories without the connecting threads of theory, of that I would have been guilty. Those fond of light reading may have found the philosophy heavy, and those fond of theory the conversations lengthy, but my aim was for complementarity. One philosopher admitted: "Most philosophers are extraordinarily dry and very dull; Descartes is neither dry nor dull, and that is because he doesn't confine himself to strict logic, but puts in picturesque materi-als of a biographical sort."[8] Although I am no Cartesian, it is nice to hear that biography is no stranger to philosophy. Dodgson's Alice complained that a book was of no use without pictures or conversations. Although readers will have to draw their own pictures (as well as their own conclusions), I hope they will agree that conversations enliven what otherwise might be "dry and dull" philosophy.

Appendix

QUESTIONNAIRE

PRELIMINARY: Name, address, age, occupation, educational background, cultural/religious background, type of vegetarian (vegan, ovo-lacto)

1. How long were you vegetarian; at what age did you begin?

2. Why did you become vegetarian? What arguments, role models or experiences convinced you?

3. When you were vegetarian, what was your view of people who ate meat?

4. How would it have made you feel if you imagined yourself eating meat?

5. What was your image of yourself as a vegetarian?

6. What was your world-view or philosophy (especially your views on our relationship to other animals and nature) when you were vegetarian?

7. Did you have a support system to help you stay vegetarian—friends, family, religion, group?

8. When you were vegetarian, did you try to convince or convert others to your way of living/eating? How and what happened?

9. Did certain books or publications help to keep you on course? What were these?

10. When you were vegetarian, how did you FEEL, emotionally, mentally, physically?

11. How did you deal with those who ate meat? Were you a bit of a pariah, or were most others interested and understanding?

12. What were the greatest benefits of following a vegetarian diet, and what were the detriments, if any?

13. Why did you begin to eat meat again? Was it conscious decision, or something you drifted into?

14. What was the first flesh food you ate? What were the circumstances, and how did you feel when you ate it?

15. How long now have you been eating meat again, what kinds and how often?

16. What have been the benefits—and detriments, if any—of adding meat to your diet?

17. How do you now FEEL, spiritually, mentally, physically? Do you feel different than when you were vegetarian?

18. What is your view now of people who eat meat? Is it different from when you were vegetarian?

19. What is your view now about people who still practice a vegetarian diet?

20. Do you ever now explain to vegetarians the benefits of adding meat to the diet or try to convert them to a more omnivorous diet?

21. Do you experience any conflicts having added meat to your diet? If so, what are these?

22. Do you have any regrets about your years as a vegetarian?

23. Has your self image and/or world view changed since you abandoned a vegetarian diet? How do you now see your relationship with other animals and with nature?

24. Have your dietary choices been made mostly on the basis of reason or feelings? Did you have intuitions or dreams?

25. Would anything inspire you to go back to a vegetarian diet? Do you think you will ever be vegetarian again?

CONCLUSION: Please add anything else you want to say.

Notes

Preface

1. My colleague, Henry Tritter, calls former vegetarians "born-again meat eaters" perhaps for this reason.

2. *The Complete Works of Swami Vivekanandada*, quoted in *Treasury of Philosophy* edit. Dagobert D. Runes (New York: Philosophical Library, 1955) p. 1204.

3. For more details on each of the two dozen interviewees, see the sketches in "Biographies."

4. The ages of the interviewees listed in "Biographies" are as of the winter of 1994-95 when the interviews were conducted and/or questionnaires collected. Other data are current as of the winter of 1994-95, although, on occasion, I included data up to the winter of 1996.

Introduction—The Sense of it All

1. Heraclitus, "Fragments." "Opposition is good. The fairest harmony comes out of differences," is Milton C. Nahm's translation from *Selections from Early Greek Philosophy* (New York: Appleton-Century Crofts, 1964) p. 171.

2. Aurelius Augustinus (St. Augustine), 354-430 A.D. *De Durabus Animus*, XIV, ii.

Chapter One—Coming to Terms

1. See Xenophon's *Recollections of Socrates* and *Socrates' Defense Before the Jury*, trans. Anna S. Benjamin (Indianapolis, IN: Bobbs-Merrill, 1965), I, 2, 3; II, 1; III, 14 ("On Table Manners"). Also see Dan Dombrowski's comments in *The Philosophy of Vegetarianism* (The University of Mass. Press, 1989) pp. 55-56. "It is not that Socrates neglected his body, for he realized that no one could exist without nourishment, nor did he praise those who did neglect their bodies; rather, he disapproved of overeating." ". . . for Socrates, 'to dine well' meant doing no harm to one's soul in the course of a meal, a Pythagorean commonplace."

2. I formulated my definition of "vegetarian" after listening to former vegetarians, but subsequently saw that the *O.E.D.* agreed, construing a vegetarian as "a person who *on principle* [emphasis mine] abstains from any form of animal food, or at least as such as is obtained by the direct destruction of life." (Vol. 12, 1978).

3. For introducing me to the useful term "retronym" I am grateful to Stan Kundra who in turn is grateful to William Safire in whose *New York Times* column "About Language" he first encountered it.

4. According to the *O.E.D.*, Darwin uses the locution "This vegetarian crab" to refer to a crustacean who subists entirely on coconuts. (T.R. Jones, *Aquarian Nat.* 342, 1856) and R. Trimen (1869) says similarly, "an order composed almost entirely of vegetarian insects." (Vol. 12, 1978).

5. According to Margaret Visser, even people who subsist almost entirely on meat, like the Arctic Innuit, "consider vegetation a delicacy and so preserve berries in seal oil for use during the winter" as well as consume the vegetable contents of carribou stomachs. "The Sins of the Flesh," in *Food. The Vital Stuff* (*Granta* 52, Winter 1995) p. 115.

6. Carol Sugarman quotes Mary Abbott-Hess in "Even vegetarians not immune to appeal of lower beef prices," *Hartford Courant* (Food Section), Wednesday, February 8, 1995.

Chapter Two—The Perils of Purity

1. Isaac Bashevis Singer, in an interview with Rynn Berry, *The New Vegetarians* (New York: Pythagorean Publishers, 1993) p. 76.

2. Heraclitus's cryptic fragment may refer to the evaporation of vice—or perhaps to the absense of alcohol. Compare "Vegetarianism . . . has always been a form of aceticism, a way of purifying its adepts." Visser p. 121. Visser sees through such claims to purity, however, calling vegetarians "sanctimonious," "ungrateful," and "joyless" and indicting their literature for "its

contempt for others." ("The Sins of the Flesh," pp. 117-118).

3. Michael Allen Fox in "Animal Experimentation: A Philosopher's Changing Views," *Between the Species. A Journal of Ethics* (Vol. 3, No. 2, Spring, 1987) p. 59. "Nor does morality consist in trying to be perfect and pure."

Chapter Three—Vegetarianism and Virtue

1. "Man cannot live by bread alone" (Matthew, IV:4) finds a new home in Marvin Harris's *The Sacred Cow and the Abominable Pig* (New York: Simon and Schuster, 1985) p. 35. Harris claims that animal foods provide "catch-up proteins" which nourish us especially in times of stress and trauma. ". . . a man weighing 176 pounds would have to stuff himself with 3.3 pounds of whole wheat bread a day to obtain sufficient protein." Compare Emerson's "Man does not live by bread alone, but by faith, by admiration, by sympathy" in "The Sovereignty of Ethics, *"The Complete Works of Ralph Waldo Emerson* Vol. II. (New York: William Wise and Company, 1929) p. 1010.

2. Acts out of context shed no light on character, but neither do virtues out of context. Thus the conceptual distinction blurs as we go into the world where actions and virtues are each contextual. Virtue ethics seems to focus attention on persons more clearly than act ethics does, however, perhaps because it is easier to abstract act from actor than character trait from character.

3. My colleague, David Makinster, in a private correspondence, January 13, 1995.

4. The epithets can, of course, be hurled from either direction. In Visser's article alone, vegetarians are called: "hostile"; "narrow"; "judgmental"; "sanctimonious"; "pale"; "unhealthy"; "tight-lipped"; "wasted"; "mean"; "unhappy"; "ascetic"; "exclusive"; "fixated on health and purity"; and their practice seen as "mere obsession" and a "manifestation of modern narcissim."

5. Frey's whole statement is: "Some people have come to believe and fear that, in the suffering and killing which occurs in commercial farming, we demean ourselves, coarsen our sensitivities, dull our feelings of sympathy with our fellow creatures, and so begin the slippery slope of torture and death, to a point where it becomes easier for us to contemplate and carry out the torture and killing of human beings." *Rights, Killing, and Suffering. Moral Vegetarianism and Applied Ethics* (Oxford: Basil Blackwell, 1983) p. 20. What he calls the "Argument from Effects on Character" seems to include both the meat eater and the meat maker. Although he says else-

where (p. 190) "... it does not follow from the fact that it is wrong to inflict undeserved pain on animals that it is wrong to eat them," he switches from a virtue ethics to an act ethics stand, for we could still hurt ourselves by knowingly consuming meat produced cruelly. Frey minimizes the "Effects on Character Argument" by emphasizing indirect duties toward other people rather than the harm we may do to our selves.

6. Plato's *Republic*, Book IV: 439 e. In Hamilton (p. 582) the translation is, "There, ye wretches, take your fill of the fine spectacle!"

7. Brigid Brophy in an interview with Rynn Berry, *The New Vegetarians*, p. 51.

8. In Classical Greece, where vegetarianism was associated with fasting, it was people with fortitude who forewent flesh. Visser says that both "fast" and "steadfast" are cognate with the German "fest" which means "firm." ("The Sins of the Flesh") p. 122.

9. See Shunryu Suzuki, *Zen Mind, Beginner's Mind* (New York: Weatherhill, 1973).

10. In *Friends Magazine* (February 1995) a "big, strong but gentle SWM" specified "no smokers, drugs, vegetarians." (p. 23).

11. Compare Mark Mathew Braunstein, "If our killing a cat which was about to kill a bird could be justified with the thought that our action saved the life of the bird, then we could justify the cat's killing the bird which was about to kill a fly—whereby we could no longer justify our killing the cat. The point is that no human is capable of such broad vision as to be able to determine who should live and who should die." *Radical Vegetarianism. A Dialectic of Diet and Ethic*, Revised Edition (Quaker Hill, CT: Panacea Press, 1993) pp. 90-91.

12. Bible. Proverbs 17:1.

13. For a full characterization, see Tom Regan's *The Thee Generation. Reflections on the Coming Revolution.* (Philadelphia: Temple University Press, 1991) p. 3.

14. Robert M. Pirsig in *Zen and the Art of Motorcycle Maintenance. An Inquiry into Values.* (New York: Bantam, 1989) p. 293.

15. Artur Schopenhauer, *On the Basis of Morality* trans. E.F.J. Payne. (Indianapolis, IN: Bobbs-Merrill Company, Inc., 1965) p. 172.

Chapter Four—A Spiritual Pragmatist

1. Admittedly, mine is a very Greek (and Western) list of virtues. For a more Eastern one, see Schopenhauer (*On the Basis of Morality*) p. 210 where he offers: "gentleness"; "leniency"; "loving-kindness and mercy instead of justice"—as well as "compassion" (*passim*).

2. SIANNA usually calls me "Karuna"—the Sanscrit word for compassion.

Chapter Five—Parameters and Plants

1. Compare Nietzsche's "But if we could communicate with the mosquito, then we would learn that it floats through the air with the same importance, feeling within itself the flying center of the world." *On Truth and Lie in an Extra Moral Sense* (1873) in *The Portable Nietzsche* edit. Walter Kaufman (New York: The Viking Press, 1965) p. 42.

2. For a discussion of orchids and mimicry, see Burkhardt et. al. in *Signals in the Animal World* trans. Kenneth Morgan (New York: McGraw-Hill Book Co., 1967) p. 85.

3. Compare Brigid Brophy, "A millenneium from now, there may well be a symposium on the rights of plants. Humans may be working out techniques whereby we could, for instance, derive our food exclusively from fruits, which display as it were a biological acquiescence about falling off into the hands of grasping animals like ourselves." *Animal Rights: a Symposium*, reprinted in *The Extended Circle* edit. Jon Wynne-Tyson (Fontwell, Sussex: Centaur Press) p. 27. Thomas Taylor parodied Mary Wollstonecraft's *Vindication of the Rights of Women* in his satire *Vindication of the Rights of Brutes* in which he joked about future treatises on the rights of vegetables. Our thinking has changed much since 1792; Brophy's vision may not be millennial but (foreseeably) eventual.

4. Compare Charles Hartshorne, "To cut down a tree is not analogous to killing a deer or even a fish, but rather to destroying a colony of paramecia or bacteria." Hartshorne quotes Aristotle ("wiser here than he knew") as saying, "A tree is like a sleeping man who never wakes up" and adds, "One must understand that the sleep is dreamless." "Foundations for a Humane Ethics" in *On the Fifth Day. Animal Rights & Human Ethics* edit. Richard Knowles Morris and Michael Fox (Washington, D.C.: Acropolis Books, ltd., 1978) p. 154.

Chapter Six—Fish out of Water

1. J. Howard Moore shares my sentiments but goes further: "No human would lounge all day about the margins of a brook, blind to the beauties of the stream and the glories of forest and sky, in order to thrust brutal hooks into the lips of those whom he deceives, and drag them from their waters to suffocate in the sun—unless he were a savage." *The Universal Kinship* edit. Charles Magel (Fontwell, Sussex: Centaur Press Ltd., 1992) p. 287.

2. David Cantor, "Victims of Apathy," *Animals' Agenda* (September/October, 1993) pp. 18-19.

3. Giving up fish is "Phase 3" in Rudolph Ballentine's *Transition to Vegetarianism: An Evolutionary Step* (Honesdale, PA: The Himalayan Institute of Yoga Science and Philosophy of the U.S.A., 1987).

4. Rabindrath Tagore, *Sadhana, The Realisation of Life* (New York: The Macmillan Company, 1914) pp. 110-111. Compare Norman MacAfee: "You catch a fish. It looks/up at you. You say/ 'How beautiful you are, but this/is the worst day of your life'" from "12 Nightingales" quoted by Mark Mathew Braunstein in *Radical Vegtetarianism*, First Edition (Los Angeles: Panjandrum Books, 1981) p. vi.

5. For a discussion of inherent value and the subject-of-a-life criterion, see Tom Regan's *The Case for Animal Rights* (Berkeley: University of California Press, 1983) pp. 243-248.

Chapter Seven—Nature and Nuance

1. Aldo Leopold, *A Sand County Almanac* (New York: Ballantine Books, Inc., 1970) p. 137.

2. Some, like Leopold, hold that ethics is all about community ("Ethics are possibly a kind of community instinct-in-the-making") and that the land is itself a community, "Foreword to *A Sand County Almanac*, p., xix; "The Land Ethic," p. 239.

3. Jane Goodall found and filmed chimpanzees killing prey and eating meat at Gombe. Jim Mason suggests that the behavior may be a stress-induced aberration. Because no other studies of "unprovisioned, untamed forest chimps" reveal evidence of predation, Mason hypothesizes that "social and territorial" factors rather than "true hunting, predation and food aquisition" best explain the chimps' behavior. *An Unnatural Order. Uncovering the Roots of our Domination of Nature and Each Other* (New York: Simon and Schuster, 1993) p. 82.

4. Compare Gary Snyder's "Other beings . . . do not mind being eaten as food but they expect us to say please and thank you and they hate to see themselves wasted." "The Etiquette of Freedom" in *The Practice of the Wild* (San Franscisco: Northpoint Press, 1990) p. 20.

5. On an atomistic view, the violence and opportunism in nature is hardly a basis for an ethic. Nietzsche said, "'Thou shalt not rob!' 'Thou shalt not kill!' Is there not in all life itself robbing and killing?" *Thus Spoke Zarathustra* in *The Portable Nietzsche* edit. Walter Kaufman p. 314. But on a holistic view, we face what Tom Regan calls "environmental fascism." See J. Baird Callicott's "The Search for an Environmental Ethic" in *Matters of Life and Death* edit. Tom Regan (New York: Random House, 1986) p. 410. A third

problem is conceptual: How are we to understand the nature of nature independently of the categories we project on it? Stephen Jay Gould says, "Our categorizations of nature also tend to favor dualistic hierarchies based upon domination. We often divide the world ecologically into predators and prey, or atomistically into complicated and controlling 'higher' animals versus simpler and subservient 'lower' forms. Dualism based on dominance may represent the imposition of a preferred human order on nature . . ." "Reversing Natural Orders," *Natural History* (9/95) p. 12.

6. For another interpretation of the relation between facts and values, see Holmes Rolston, III., *Philosophy Gone Wild* (Buffalo: N.Y.: Prometheus Books, 1989) and "Challenges in Environmental Ethics" in *Ecology, Economics, Ethics: The Broken Circle* (New Haven: Yale University Press, 1991).

7. Compare Tagore: "When science collects facts to illustrate the struggle for existence that is going on in the kingdom of life, it raises a picture in our minds of 'nature red in tooth and claw.' But in these mental pictures we give a fixity to colours and forms which are really evanescent." "Life as a whole never takes death seriously. It laughs, dances, and plays, it builds, hordes and loves in death's face." *Sadhana. The Realisation of Life* (New York: The Macmillan Company, 1914) pp. 49 and 50.

8. Edna St. Vincent Millay, "Dirge without Music," *The Buck in the Snow* (New York: Harper and Brothers Publishers, 1928) p. 43.

Chapter Eight—Attitudes and Animals

1. See Henry S. Salt, "The Logic of the Larder," *The Humanities of Diet* (Manchester: The Vegetarian Society, 1914) reprinted in *Animal Rights and Human Obligations*, First Edition, edit. Tom Regan and Peter Singer (Englewood Cliffs, N.J., 1976) pp. 185-189.

2. ". . . it was an era of terrific abuses, both in animal experimentation and in the management of farms and slaughterhouses," according to Temple Grandin in the title essay from Oliver Sacks' *An Anthropologist from Mars* (New York: Alfred A. Knopf, 1995) pp. 267-268.

3. Temple Grandin's use of the phrase "stairway to Heaven" should be understood in the context of the cruelty to farm animals which she has documented. Some slaughterers work mechanically, she says, but others "start to enjoy killing and . . . torment the animals on purpose." (p. 280). Also see her "Behavior of Slaughter Plant and Auction Employees Toward the Animals," *Anthrozoos. A Multidisciplinary Journal of the Interactions of People, Animals, and Environment* 1(4) (Spring 1988) pp. 205-213.

4. Grandin, p. 268.

5. Grandin, p. 267.

6. Ann Landers publicized this (and other) recent cruelties to farm animals in columns such as "Cruel death of pig at county fair takes on life of its own" (May 3, 1995) and "What won't people do to yield 'prize-winning' animals" (November 5, 1995).

7. Karen Davis, Ph.D., Lecture, "Genetic Engineering: The Ultimate Degradation of Farm Animals" (presented July 28, 1995 NAVS Summerfest, Byrant College, Smithfield, Rhode Island.) Also see her "Thinking like a Chicken: Farm Animals and the Feminine Connection" in *Animals and Women*, edit. Carol J. Adams and Josephine Donovan (Durham: Duke University Press, 1995) pp. 192-213 and "Viva, The Chicken Hen," in *Between the Species. A Journal of Ethics* (Vol. 6, No. 1, Winter 1990) pp. 33-36. For chickens and the masculine connection, see Geoffrey Beatties' "Men as Chickens" in *Food. The Vital Stuff* (*Granta* 52, Winter 1995) pp. 203-213.

8. TONY admitted that he had never actually beheld this phenomenon himself.

9. Annie Dillard, *Pilgrim at Tinker Creek* (New York: Harpers Magazine Press, 1974) p. 4.

Chapter Nine—Bloody Epiphanies

1. Kavi Yogi Maharshi Shuddhananda Bharat, *The Vegetarian Way* (XXIV World Vegetarian Conference, 1977) quoted in *The Extended Circle. A Dictionary of Humane Thought* edit. Jon Wynne-Tyson p. 19.

2. Dr. Alan Long in an interview with Rynn Berry in *The New Vegetarians* p. 110.

3. Compare "There *are* no beings in the universe, according to human beings, except ourselves. All others are *commodities*." (J. Howard Moore, *The Universal Kinship*) p. 274.

4. Tom Regan often uses this phrase in his lectures. "Animals Are Not Our Tasters; We Are Not Their Kings" is the title of his fourth chapter in *The Struggle for Animal Rights* (Clarks Summit: PA, International Society for Animal Rights, Inc. 1987) pp. 83ff.

Chapter Ten—Thinking with the Body

1. KIVA's teacher was Annemarie Colbin, author of *Food and Healing* (New York: Ballentine Books, 1986). For an interesting rebuttal of "iron-clad logic as a defense of vegetarianism," see pp. 120-122.

2. See Georges Ohsawa, *Zen Macrobiotics* (Los Angeles: The Ohsawa Founda-

tion, 1965).

3. Marvin Harris says that certain Peruvian forest women tug at the shirts or belts of their men and sing, "We are sending you to the forest, bring us meat"—and will not sleep with them unless they do. Amazonian natives, according to Harris, have one expression to denote hunger and another to denote hunger for meat. Natives of the Malaysian rain forests say "I have not eaten for days" when they have eaten their fill of foods other than meat. See pages 25-27 in his chapter "Meat Hunger" in *The Sacred Cow and the Abominable Pig*.

4. Harris, pp. 29-30. "Some monkeys simply ignore the fruits that show no sign of insect-induced decomposition. They open a weevil infested fig, eat the weevil, and discard the fig."

5. Interestingly, Pythagoreans were called by their fellow Greeks who mocked them not only "pale, foolish, self-righteous" and "hilariously solemn" but also *smelly* [emphasis mine] according to Margaret Visser in "Sins of the Flesh" p. 125.

Chapter Eleven—Meat as Medicine

1. Ralf Norrman, *The Insecure World of Henry James's Fiction* (London: 1982) p. 138 quoted in *Solitude: A Return to the Self* by Anthony Storr (New York: The Free Press, 1988) p. 181. The phenomenon is: "A changes and becomes what B has been while B changes and becomes what A has been."

2. See Dr. Ronald Hoffman, *Tired all the Time. How to Regain Your Lost Energy* (New York: Poseidon Press, 1993).

3. See Michio Kushi, *The Book of Macrobiotics. The Universal Way of Health and Happiness* (Tokoyo: Japan Publications, 1977) and *Natural Healing through Macrobiotics* (Tokoyo: Japan Publications, 1989).

4. See Donald Kelley, M.D., D.D.S., *Metabolic Types* (Winthrop, WA: International Health Institute, 1982) and "Dr. Kelley's Self Test for the Different Metabolic Types," *Healthview Newsletter* (Charlottesville, VA, 1971).

5. Luke 4:23. [emphasis mine]

6. For a discussion of blood types and other biological barriers to vegetarianism (by a former vegetarian) see Ann Louise Gittleman *Your Body Knows Best* (New York: Pocket Books, 1996). A nutritionist based in Bozeman, Montana, Gittleman has spent two decades counseling more than 7,000 clients many of whom also gave vegetarianism up in return for good health. "My mind was dictating how healthy my body was supposed to be by eating this way, but my body knew better . . . I was wasting away." (p. xvii). "It has been a long and difficult path, trying to understand the difference between

spiritual beliefs and the biological needs of the human body." (p. 71). Physician Michael Klaper, director of the Institute of Nutrition Education and Research, Manhattan Beach, California, is conducting a Vegan Health Survey in part to determine whether "failed vegans" are in a distinct metabolic category of humans, what the animal-derived nutrient that improves their feelings of well-being might be, and whether this nutrient could be supplied through plant-derived sources.

7. For a discussion of "Mad Cow Disease" (Bovine Spongiform Encephalopathy—BSE) and its relation to CJD (Cruetzfeldt-Jakob Disease) in humans, see Joel Bleifuss "Killer Beef: Why Americans Should be Worried about Mad Cow Disease," *Hartford Advocate* (June 17-23, 1993) pp. 6-7. For a discussion of BIV (Bovine Immunodeficiency Virus) see Keith Schneider "AIDS-like virus found at unexpectedly high rate," *New York Times* (June 1, 1991). For a discussion of BSE, CJD, BIV, and BLV (Bovine Leukemia Virus) see Jeremy Rifkin, *Beyond Beef. The Rise and Fall of the Cattle Culture* (New York: Dutton, 1992) pp. 143-144. For a discussion of BLV and the connection between scrapie disease in animals and human AIDS see Laurie Garrett *The Coming Plague. Newly Emerging Diseases In a World out of Balance* (New York: Farrar, Strauss and Giroux, 1994) pp. 381-383 and p. 323. It is unsettling to learn that the USDA doesn't know whether exposure to BIV can make humans HIV positive; that BLV and the first human retrovirus known to cause cancer share a common gene, and that human cells have been successfully infected with BIV. In March and April 1996 news stories about BSE appeared almost daily. Neal Barnard (president of Physicians for Responsible Medicine) wrote a March op-ed piece "Mad Cow: The Risk of Meat Diets" and *Animal People* featured "Mad cow disease panic hits beef-eaters" in April. (The USDA has banned beef from countries with BSE since 1989, and other nations are now following suit.) The species barrier is also broken by other diseases. In 1994, *Newsweek* reported that "a stomach parasite that was seen as nothing more than a cow disease . . . is now surfacing with alarming frequency in humans (reprinted in the *Hartford Courant*, Thursday, November 24, 1994.) The debate over recombinant Bovine Growth Hormone continues. *Vegetarian Times* (March 1996) featured Amy O'Connor's "BGH Linked to Cancer in Humans" (p. 18). Salmonella risks and the tragedy of E. Coli 0157 in Jack-in-the-Box hamburgers in 1993 are widely known; less widely known are other bacterial contaminants in meat. For a discussion of these, see "Contaminated Meat Poses Serious Health Risks" in *Vegetarian Voice* Vol. 20, No. 4 (Winter 1994) p. 22-23. Classic discussions of antibiotics, hor-

mones, and other pharmaceuticals used in meat production are Orville Schell's *Modern Meat* (New York: Random House, 1984) and *Animal Factories* by Jim Mason and Peter Singer (New York: Crown Publishers Inc., 1980). *Animal People* (April 1996) revealed the use of the illegal drug Clenbuterol in veal. For more information see David Steinman's *Diet for a Poisoned Planet. How to Choose Safe Foods for You and Your Family* (New York: Harmony Books, 1990) and John Robbins' *Diet For a New America* (Walpole, N.H.: Stillpoint Publishing, 1987).

8.   It is difficult to profitably compare vegetarian and omnivore diets if we only compare diets which exclude flesh to diets which include it. In the absence of other nutritional data (caloric intake, frequency of meals, variety of foods, and any supplementation) we learn very little.

Chapter Twelve—Convenience and Conscience

1.   Compare David Makinster's: "I knew a couple who were real lovebirds. He was a vegetarian, and she was not. He was also a great cook and she was not, so she gladly became a de facto vegetarian to avoid culinary duty. As the romance began to fade, she began to sneak out for burgers, guiltily at first, then defiantly as the couple began to argue more. She began leaving him evidence to find . . . McDonald's wrappers on the car floor, and so forth. Clearly this was beyond diet—it was a death wish for the romance. Finally, when they agreed to scuttle the relationship, she went out on a carnivorous binge, not so much because she felt flesh-deprived, but more as an "In your face, Buster" sort of gesture. (Private correspondence, April 3, 1996).

2.   R.G. Frey says ". . . to go ahead and eat meat on social occasions rather than cause embarrassment is, I suspect, a serious temptation to many vegetarians which, if indulged, other vegetarians condemn as a form of hypocrisy." (*Killing, Rights, and Suffering*) p.7.   Frey, however, thinks the issue here is one of trying to keep oneself "pure" rather than one of ethics.

Chapter Thirteen—Travelogues

1.   The other vegetarian voyager is Jeff Meyerhoff, quoted by Drew DeSilver in "Putting Meat Back on Their Menu," *Vegetarian Times* (January 1995) p. 68.

2.   If he saw the "atmosphere" in which canines and felines are killed in China (as aired on HBO's 4/8/96 "To Love or Kill: Man vs Animal") INGRID's father might have changed his mind.

3.   Richard Sterling in *Dining With Headhunters. Jungle Feasts and Other Culinary Adventures* (Freedom, CA: The Crossing Press, 1995) p. 163.

4.   Sterling, p. 143.

5. Sterling, pp. 165-166. Also see an account of trepanning a live vervet monkey at the table at a Hong Kong restaurant so that patrons can "spoon out the warm brains" in J. M. Croetzees' "Meat Country" (*Granta* 52, p. 48) and in the same issue, an account of tasting whale in Iceland (". . . in dark, gleaming strips [with] a rich, fatty taste, somewhere between tuna and fillet steak") in Sean French's "First Catch Your Puffin" p. 201.

6. Gary himself experimented with vegetarianism as a high school senior because he was "into Buddhism" (perhaps intuiting that he would move to Thailand) but he "didn't feel good" (physically) and after three weeks, regarding himself in the mirror, concluded: "I am an omnivore; I have canines." Now he has his Buddhism and his omnivorism, too.

Chapter Fourteen—The Way They Were

1. "Nothing Gold Can Stay" in *Modern American Poetry* edit. Louis Untermeyer (New York: Harcourt, Brace and Company, 1942) p. 229.

2. INGRID may have remembered *Hackepeter* as ground beef, but according to *The New Cassell's German Dictionary*, *Hackepeter* is "minced pork." (p. 212).

3. Compare Millay's "Happy are the toothless old and the toothless young/ That cannot rend this meat" from "The Anguish" in *The Buck in the Snow* (New York: Harpers and Brothers Publishers, 1928) p. 31.

Chapter Fifteen—Reasons and Rationalizations

1. R.G. Frey (*Killing, Suffering, and Rights*) p. 5.

2. Compare Samuel Butler's "To live is like love, all reason is against it and all healthy instinct for it" and "Life is the art of drawing sufficient conclusions from insufficient premises." (*Notebooks. Life and Love* and *Life* ix.)

3. Dostoevsky, *The Possessed*.

4. Darwin says: "It is absurd to talk of one animal being higher than another." (*Notebook B74*) and "When we talk of higher orders, we should always say, intellectually higher.—" (*Notebook B252*). For Darwin, 'higher' and 'lower' are relative, e.g., to intelligence, and are not absolute categories. *Darwin's Notebooks* ed. Paul H. Barrett et. al (Ithaca: Cornell University Press, 1987) pp. 189 and 23.

5. I am grateful to my friend Marie Dick for this colorful expression.

6. See Kant's "Idea for a Universal History" in *On History* edit. Lewis White Beck (Indianapolis, IN: Bobbs-Merrill Publishing, 1963) p. 16. "Man wishes concord; but Nature knows better what is good for the race; she wills discord."

Chapter Sixteen—Consistency and the Coherent Life

1. For the other side, see *Vegetarian Cats & Dogs*, Second Edition, by James A. Peden (Troy: MT, Harbingers of a New Age, 1995).

2. See Kant's "What is Enlightenment?" (*On History*) p. 3. Kant says that "*Sapere Aude!*" ("Have the courage to use your own reason!") is the "motto of the Enlightenment."

3. See Carol Wiley, "Why it's impossible to be a vegetarian," *Vegetarian Times* (May 1991) pp. 59 ff. to learn how animal by- products find their ways into the wax on fruits and vegetables; bread flours (which can contain hog enzymes); sugar (filtered through charred animal bones); biodegradable trash bags (containing lactic acid from cheese processing); and even cotton, for "animal products are used in almost every step of cloth manufacturing." (p. 62). My students are always amazed to learn that marshmallows contain animal products (gelatin from bones, horns, hooves, feathers, and other connective tissue) and that even beer foam can contain animals' intestinal enzymes. Also see Max Friedman's *Vegetarian Times* article "More Vegetar-ian Than Thou" (September 1995) pp. 59-64 for a realistic look at consis-tency, purity, and fanaticism.

Chapter Seventeen—Morals and Moralizing

1. In a discussion of "contextual moral vegetarianism," Deane Curtin recog-nizes that "the reasons for moral vegetarianism may differ by locale, by gender, as well as by class." "Toward an Ecological Ethic of Care" in *Beyond Animal Rights. A Feminist Caring Ethic for the Treatment of Animals* edit. Josephine Donovan and Carol J. Adams (New York: Continuum, 1996) p. 69. Compare to Kathryn Paxton George's "Discrimination and Bias in the Vegan Ideal" in which she warns us against holding vegetarianism as an "ideal for all" (from the perspective of the "powerful" rather than that of the "vulnerable") thus creating a "moral underclass of beings . . . not capable of being fully moral" but only doing the right thing "in their contexts." *Journal of Agricultural and Environmental Ethics* 7(1) (1994) pp. 9-28.

2. See Marjorie Spiegel, *The Dreaded Comparison. Human and Animal Slavery* (New York: Mirror Books, 1989).

3. R. G. Frey (*Killing, Rights, and Suffering*) reduces the demand for moral consistency to absurdity, asking whether buying an Israeli orange amounts to approving of the dispossession of the Palestinians; buying a shirt from China the approval of communism; or attending a concert by the Lennin-grad Philharmonic Orchestra the approval of the suppression of Jews in the [former] Soviet Union. Gestures such as a Jew's refusing to listen to Wagner

may be symbols, says Frey, but are not instances of moral consistency. "One simply cannot be on the side of the angels with an accusation as cosmic in its application." (p. 229).

4. Mark Sagoff, quoted by Gary Varner in "What's Wrong with Meat By-Products?" in *JAEE* Special Issue "Might Morality Require Vegetarianism?" 7(1) 1994 p. 13.

5. See "Paving Moratorium Update and Auto-Free Times" published by the Alliance for a Paving Moratorium (Box 4347, Arcata, CA 95521).

6. For a discussion of vegetarianism as supererogatory, see Dan Dombrowski's *The Philosophy of Vegetarianism* pp. 121 ff.

7. J. Howard Moore says that altruism ("the recognition of and regard for others") "shows itself in *feelings* of justice, goodwill, tenderness, charity, pity, public spirit, sympathy, fraternity and love, and in *acts* of kindness, humanity, mercy, generosity, politeness, philanthropy and the like." [emphasis mine]. *The Universal Kinship* edit. Charles Magel (Fontwell, Sussex: Centaur Press, 1992) p. 284.

8. This is not to say that other-regarding motives are foreign to human nature. Moore says, "Altruism (other-love) is just as natural as egoism (self-love) is. There is not so much of it as there is of egoism." (*The Universal Kinship*) p. 284.

9. Moore says "True altruism and solidarity—true expansion and universalization of the self—are found in sympathy" (p. 297) and enjoins us to "ACT TOWARD OTHERS AS YOU WOULD ACT TOWARD A PART OF YOUR OWN SELF" (p. 325). Compare to Schopenhauer's "The others are not a non-ego . . . but an 'I once more.' (*On the Basis of Morality*) p. 211.

10. Schopenhauer quotes Calderón (*Jornale*, II, p. 229) ". . . there is no difference between suffering and seeing suffering." (*On the Basis of Morality*) p. 165.

Chapter Eighteen—The Correctly Politic Vegetarian

1. R.G. Frey says, "If I want hogs to have straw bedding, then presumably, I must on Singer's view give up eating them; I am not to rectify the matter by ensuring that they have straw bedding." (*Killing, Rights, and Suffering*) p. 209. Frey is taking a welfarist not an abolitionist stand.

2. George Bernard Shaw, quoted in Peter Singer's *Animal Liberation*, Revised Edition (New York: Avon Books, 1990) p. 163. "George Bernard Shaw once said that he would be followed to his grave by numerous sheep, cattle, pigs, chickens, and a whole shoal of fish, all grateful at having been spared because of his vegetarian diet." Singer, like Shaw, believes that vegetarians,

collectively at least, do affect the meat industry; but our "sparing" an animal and that animal's being spared are not the same. One vegan I know, however, insists that if a steer could feed fifty people, but only forty-nine eat him (the fiftieth being a vegetarian), then "all those forty-nine fiftieths add up to one cow." (Mark Reinhardt, vegetarian columnist and contributor to *Vegetarian Voice*, in a private conversation, June 4, 1996). Yet even if they do, by some magic of mathematics, make a statistical steer, no new cow is allowed to live although (perhaps) one will not be bred to die. Thus we equivocate when we speak of "sparing" (refusing to eat) an animal, for as vegetarians, at best we spare not animal lives but only animal deaths. Strictly, we spare animals not by refusing to eat them, but by refusing to kill them.

3. See *Acres U.S.A.: A Voice for Eco-Agriculture* (Acreas U.S.A., 1008 E. 60th Terrace, Kansas City, MO 64133).

4. Tamara R. D'Agnati, in a letter to *Vegetarian Times* (March 1995) p. 10.

5. Dave Taylor, in a letter to *Vegetarian Times* (April 1995) p. 8.

6. Jan Craig-Olinger, in a letter to *Vegetarian Times* (March 1995) p. 10.

7. Amy Clark, quoted in "Some meatless competition hasn't hurt *Vegetarian Times* by Carole Sugarman, *Hartford Courant* (Food Section) Wednesday, July 12, 1995.

8. Karen Lee and Diana Porter, *The Occasional Vegetarian* (New York: Warner Books, 1995); Diana Shaw, *The Almost Vegetarian* (New York: Clarkson Potter, 1994); Lisa Tracy, *The Gradual Vegetarian* (New York: Dell, 1986). Also see Sarah Fritschner, "The New Vegetarians" in *Food and Wine* Vol. 18, No. 9 (September, 1995) pp. 56-62.

9. Carole Sugarman, "Some meatless competition hasn't hurt *Vegetarian Times*."

10. Mark Mathew Braunstein takes credit for the epithet "Outdoor Death."

Chapter Nineteen —Eating Animals Again

1. Carol J. Adams, *The Sexual Politics of Meat: A Feminist Vegetarian Critical Theory* (New York: Continuum, 1990) pp. 40-62.

2. This is Frey's eighth argument against vegetarianism. "Social life will be seriously affected." Frey offers as examples teens not able to enjoy burgers, restaurants and caterers losing business, and suburban life lacking character in the absence of outdoor barbecues. "To appreciate this," he says, "think only of the many roles the sandwich plays in our lives and then think of the role meat plays in the sandwich." (*Killing, Rights, and Suffering*) pp. 199-200.

3. Lawrence Shamblin, in a letter to *Tricycle. The Buddhist Review* (Summer,

1995) p. 8. Compare with Deane Curtin who says, "Tibetans, who as Buddhists have not generally been drawn to vegetarianism, nevertheless give their bodies back to the animals in an ultimate act of thanks by having their corpses hacked to pieces as food for the birds" in "Toward an Ecological Ethics of Care" in *Beyond Animal Rights. A Feminist Caring Ethic for the Treatment of Animals* p. 71. Whether the act is one of reverence or one of economics is, however, moot. Curtin reveals (p. 76) that the practice saves "the enormous expense of firewood for cremation"—an explanation anthropologist Marvin Harris would no doubt favor.

4. Although there is nothing obscene about killing per se (for example, euthanasia), there may be something obscene about a system in which eating depends on killing. For a fascinating (fictional) exposition of *eating* as obscene, see Olaf Stapledon's 1920 *Last Men in London* (Baltimore, MD: Penguin, 1972) p. 414. "Eating became at once a sin and an epitome of the divine power; for in eating does not the living body gather into itself lifeless matter to organize it, vitalize it? The mouth was, of course, never exposed to view. The awful member was concealed behind a little modesty apron, which was worn below the nose."

5. John McClellan in "Meat: To Eat It Or Not. A Debate on Food and Practice," *Tricycle. The Buddhist Review* (Winter, 1994) p. 52. McClellan writes, ". . . some might wish to resume eating meat—out of compassion—to take further painful responsibility for the suffering of all beings . . . "

6. Compare to Schopenhauer's third "fundamental incentive of human action": "Compassion: this desires another's weal (goes the length of nobleness and magnanimity)." (*On the Basis of Morality*) p. 145. Later he says, "Nothing shocks our moral feelings so deeply as cruelty does. We can forgive every other crime, but not cruelty. The reason for this is that it is the very opposite of compassion . . . Thus it is the greatest lack of compassion that stamps a deed with the deepest moral depravity and atrocity. Consequently, compassion is the real moral incentive. (pp. 169-170).

7. I say this somewhat tongue in cheek (my own tongue in my cheek, not a cow's!) because I believe it is not meatlessness but living with compassion and "harmlessness" which would be an antidote to violence. Perhaps because carnivorous animals are "fierce" and herbivores docile, we associate flesh eating with aggression, but neither anecdotal nor anthropological evidence clearly bears this out. One of my students narrowly escaped being raped by a vegan and most of us had seen vegans with frighteningly confrontational dispositions at demonstrations. The Kurgan peoples with their vast herds and lust for more cows decimated pastoralist cultures, but the

nearly carnivorous Innuit seem peaceful. Even if there is a correlation between hormones, meat, and aggression, aggression probably stems from attitudes within a culture spilling into harms against human and nonhuman others. There have been vegan bombers and arsonists, and psychologists who study us find aberrations. For references to such studies, see Judith *Dyer's Vegetarianism: an Annotated Bibliography* (Metuchen, N.J.: Scarecrow Press, 1982). Nevertheless, with respect to candidates for office, one can only wonder about the source of folk traditions linking psychology to meat. Carol Adams offers insightful analyses in *The Sexual Politics of Meat* and even Shakespeare makes such references, for example, having Sir Andrew Aguecheek (tongue in cheek?) say in *Twelfth Night*, "Methinks sometimes I have no more wit than a Christian or an ordinary man has; but I am a great eater of beef, and I believe that does harm to my wit." (Act I, Scene 3).

Chapter Twenty—An Appetite for Accommodation

1. Cathleen Schine, *The Love Letter* (New York: Houghton Mifflin Company, 1995) p. 78.
2. A former vegetarian I met recently said, "I have a vegetarian philosophy, but I can't eat a vegetarian diet." We can, of course, "have" (in the sense of being sympathetic to) a vegetarian philosophy without living it as a philosophy of life.
3. Daniel C. Dennett, *Consciousness Explained* (Boston: Little, Brown and Company 1991) p. 177.

Postface

1. J. Krishnamurti, *Beyond Violence* (New York: Harper and Row, 1973) p. 44.
2. Dudley Giehl distinguishes "inconstants" (Bryon, Shelley, and Thoreau); "apostates" (Seneca, Plutarch, Tennyson, and Mahler); as well as "advocates who did not practice what they preached" (including Voltaire and Wagner) and summarizes their reasons and stories. *Vegetarianism: A Way of Life* (New York: Harper and Row, 1979) pp. 145-155.
3. Celeste Turner Wright, "Much Taboo About Nothing," *Hygeia* 18 (December, 1940) pp. 1088-1090. "Vigilance is the price for purity," she said, explaining how vegetarianism did her "psychological harm." Finally she broke a "chain of overgrown habits" which she came to see as "prejudices" and "fetishes." No account I heard was as sad as this which I read, for its writer concludes, almost gaily, that her new freedom was cause for celebration as she traded new taste sensations for outdated spirituality.
4. Drew DeSilver includes cases of lapsing from vegetarianism while living

abroad; during pregnancy; "on the road"; and for philosophical (what he calls "personal") reasons. "Putting Meat Back On Their Menu" *Vegetarian Times* (January 1995) pp. 67 ff.

5. Rupert Sheldrake, *A New Science of Life. The Hypothesis of Formative Causation* (Los Angeles: J. P. Tarcher, 1981).

6. Marvin Harris, *The Sacred Cow and the Abominable Pig*, pp. 22-23.

7. Robert M. Pirsig, *Lila. An Inquiry Into Morals* (New York: Bantam, 1992) p. 62.

8. Bertrand Russell, *Descartes' Discourse on Method* (New York: Random House, 1942) reprinted in *Mind, Matter and Morals* (New York: Philosophical Library, 1952) p. 179.

Select Bibliography

Adams, Carol J. "Eco-feminism and Eating of Animals." *Hypatia* 6 no. 1 (spring 1991): 125-146.

______. *The Sexual Politics of Meat: A Feminist-Vegetarian Critical Theory.* New York: Continuum, 1990.

Adams, Carol J. and Marjorie Procter-Smith. "Taking Life or 'Taking on Life'?" In *Ecofeminism and the Sacred* ed. Carol J. Adams, New York: Continuum, 1993.

Adams, Carol J. and Josephine Donovan, eds., *Animals and Women: Feminist Theoretical Explorations.* Durham: Duke University Press, 1995.

Aiken, William and Hugh LaFolette, eds., *World Hunger and Moral Obligation.* Englewood Cliffs, N.J.: Prentice-Hall, 1977.

Ballentine, Rudolph, M.D. *Transition to Vegetarianism.* Honesdale: The Himalayan International Institute of Yoga Science and Philosophy of the U.S.A., 1987.

Beattie, Geoffrey. "Men as Chickens." *Granta* 52 (winter 1995): 203-213.

Berry, Rynn. *Famous Vegetarians and Their Favorite Recipes: Lives and Lore from Buddha to Beatles.* New York: Pythagorean Publishers, 1993.

______. *Food for the Gods: Vegetarianism and the World's Religions.* New York, Pythagorean Publishers, 1996.

______. *The New Vegetarians*, rev. ed. New York, Pythagorean Publishers, 1993.

Braunstein, Mark Mathew. *Radical Vegetarianism: A Dialectic of Diet and Ethic.* rev. ed. Quaker Hill, CT: Panacea Press, 1993.

Callicott, J. Baird. "Animal Liberation: A Triangular Affair." *Environmental Ethics* 2 no. 4 (winter 1980): 311-338.

Cantor, David. "Victims of Apathy." *Animals' Agenda* (September 1993): 12-19.

Clark, Stephen, R.L. *The Moral Status of Animals.* Oxford: Clarendon Press, 1977.

Coetzee, J.M. "Meat Country." *Granta* 52 (winter 1995): 41-53.

Colbin, Annemarie. *Food and Healing.* New York: Ballentine Books, 1986.

Comstock, Gary. Introduction to "Might Morality Require Veganism?" *Journal of Agricultural and Environmental Ethics* 7 no. 1 (1994): 1-7.

Curtin, Deane. "Toward an Ecological Ethic of Care." *Hypatia* 6 no. 1 (1991): 60-74. Reprinted in *Beyond Animal Rights: A Feminist Caring Ethics for the Treatment of Animals* ed. Josephine Donovan and Carol J. Adams. New York: Continuum, 1996.

Davis, Karen. "Thinking like a Chicken: Farm Animals and the Feminine Connection." In *Animals and Women* ed. Carol J. Adams and Josephine Donovan. Durham: Duke University Press, 1995.

———. "Viva, the Chicken Hen (June?-November 1985)." *Between the Species: A Journal of Ethics* 6 no. 1 (winter 1990): 33-36.

DeSilver, Drew. "Putting Meat Back on Their Menu." *Vegetarian Times* (January 1995): 65-72.

Devine, Philip. "The Moral Basis of Vegetarianism." *Philosophy* 53 (1978): 481-505.

Dombrowski, Daniel A. *The Philosophy of Vegetarianism.* Amherst: The University of Massachusetts Press, 1984.

Donovan, Josephine and Carol J. Adams, eds., *Beyond Animal Rights: A Feminist Caring Ethic for the Treatment of Animals.* New York: Continuum, 1996.

Dyer, Judith. *Vegetarianism: An Annotated Bibliography.* Metuchen, N. J.: Scarecrow Press, 1982.

Ferré, Frederick. "Moderation, Morals, and Meat." *Inquiry* 29 (December 1986): 391-406.

Food: The Vital Stuff. Granta 52 (winter 1995).

Fox, Michael Allen. "Environmental Ethics and the Ideology of Meat Eating." *Between the Species: A Journal of Ethics* 9 no. 3 (summer 1993): 121-132.

———. *Farm Animals, Husbandry, Behavior, and Veterinary Practice*, Baltimore, University Park Press, 1984.

French, Sean. "First Catch Your Puffin." *Granta* 52 (winter 1995): 195-203.

Fritschner, Sarah. "The New Vegetarians." *Food and Wine* 18 no. 9 (September 1995): 56-62.

Frey, R.G. *Rights, Killing, and Suffering: Moral Vegetarianism and Applied Ethics.* Oxford: Basil Blackwell, 1983.

Friedman, Max. "More Vegetarian Than Thou." *Vegetarian Times* (September 1995): 59-64.

George, Kathryn Paxton. "Discrimination and Bias in the Vegan Ideal." *Journal of Agricultural and Environmental Ethics* 7 no. 1 (1994): 19-28.

______ "So Human an Animal . . ., Or the Moral Relevance of Being an Omnivore." *Journal of Argicultural Ethics* 1 (1990) : 175-192.

______. "Use and Abuse Revisited: Response to Pluhar and Varner." *Journal of Agricultural and Environmental Ethics* 7 no. 1 (1994): 41-77.

Giehl, Dudley. *Vegetarianism: A Way of Life.* New York, Harper and Row, 1979.

Gittleman, Ann Louise, with James Templeton and Candelora Versace. *Your Body Knows Best.* New York, Pocket Books, 1996.

Godlovitch, Stanley and Rosalind, and John Harris, eds., *Animals, Men and Morals.* New York: Grove, 1974.

Grandin, Temple. "Behavior of Slaughter Plant and Auction Employees Toward the Animals." *Anthrozoos: A Multidisciplinary Journal of the Interactions of People, Animals, and Environment* 1 no. 4 (spring 1988): 205-213.

Gruen, Lori. "Another Bridge to Cross." Review of *The Sexual Politics of Meat* by Carol J. Adams. *Between the Species: A Journal of Ethics* (spring 1993): 96-116.

Gruzalski, Bart. "The Case Against Raising and Killing Animals for Food." In *Ethics and Animals* ed. Harlan B. Miller and William H. Williams. Clifton, N.J.: Humana Press, 1983.

Harris, Marvin. *Cannibals and Kings: The Origins of Cultures.* New York: Random House, 1975.

______. *The Sacred Cow and the Abominable Pig: Riddles of Food and Culture.* New York: Simon and Schuster, 1983.

Harrison, Ruth. *Animal Machines.* London: Vincent Stuart, 1964.

Hill, John Lawrence. *The Case for Vegetarianism: Philosophy for a Small Planet.* Lanham, MA: Rowman and Littlefield, 1996.

Hudson, Hud. "Collective Responsibility and Moral Vegetarianism." *Journal of Social Philosophy* 24 no. 2 (fall 1993): 89-104.

Hyland, J.R. *The Slaughter of Terrified Beasts: A Biblical Basis for the Humane Treatment of Animals.* Sarasota, FLA: Viatoris Ministries, 1988.

Irvine, William B. "Cannibalism, Vegetarianism and Narcissism." *Between the Species: A Journal of Ethics* 5 no. 1 (winter 1989): 11-17.

Linzey, Andrew. "The Bible and Killing for Food." *Between the Species: A Journal of Ethics* 9 no. 1 (winter 1993): 1-19.

Luke, Brian, "Justice, Caring and Animal Liberation." *Between the Species: A Journal of Ethics* 8 no. 2 (spring 1992): 100-108. Reprinted in *Beyond Animal Rights* ed. Josephine Donovan and Carol J. Adams. New York: Continuum, 1996.

______. "Stopping the Slaughter: From Virtuous Vegetarianism to Radical Subversion." Unpublished manuscript, Department of Philosophy, University of Dayton, April 28, 1995.

Magel, Charles. *A Bibliography of Animal Rights and Related Matters.* Washington, D.C.: University Press of America, 1981.

______. "Journey from Iowa Farm Boy to Animal Rights Bibliographer." *Between the Species: A Journal of Ethics* 4 no. 4 (fall 1988): 286-289.

Mason, Jim. An Unnatural Order: Uncovering the Roots of our Domination of *Nature and Each Other.* New York: Simon and Schuster, 1993.

Mason, Jim and Peter Singer. *Animal Factories.* New York: Crown Publishers, Inc., 1980.

"Meat, To Eat It or Not: A Debate on Food and Practice." *Tricycle: The Buddhist Review* (winter 1994): 49-63.

Midgley, Mary. *Animals and Why They Matter: A Journey Around the Species* Barrier. Athens: University of Georgia Press, 1983.

Miller, Harlan B. and William H. Williams, eds., *Ethics and Animals.* Clifton, N.J.: Humana Press, 1983.

Moore, Howard J. *The Universal Kinship* ed. Charles Magel. Fontwell, Sussex: Centaur Press, 1992.

Moran, Victoria. *Compassion the Ultimate Ethic: An Exploration of Veganism.* Wellingborough, Northants, Thorsons, 1985.

Morris, Richard Knowles ed. *On the Fifth Day: Animal Rights and Human Ethics.* Washington, D.C.: Acropolis Press, 1978.

Narveson, Jan. "A Defense of Meat Eating." In *Animal Rights and Human Obligations* sec. ed., ed. Tom Regan and Peter Singer. Englewood Cliffs, N.J.: Prentice-Hall, 1989.

Parham, Vistara. *What's Wrong With Eating Meat?* Denver, CO: PCAP Publications, 1979.

Patterson, David and Richard Ryder, eds., *Animal Rights: A Symposium.* Fontwell, Sussex: Centaur Press, 1979.

Pluhar, Evelyn B. *Beyond Prejudice: The Moral Significance of Human and Non-human Animals.* Duke University Press, 1995.

______. "On Vegetarianism, Morality and Science: A Counter Reply." *Journal of Agricultural and Environmental Ethics* 6 no. 2 (1993): 185-213.

______. "Veganism, Morality and Science Revisited." *Journal of Agricultural and Environmental Ethics* 7 no. 1 (1994): 77-83.

______. "When is it Morally Acceptable to Kill Animals?" *Journal of Agricultural and Environmental Ethics* 3 no. 3 (1990): 211-224.

______. "Who Can Be Morally Obligated to be a Vegetarian?" *Journal of Agricultural and Environmental Ethics* 5 no. 2 (1992): 89-215.

Rachels, James. *Created from Animals: The Moral Implications of Darwinism.* Oxford University Press, 1990.

______ . "Vegetarianism and 'The Other Weight Problem.'" In *World Hunger and Moral Obligation* ed. William Aiken and Hugh La Follette. Englewood Cliffs, N.J.: Prentice-Hall, 1977.

Regan, Tom. *All That Dwell Therein: Essays on Animal Rights and Environmental Ethics.* Berkeley: University of California Press, 1982.

______. *The Case for Animal Rights.* Berkeley, CA: University of California Press, 1983.

______. "The Moral Basis for Vegetarianism." *Canadian Journal of Philosophy* 5 no. 2 (October 1975): 181-214.

______. *The Struggle for Animal Rights.* Clarks Summit, PA: International Society for Animal Rights, Inc., 1987.

______. *The Thee Generation.* Philadelphia: Temple University Press, 1991.

______. "Utilitarianism and Vegetarianism Again." *Ethics and Animals* 2 (1981): 2-27.

______. "Utilitarianism, Vegetarianism, and Animal Rights." *Philosophy and Public Affairs* 9 (1980): 305-324.

Regan, Tom and Peter Singer, eds., *Animal Rights and Human Obligations.* Englewood Cliffs, N.J.: Prentice-Hall, 1976.

Richards, Stewart. "Forethoughts for Carnivores." *Philosophy* 56 (1981): 73-87.

Rifkin, Jeremy. *Beyond Beef: The Rise and Fall of the Cattle Culture.* New York: Dutton, 1992.

Robbins, John. *Diet For a New America.* Walpole, N.H.: Stillpoint, 1987.

Rollin, Bernard E. *Animal Rights and Human Morality.* Buffalo, N.Y. Prometheus, 1981.

Sacks, Oliver. Title essay. *An Anthropologist on Mars: Seven Paradoxical Tales.* New York: Alfred A. Knopf, 1995.

Salt, Henry S. *Animals' Rights.* Clarks Summit, PA: Society for Animal Rights, 1980.

______. *The Humanities of Diet.* Manchester: The Vegetarian Society, 1914.

Sapontzis, Stephen F. "Animal Liberation and Vegetarianism." *Journal of Agricultural Ethics* 1 no. 2 (1988): 139-153.

______. "A Reply to Weir: Unnecessary Pain, Fear, Nutrition, and Vegetarianism." *Between the Species: A Journal of Ethics* 7 no. 1 (winter 1991): 33-35.

______. *Morals, Reason and Animals*. Philadelphia, PA: Temple University Press, 1987.

Schell, Orville. *Modern Meat*. New York: Random House, 1984.

Schlieffer, Harriet. "Images of Life and Death: Food Animal Production and the Vegetarian Option." In *In Defense of Animals* ed. Peter Singer, New York: Basil Blackwell, 1985.

Singer, Peter. *Animal Liberation* rev. ed. New York, Avon Books, 1990.

______. "Killing Humans and Killing Animals." *Inquiry* 22 (1979): 145-156.

______. Practical Ethics. Cambridge University Press, 1979.

______. "Utilitarianism and Vegetarianism." Philosophy and Public Affairs 9 (1980): 325-337.

Singer, Peter, ed. *In Defense of Animals*. New York, Harper and Row, 1985.

Sorabji, Richard. *Animals and Human Morals: The Origins of the Western Debate*. Ithaca, N.Y.: Cornell University Press, 1994.

Speigel, Marjorie. *The Dreaded Comparison: Human and Animal Slavery*, rev. ed., New York: Mirror Books, 1996.

Steinman, David. *Diet for a Poisoned Planet: How to Choose Safe Foods for You and Your Family*. New York: Harmony Books, 1990.

Stephens, William O. "Five Arguments for Vegetarianism." *Philosophy in the Contemporary World* 1 no. 4 (winter 1994): 25-39.

VanDeVeer, Donald. "Interspecific Justice." *Inquiry* 22 Nos. 1-2 (summer 1979): 55-70. Reprinted in *People, Penguins, and Plastic Trees: Basic Issues in Environmental Ethics* ed. Donald VanDeVeer and Christine Pierce. Belmont, CA: Wadsworth Publishing Company, 1986.

Varner, Gary E. "In Defense of the Vegan Ideal: Rhetoric and Bias in the Nutrition Literature." *Journal of Agricultural and Environmental Ethics* 7 no. 1 (1994): 29-41.

______. "What's Wrong With Animal By-Products?" *Journal of Agricultural and Environmental Ethics* 7 no. 1 (1994): 7-19.

Visser, Margaret. "The Sins of the Flesh." *Granta* 52 (winter 1995): 111-133.

Watson, Richard. *The Philosopher's Diet: How to Lose Weight and Change the World*. Boston: The Atlantic Monthly Press, 1985.

Weir, Jack. "Unnecessary Pain, Nutrition, and Vegetarianism." *Between the Species: A Journal of Ethics* 1 (winter 1991): 13-26.

Wenz, Peter S. "An Ecological Argument for Vegetarianism." *Ethics and Animals* 5 (March 1984): 2-9.

Wiley, Carol. "Why It's Impossible to be a Vegetarian." *Vegetarian Times*, May, 1991, 59 ff.

Williams, Howard. *The Ethics of Diet*. London: Richard James, 1907.

Wright, Celester Turner. "Much Taboo About Nothing." *Hygeia* 18 (December 1940): 1088-1090.

Wynne-Tyson, Jon. ed. *The Extended Circle: A Dictionary of Humane Thought.* Fontwell, Sussex: Centaur Press, 1985.

Biographies

AVA, 53, from Australia, is as outspoken against vegetarianism as most vegetarians are outspoken in its favor, convinced that a decade of meatlessness contributed to her ill health. A practicing Taoist and disciple of Master Hua-Ching Ni (author of an especially beautiful translation of the *Tao Teh Ching* and the *Hua Hu Ching*), AVA pursues the Integral Truth "Down Under" where she and her husband, a psychologist, run a health clinic. AVA divines deep wisdom not only in Chinese philosophy but also in Chinese medicine to which she attributes her and her spouse's recovery from serious illness. Although she rejects Western medicine, she accepts the mainstay of Western diet, believing that meat is an essential ingredient in the recipe for their vibrant good health today.

BARBARA, 42, began her transition to a nearly vegan diet as a student, convinced by insights into the environmental consequences of meat production. Her vegetarianism later became deeply spiritual, and her example inspired her husband to become a vegetarian as well. BARBARA has an M.A. in political science from SUNY, Binghampton, and worked for a decade as an academic advisor to college adults. Now resting and recuperating, she works as a house-sitter in northern New York State. From an Irish Catholic background and one of thirteen children, BARBARA chose to have none of her own, having fledged enough younger brothers and sisters already. BARBARA ended seventeen years of vegetarianism tearfully (and temporarily) on the advice of a Buddhist vegetarian acupuncturist who subsequently cured her of some life-long health problems.

*D*AVID, 42, a physician from a Jewish background, has an undergraduate degree from Harvard and an M.D. degree from the University of California at San Francisco. DAVID did his residency in Lancaster, Pennsylvania, and practiced emergency medicine in rural Vermont. Recently transplanted, DAVID is now head of the Emergency Medicine Department at an urban hospital in Connecticut. A practicing Zen Buddhist, DAVID identifies with his role as a healer and calls himself "a latent shaman." (He also identifies with his role as a father and takes his two daughters, one and a time, for rides on his bicycle built for two.) A collector of Asian art, DAVID lives right on the beach where he can burn incense to his Buddhas and watch the waves roll in. DAVID was vegetarian for six years for moral reasons, but lapsed after finding something wrong with the concepts of "right" and "wrong."

*E*LLY, 43, originally from Rhode Island, is a community advocate with a B.A. in religion from Trinity College and an almost complete Ph.D. in anthropology from Columbia. Moved by the plights of battered women and abused animals, the disenfranchised and the disabled, ELLY is a humanitarian with a tortured soul and an outrageous sense of humor—a Jewish intellectual as sharp-witted as she is tender-hearted. ELLY traces the roots of her vegetarianism to age seven when her mother told her chickens come from Chicken Old Age Homes. ELLY lives with her vegetarian daughter and an assortment of rescued canines and felines in a rambling, book-filled farmhouse in Connecticut. A vegetarian for twenty-four years for philosophical reasons, ELLY recently began eating some meat to off-set otherwise intractable health problems.

*F*RANK, 39, from a Jewish background, holds a B.A. in biology from Yale (where he also did his graduate work in Far Eastern Studies) and became a near-vegetarian there after seeing unsettling anatomical similarities between humans and other mammals. FRANK knows Chinese and Japanese and has lived in Japan. He teaches science to children from age three through the ninth grade, and delights them with science parties at their homes as well. FRANK has made over thirty live science presentations on Fox's celebrity-variety show "Breakfast Time," and was sent around the country on tour by Random House/Knopf to promote their line of science books with his wizardry. A student of life with eclectic interests, FRANK is a charismatic conversationalist, guitarist, and gentle genius, likely to be found among microscopes, lightning generators, and rainbow machines.

*G*AIL, 46, is a retail natural foods buyer with a long history in the health foods industry. She has a B.A. in English from the University of Connecticut and grew up Catholic, attending Catholic schools. GAIL experimented with a vegetarian lifestyle in California after graduating from college. Choosing meatless meals for health rather than for animal rights or spiritual reasons, GAIL adopted and then abandoned vegetarianism six times. With a gypsy-like soul that needs to roam, GAIL is most at home when not at home, in wide-open spaces. She says she prefers a small house to a large so that she will want to go outside. GAIL can be found outside at Rainbow Gatherings, folk and peace festivals, pow wows, and in the woods, exploring people and places near or far from her New England roots.

*I*NGRID, 26, is a massage therapist from Western New York State, with a B.S. in geology from Tufts. INGRID grew up Unitarian Universalist with old-country traditions including lighted candles on the Christmas tree and St. Nicholas Day. From the age of ten she refused to eat red meat after seeing a whole pig on a buffet table. She became ovo-lacto at the end of high school, but stopped after a few years when she developed an eating disorder. INGRID is now considering a degree in naturopathic medicine or polarity training and has discovered the joys of organic farming which she wants to do every summer forever. Soft spoken and spiritual, INGRID may return to vegetarianism, but for now she believes eating some meat is essential to her well being.

JOHN, 41, grew up in New Jersey in the suburbs on a diet of junk food, mostly cold cuts and cola. He has two years of college, studying English at Montclair State in New Jersey and comes from a loosely Protestant family background. JOHN has been vegetarian twice, once in his twenties for four years and then again in his mid-thirties for two. He says he met his wife over a "god-awful" dish of bulghar and boiled onions—but she's loved him ever since. They have a daughter and a poodle—the one animal JOHN is not allergic to. JOHN manages a used bookstore in an old red barn, and writes incisive film reviews for an alternative newspaper—the *Advocate*. He has a wonderfully wry sense of humor, and a dramatic sense of life influenced no doubt by endlessly watching movies.

JONATHAN, 39, is a world traveler and importer of drums. With a B.A. in botany and an M.S. in nutrition (from Connecticut College and the University of Connecticut respectively), he can not only name every plant he passes on a hike, but prescribe panaceas for health problems as well. Expanding his Jewish traditions, JONATHAN also embraces the pagan and can be found at Rainbow Gatherings and New Age workshops of all kinds. JONATHAN has been vegetarian (and occasionally vegan) for nineteen years, but lapses when traveling abroad. When in North America, he lives in a cottage on a lake in Massachusetts. A brave and daring spirit, JONATHAN is drawn to distant places, arriving by camel, bush plane, or dugout canoe, and has even climbed a live volcano or two. He is an engaging conversationalist, seasoning wide knowledge with tales of high adventure.

*K*EN, 43, never went to college, but is the Horatio Alger of the vegan cooking world. From the age of eighteen, he was a vegetarian on and off three or four times for six months at a time, but has been ovo-lacto for the last fourteen years. KEN's mission is to dispel the image that vegetarian food is not delicious. With his mentor, Ron Pickarski (author of *Friendly Foods* and *Eco-Cuisine*), KEN trained for international competitions and won the first Gold Medal for all-vegan fare at the Culinary Olympics in Germany in 1992 with an around-the-world theme featuring a course for each continent (wildflower sorbet for Antarctica, of course!) KEN has owned restaurants including the all-vegan It's Only Natural where he was sole proprietor for five years. Now consulting for colleges and food services, KEN believes each time he serves a meatless dish he helps to change the world. Apprenticing in the old fashioned manner with no Chef's School behind him, KEN is an inspiration for all who have aspirations. His all-vegan cookbook will be published this year.

*K*IVA, 20, finished her undergraduate degree in cultural and women's studies and in theater at NYU and studied with Annemarie Colbin (author of *Food and Healing* and *The Book of Whole Meals*) at the Natural Gourmet in New York City. KIVA was vegan from the age of twelve to nineteen, but returned to eating fish and chicken for health reasons. It was KIVA's plaintive, "Since I stopped being a vegan, I don't know who I am anymore!' which I heard, literally, in passing, that stopped me, literally, in my tracks. Her fascinating story led to another and another . . . and thus was her consternation turned into a book. Residing in Seattle, Washington at the time of her interview, KIVA is now on her way to Boulder, Colorado to study herbal healing. Beautiful in every way, KIVA is bound to bring much light into the world.

$\mathscr{L}$EONARD, 77, is a health food store owner and organic farmer. Son of Polish immigrants, LEONARD has only a grammar school education, but that never stopped him from chasing his dreams. A WWII veteran, army cook, welder, and shipyard worker, LEONARD went on to help launch the natural foods revolution. (In the 1950's, he told me that fruit was no good unless it had a "critter" in it.) Inspired by his naturopathic physician, Max Warmbrand (author of *The Encyclopedia of Natural Health*), LEONARD became a vegan in his early forties, and then remained near-vegetarian for life. Tall, gaunt, with blazing blue eyes, a shock of white hair and a mein of being immortal, LEONARD is the prototype of The Wise Old Man. Widely read and well-informed, LEONARD is as likely to ask you whether the government is covering up the discovery of sphinxes on Mars as he is to share the secrets of organic gardening or his recipe for split pea soup.

$\mathscr{L}$INDA, 36, says she's had a weird life: she even lived alone in a tent in the mountains of Vermont for some time and forwent a car even after she found a more solid dwelling. From a Lutheran background, LINDA calls herself a WASP, an English-Swedish mix. She was ovo-lacto from the age of fifteen until recently when mothering led to her break with twenty years of vegetarianism. LINDA has a high school education and some college, and now lives in rural Massachusetts with her son and husband, an organic vegetable farmer. Feisty, earthy, and direct, LINDA has negotiated many sharp twists and turns in her life and is a real survivor. She looks back on her foibles and failures with a devastating sense of humor, and laughed more than anyone else I interviewed.

$\mathscr{M}$ARCIA, 50, originally from North Dakota, is now far from her roots on the farm. She holds a B.A. in French and mathematics from the University of North Dakota and an interdisciplinary M.A. and Ph.D. from the University of Chicago. MARCIA stopped eating mammals and birds as a graduate student, inspired by her roommate who had taught English in Bombay, India. (The roommate returned to meat, but MARCIA didn't.) Now a philosophy professor at a small New England University, MARCIA can usually be found surrounded by students to whose betterment she is deeply devoted. Also devoted to critical thinking, MARCIA is still pondering whether to draw the line at eating fish. She lives with her omnivorous husband (also a philosophy professor), two carnivorous felines, and thousands of books in a picture-perfect small town in Connecticut.

*M*ICHAEL, 53, hails from the British Isles. An Englishman with a B.A., M.A., and Ph.D. in mathematics from King's College, London University, MICHAEL also has a law degree from Stanford. MICHAEL has taught on the mathematics faculties at Ohio State and Caltech and on the law faculty at the University of Pennsylvania. He has published three books on computers and one on evidence law and has written an (as yet unpublished) mystery novel. A man of musical and mechanical talents as well, MICHAEL is a multi-talented savant with a mind like a laser and takes great pleasure in intellectual riposte. He recently moved from Portugal to the United States to teach International Law in Washington, D.C. where he lives with his wife, also a J.D. Michael stopped eating mammals in 1988, "out of a general distaste with moral overtones"—overtones not altogether overlooked in the case of his continuing to eat fish and chicken.

*N*ANCY, 46, is a natural foods retailer and vegetarian caterer and chef. Originally from Brooklyn she earned a B.A. in education and was an ovo-lacto vegetarian for more than twenty years before lapsing for reasons of health. Recently remodeling the health food store she runs with her nutritionist husband, NANCY appeared for weeks paint-smeared, looking like a work of modern art. NANCY has a can-do attitude and even learned to navigate the narrow aisles in a wheelchair after breaking her ankle dancing. When she is not recuperating, she practices the less risky arts of basketry and confectionery and displays her edible wares in her store. NANCY lives in the

Connecticut woods with her husband and has a grown daughter. Vegetarian or not, she is on a spiritual path, inspired by the Course in Miracles.

*P*ATCHRI, 25, lives in Thailand. Raised as a vegan and a Buddhist by Chinese grandparents, PATCHRI moved from a remote village to Bangkok to become a ninth grade student in a special school for people who have not gone straight through the grades at a younger age. PATCHRI ended her veganism of a dozen years as soon as she relocated, dropping it as part of her cultural assimilation. When a vegan, she could not eat meat because of the smell (even though she believed it was good for her) but has learned to overcome her aversion in order to adopt new traditions and new nutrition. Western Connecticut State University student, Wutthisak Thabthim, translated my questionnaire into Thai and Patrichi's responses into English, and my student Gary Meier, who had recently moved to Thailand, not only did research for me on tiger ranching there, but also found PATCHRI and arranged the interview.

*P*ETER, 43, is a chiropractor who came of age in the West, Southwest, Midwest and in Israel, far from his beginnings in New York City. He holds a B.A. in philosophy and mathematics from St. John's College (The Great Books School) in New Mexico, a master's degree in philosophy from the University of Texas at Austin, and a doctorate in chiropractic from Palmer College, Davenport, Iowa. PETER was a strict vegetarian in his twenties while living on an ashram in California, essentially ovo-lacto for a decade after, and then macrobiotic, trading pasteurized dairy for raw fish. PETER has been a teacher of holistic lifestyle and of yoga, and now lives in rural Connecticut with his wife and two sons. When he is not adjusting spines and easing pains, PETER can be found opening his home to appreciative macrobiotic guests, giving poetry readings, or running Enlightenment Intensives for those interested in spiritual growth.

*R*OBBAN, 37, is from Ohio where she grew up on a farm. She has an undergraduate degree in biology from the University of Toledo and an M.D. from the Medical College of Ohio. She did residencies both in holistic therapies and in psychiatry, and studied nutrition at the Interface Foundation and the Kushi Institute in Boston. ROBBAN was "pretty much a vegetarian" for only nine months, returning to meat when she started shivering and shaking. When not healing the sick or helping the well to stay well, ROBBAN gives public lectures on environmental illness, attends conferences on clinical ecology, and can often be found relaxing at the Omega Institute in New York or in the Caribbean. She lives in Connecticut with her two children.

*R*OCKY, 43, was vegetarian as a night-shift factory worker. He has a high school education and needed only a course in business management at the University of Bridgeport to launch himself into a career in retail sales, third generation in his family's paints and wallcoverings business. ROCKY was raised Catholic in a Catholic/ Jewish household and was vegetarian in the late 60's and early 70's for religious reasons, but lapsed when he found himself alone with it and his friends thought they were losing him. Even though he added meat to his diet, ROCKY still cooks with tofu and enjoys oriental noodle dishes. ROCKY values vegetarianism and says he would return to it if he found someone with whom to share it.

*R*OLF, 54, grew up in a middle class, midwestern, middle of the road Methodist family in the middle of Illinois, and became a near vegetarian in the middle of his life. He has a B.A. in philosophy from Northern Illinois University, an M.A. in philosophy from the City College of New York, and a Ph.D. in philosophy from the City University of New York. He is a professor of philosophy specializing in the philosophy of love and eco-philosophy. ROLF is as physically graceful as he is mentally agile, and will even do headstands for his students if they ask him nicely, demonstrating that philosophers use their heads in more ways than one. ROLF is a dancer with Kathryn Kollar and Company and has improvised in art galleries, sculpture gardens, churches, museums, bookstores, and bars. He hopes to see his book, *The Meanings of Love*, published this year.

*S*IANNA, 47, is your basic rainbow walking around in the shape of a human being. She was conceived in Florence, Italy and brought up in Europe and Massachusetts. She calls her present occupation "aspiring to be a human being" but is also aspiring toward a desktop publishing business, assuming the two are compatible. SIANNA was educated as an artist in Italy and Hawaii, and lived for a time in a loft in Paris. She has worked in art galleries and in cottage industry, making and selling jewelry. She was a strict vegetarian and then ovo-lacto in her twenties, but has been eating meat on occasion for twenty years, for health reasons. Beset with chemical sensitivities and chronic fatigue, SIANNA lives in seclusion with a feline and a canine companion on Cape Cod where she can be seen walking by the ocean, gratefully inhaling the bracing, less polluted air.

*T*ONY, 59, calls himself a philosopher, poet, and woodcutter, and has worked as a gardener. For variety, he acquired a real estate license. Before moving from New York City to rural Connecticut (where he soon ended his vegetarianism of five years), he was a tenor in the New York City Opera and traveled with the road show "Carnival!" He has a grammar school education, some high school, and then went on to the American Theater Wing for training in classical theater. TONY grew up in an Italian, Catholic family, but considers himself a citizen of the universe. He can be found in or around his modest dwelling on several wooded acres, working the land and being much more self-sufficient than the rest of us. Self-educated and widely read, and of a very independent spirit, TONY has a vision of what the earth could be like if only we could listen to its wisdom.

VICKY, 32, is a graphic designer with a BFA degree from the University of Hartford. She was raised in a very conservative, Protestant New England family, and now lives in New Hampshire with her omnivorous husband in a spacious Victorian home. VICKY experimented with vegetarianism for several years as a college student, but did not stay with it out of what she admits is weakness. VICKY is now passionate about natural habitat gardening and supports national wildlife and conservation organizations. When she is not planting "weed seeds" or watching her sunflowers, berries, or echinacea grow, she can be found canoeing, hiking, or climbing Mt. Washington. On a spiritual journey, VICKY has been inspired by Mother Teresa, Peace Pilgrim, and Christ, but said recently that she is happier "just living" without worrying about what her moral mentors might think of her. VICKY is a talented painter who has shown her work at exhibitions.

Rynn Berry epitomizes "gentleman and scholar." Born in Hawaii and educated in boarding schools, he has lived in France, England, Italy, and India. He did his undergraduate work in archeology and European literature at the University of Pennsylvania, post graduate work in classical philology at Columbia, and has taught at Baruch College in New York City. He became a strict vegetarian in 1966 during a college course on the Romantic poets, inspired, like George Bernard Shaw, by the lives of Shelley and Byron. Drawn to unearthing vegetarian lore, among his treasures are the recipes of Leonardo da Vinci which he translated from the Medieval Latin. Deciphering Greek and Latin for pleasure, he has also rendered Plutarch, Porphyry, and Pliny, among others. Author of *The New Vegetarians*, *Famous Vegetarians and Their Favorite Recipes*, and *Food for the Gods*, Rynn Berry is a vegetarian becoming famous for his interviews with famous vegetarians. He is also well known on the lecture circuit where he puts his knowledge of the classics and of Eastern religions to good use.

Index of Names

About the Author

Kristin Aronson received her doctorate in ethics from The Ohio State University in 1983. She has taught philosophy, specializing in applied ethics, for nearly thirty years. Also a playwright and poet, she has had a full length play (with a vegetarian theme) and two one act plays produced, one under an Ohio Grant for the Humanities. Her poetry has appeared in *The Antigonish Review, Between the Species: A Journal of Ethics, McCann's Journal of Poetry and Political Writing, Long River Run,* and *American Poetry Anthology.* She has served as editor for *The Connecticut River Review* and is a staff book reviewer for *The SMALL POND Magazine of Literature.* She is a board member of Earth Rebirth and the Ecological Health Organization, and has been a vegetarian for more than twenty years. She is an Assistant Professor of Philosophy and Humanistic Studies at Western Connecticut State University in Danbury, Connecticut.

This book was written entirely by hand
(with an old fountain pen and not on a computer) and printed
with soy ink on recycled paper milled without elemental
chlorine or detectable dioxins. Trees still stand that
might have been these pages.

**By day,
they
spoke
of**

*Ahimsa,
tofu,
macrobiotic justice*

**But
when the full moon rose,**

they thirsted for blood!
**THEY LONGED TO FEEL HOT FLESH THROB BETWEEN
THEIR TEETH!**

Hide your pets!
Guard your children!
Lock Your Doors!
BAR YOUR WINDOWS!

IT'S THE

NIGHT

of the

APOSTATE

VEGETARIANS

And YOU may be their next VEAL!

A NEW THRILLER BY KRISTIN ARONSON – SOON TO BE A MAJOR MOTION PICTURE!

dpm '95